Curriculum Patterns in
Elementary Social Studies

Curriculum Patterns in Elementary Social Studies

R. Murray Thomas
University of California, Santa Barbara

Dale L. Brubaker
University of North Carolina, Greensboro

Wadsworth Publishing Company Inc., Belmont, California

ISBN: O-534-00045-2

L.C. Cat. Card No.: 74-146056

Printed in the United States of America

1 2 3 4 5 6 7 8 9 10—75 74 73 72 71

To
Lissa and Carol
Rob, John, and Mike

Preface

Curriculum Patterns in Elementary Social Studies is directed to those persons who would like to know what options are available when they seek to initiate a social-studies program or to improve an existing one.

Since books and journal articles on elementary social-studies curricula have been appearing for some years, you may ask what further contribution this book hopes to make. In reply we point out that the writings published in recent years have been either cursory surveys of a range of programs or detailed descriptions of a single type. We think that something different is now needed and believe that many teachers and administrators would appreciate a new book that combines features of both the survey and the in-depth approaches. We have tried to produce a book that offers breadth by describing a variety of programs and at the same time that presents some degree of depth by analyzing each program in sufficient detail to make clear both its theoretical foundations and its application in the classroom situation.

We wish to express our appreciation to the authors of the curricula included in this book for their willingness to have their contributions described in detail. In addition we wish to thank Richard L. Greenberg and Mary Noll of Wadsworth Publishing Company for the wisdom they brought to the editing of this book.

Contents

Curriculum Patterns in
Elementary Social Studies

One

Backgrounds for Analyzing Programs

The function of Part One is to suggest a perspective, a kind of vantage point from which to view the social-studies programs described in Parts Two and Three.

Chapter 1 introduces this function by chronicling some of the more notable campaigns launched by innovators in recent centuries as they have sought to replace existing social-studies practices in American elementary schools. The chapter reviews several programs of the past, suggests why critics became dissatisfied with them, and points out traditional elements still prominent in curriculum patterns today.

If you wish to understand the historical backgrounds of present-day social-studies curricula, you can profit from beginning with Chapter 1. However, if you are more interested in how to analyze present-day programs than in the antecedents of today's curricula, you may wish to skip the first chapter and begin reading the second. The purpose of Chapter 2 is to propose a series of criteria useful for comparing one social-studies program with another. This set of measures is then employed throughout the rest of the book as the framework against which the illustrative social-studies curriculum patterns are displayed.

As the title of Part Two (Complete Programs) suggests, a curriculum proposal can be in the form of a thorough plan intended to provide an array of social-studies goals, methods, materials, and evaluation techniques for use over a range of several grades. The chapters composing Part Two illustrate five such plans found in present-day schools.

In contrast, other curriculum proposals are more appropriately labeled *partial programs*, since they provide for only a portion of children's overall social-studies experiences. Five partial programs are illustrated in Part Three.

Parts Two and Three furnish detailed analyses of only 10 of the many scores of social-studies designs available today for elementary classrooms. Limitations of space prevent us from inspecting other varieties in the same detail. However, in order to give some impression of key features of a number of other innovative plans that have gained national attention over the past decade, in Part Four we provide a brief survey of 11 more curriculum patterns. The survey is intended to supplement the descriptions of Parts Two and Three.

A school system or an individual teacher does not always adopt a single curriculum design. Some combine what they believe are desirable features of several proposals, thereby forming an eclectic pattern of their own. We trust that this book will serve the purposes of such curriculum planners. Even though they may not wish to adopt outright a specific program described in these pages, they may well find among our array of curriculum patterns a variety of ideas they can profitably incorporate into their own eclectic plan.

1

Historical Perspectives

In setting out to identify several highlights of social-studies curriculum development over recent centuries, we may begin by recognizing that *curriculum* and *social studies* are terms that can mean different things to different people.

For some people, *curriculum* means a written document that describes what is to be taught and sometimes how to teach it. This document can assume several forms. It may be simply a list of goals and an outline of topics to be studied throughout the year or over a sequence of years. Or it may be both an outline of topics and a series of suggested books, charts, films, and recordings that will assist students in attaining the goals. In still other cases the document is a textbook or a series of texts whose contents the pupils are to master.

In contrast, other educators believe it improper to call a written or printed document the curriculum. They believe that the learning experiences that the pupils encounter are the true curriculum, whether or not these experiences correspond closely to a printed course of study or textbook.

Both of these concepts—that of the printed document and that of the actual experiences of the pupils—are useful, and we shall employ each of these meanings of curriculum throughout this volume. However, we shall try to make clear which meaning is intended in each instance by including a distinguishing noun or adjective or by using a synonym. So to denote the curriculum as a written plan, we shall employ such terms as *curriculum guide*, *curriculum design*, *printed curriculum*, *teaching manual*, *course of study*, and *program guidebook*. To denote curriculum as the learning experiences that the pupils encounter, we shall use such labels as *sequences of activities*, the *curriculum in practice*, and *pupil experiences*. It should be apparent that when a teacher adheres closely to the recommended topics and methods from a guidebook, the foregoing two meanings for curriculum become identical. But when a teacher either chooses to deviate from the printed suggestions or is incapable of carrying them out effectively, then the two uses of curriculum refer to quite different matters.

Next, let us consider *social studies*. In the long historical view, this term is something of a newcomer to education. Prior to the early twentieth century, those school subjects that today fall in the realm of social studies were identified first by their individual titles—religion, history, geography, civil government—and later by the inclusive term *social science* or *social sciences*. Then in 1916 a committee of the National Education Association adopted the label *social studies* to represent all subjects treating human relationships, and the National Council for the Social Studies was formed by teachers of these subjects in 1921. Formation of the Council hastened the acceptance of *social studies* as the standard designation for curricula treating man in society.

During the 1960s the popularity of the term *social studies* diminished in some quarters as certain members of the educational community readopted the phrase *social science*. They were attempting to emphasize that they taught scientific inquiry into social phenomena through the use of concepts and generalizations from such disciplines as anthropology, economics, political science, social psychology, and sociology. Today the debate continues over which term—social *studies* or social *science*—better represents what should occur in elementary-school classrooms. Some typical elements of the debate are illustrated in passages from two leading books in the field: *Teaching Social Studies in Elementary Schools* by Edgar B. Wesley and William H. Cartwright, who represent the more established tradition, and *Strategies for Elementary Social Science Education* by Bruce R. Joyce, who represents a more recent trend.

In the opinion of Wesley and Cartwright:

> A few people persist in calling the social *studies* the social *sciences*. . . . The substitution of the term *social sciences* for *social studies* results not merely in a misnomer; it leads to confusion with regard to many curricular issues and practices. . . .
>
> The social *sciences* are the organized bodies of knowledge that deal with human relationships. Families, states, tribes, organizations—in fact, all groups and institutions—are the phenomena of the social sciences. In their content the social studies, which are derived principally from the social

sciences, resemble them. But the two terms describe different entities. The *social sciences* are scholarly disciplines; the *social studies* are school subjects.

The social sciences are concerned with *research*, *discovery*, and *experimentation*. . . . The social scientist owes the highest loyalty to his subject and to the standards of scholarship. . . . His report may be intricate and involved, but he is under no obligation to write for the hasty reader, the tired businessman, or the school child.

On the other hand, the writer of materials for the social studies must be understood by the learner; otherwise he fails in his primary purpose, which is to facilitate instruction. Thus, relative to the social sciences, the social studies must be simple, appealing, interesting, learnable. The two do not differ in kind of subject matter; they differ in level of difficulty and in primary purpose.[1]

Joyce accepts the term *social studies* as a proper designation for school subjects treating human relationships, but he believes that, through teaching pupils techniques of social-science analysis, teachers can best achieve the three goals he believes characterize the social studies. We may note that the distinctions Wesley and Cartwright drew between the social studies and social sciences is not evident in Joyce's discussion. He states that:

Three goals direct the social studies:

Humanistic education is the first goal. The social studies should help the child comprehend his experience and find meaning in life.

Citizenship education is the second goal. Each child must be prepared to participate effectively in the dynamic life of his society. . . .

Intellectual education is the third goal. Each person needs to acquire the analytic ideas and problem-solving tools that are developed by scholars in the social sciences. . . .

The point of view of this book is that these three goals are compatible and that educational activities can be designed to strive for all three goals concurrently—even though, in the past, the activities for the three have often been unrelated and conflicting. . . .

The tools for accomplishing the threefold objective reside in the social sciences. As we help the child to learn the tools of social, economic, and political analysis prevailing in the social sciences, we also help him to examine the social world around him, lead him to face social problems, and help him to comprehend his experience. . . . [The child] . . . should be helped to

---

[1] Edgar Bruce Wesley and William H. Cartwright, *Teaching Social Studies in Elementary Schools*, third edition (Boston: D. C. Heath, 1968), pp. 2-3. Reprinted by permission of the publisher.

examine social topics in such a way that he progressively learns to *apply*—not merely memorize—the intellectual tools of the social sciences.[2]

And thus the debate runs. In the present volume we do not favor one side over the other; we attempt simply to reflect, in the case of each program illustrated in the book, the particular interpretation of the terms *social studies* and *social science* that is implied in each curriculum design. When selecting the title for this book, we decided to use the label *social studies*, since it continues to be more inclusive and more popular than *social science* for describing programs in elementary schools.

Keeping these issues of terminology in mind, let us now turn back more than three centuries and identify a few of the prominent changes that have occurred in social-studies curricula since the early days of the American colonies. Our intention is not to offer a detailed review of the program patterns in various parts of the land as the United States grew from the early 1600s until the present day. Rather, our purpose is to describe only a few of the major influences on these programs so that the historical foundations for the patterns described in Parts Two, Three, and Four can be more readily understood. For convenience of discussion, we have divided this brief survey into three periods: (1) the era of the colonies and the new republic until 1876, (2) the progressive era, from 1876 to 1957, and (3) the post-progressive era, from 1957 to the present.[3]

The Colonies and the
New Republic—the 1600s to 1876

When the Puritans settled New England in the early seventeenth century, they brought with them the strong Protestant conviction that every person is to be his own intermediary with God. In order to carry out this obligation, each person had to learn to read the Bible. Instruction in school and home focused on this goal.

---

[2]Bruce R. Joyce, *Strategies for Elementary Social Science Education* (Chicago: Science Research Associates, 1965), pp. 3-4. ©1965, Science Research Associates, Inc. Reprinted by permission of the publisher.

[3]Our choice of 1876 and 1957 as the boundary lines for the progressive era follows the distinction made by Lawrence A. Cremin in *The Transformation of the School* (New York: Vintage Books, 1961).

The curricular materials that formed the core of children's study were first a hornbook, later a primer, then such items as the Psalter (Old Testament Psalms), sermons, and the Bible itself. The earliest introductory reading material was the hornbook, so named because it consisted of a flat paddle-like board on which was pasted a sheet of printed matter covered with a thin layer of horn to keep it clean. The alphabet and the Lord's Prayer typically formed the initial lesson.

In 1690 a volume entitled *The New England Primer* was first published, and its appeal was so great that it replaced the hornbook and became the basic text in schools for decades to come, reputedly selling three million copies before newer texts rendered it obsolete. The *Primer* offered a diverse selection of reading matter, all of which included some social-studies content—an illustrated rhyming alphabet, religious verse, the Westminster Catechism (religious material in question-and-answer form), and John Cotton's "Spiritual Milk for American Babes, Drawn out of the Breasts of Both Testaments, for their Soul's Nourishment."

The following excerpts from the *Primer* suggest the tenor of the social-studies ideas that the reading matter conveyed—ideas about the nature of man, his relation to God, and the manner in which he is to conduct his life.

From the illustrated alphabet:

A   In *Adam's* fall
     We sinned all.
B   Thy life to mend,
     This *Book* attend. (Bible)
F   The idle *Fool*
     Is whipt at school.
G   As runs the *Glass*   (hourglass)
     Man's life doth pass.
H   My Book and *Heart*
     Shall never part.
J   *Job* feels the rod,
     Yet blesses God.[4]

From the shorter catechism:

Q.   What is the chief end of man?
A.   Man's chief end is to glorify God and enjoy Him forever.

---

[4] H. G. Good, *A History of American Education* (New York: Macmillan, 1962), p. 54.

Q. What rule hath God given to direct us how we may glorify and enjoy Him?

A. The word of God which is contained in the scriptures of the Old and New Testament is the only rule to direct us how we may glorify and enjoy Him.

Q. What do the scriptures principally teach?

A. The scriptures principally teach what Man is to believe concerning God, and what duty God requires of Man.

Q. What is God?

A. God is a Spirit, Infinite, Eternal and Unchangeable, in his Being, Wisdom, Power, Holiness, Justice, Goodness, and Truth.[5]

As the American colonies grew, the citizenry represented a greater diversity of religious convictions and an increasing concern for matters secular. Goals of the elementary school expanded beyond the original two objectives of preparing all young people for membership in the church and of building a firm foundation for the subsequent education of ministers.

Textbooks continued to reflect most faithfully the nature of the curriculum in practice. It was the child's task to learn to read the primer and subsequent volumes and to commit to memory as much of the material as possible. Teaching methods consisted chiefly of having children read passages aloud and recite memorized portions of the text. Older children were also required to give reports on the contents of the previous Sunday's sermon. The principal techniques used by teachers for motivating pupils to study were scolding, the threat of the whip, and threat of God's wrath.

The advent of the American Revolution brought changes to the schools and particularly to the social studies. Again the textbook was the strongest factor in determining the curriculum in practice, and factors that affected authorship, production, and distribution determined which texts the pupils would study. During the colonial era the authorship had been almost exclusively English. Likewise, book production was also centered in England, though some reprinting of English texts was done in America. Pupils bought their books from either the general store or the house-to-house peddler, so that merchants had as much to do with determining which books children of the community used as did the schoolmaster or the school committee.[6] Shortly after the American Revolutionary War, a number of native American textbooks began to appear, chiefly because the war cut off the English supply and thus stimulated American authorship and because American patriots sought to create distinctively American texts for their schools.

---

[5] Ellwood P. Cubberley, *Public Education in the United States* (Boston: Houghton Mifflin, 1947), p. 44.

[6] *Textbooks in Education* (New York: The American Textbook Publishers Institute, 1949), pp. 28-29.

This Americanization of textbooks was encouraged by such statesmen as Benjamin Rush, who, in his *Thoughts upon the Mode of Education Proper in a Republic*, published in 1798, contended that:

1. Education should be indigenous to the United States, not a copy of any foreign country's system.
2. Education must inculcate national loyalty.
3. Amusements must educate for democracy.
4. Latin and Greek are not suited for American education.
5. Science should be substituted for Latin and Greek.
6. Education should make possible development of national resources.
7. Emphasis should be put on history to support nationalistic culture.
8. Schools should be supported liberally to attract good and well-trained teachers.[7]

Geography was the first social science to have an impact on the elementary curriculum. In 1795 the Reverend Jedediah Morse published his *Elements of Geography*, consisting of 144 pages of descriptive physical geography, two small maps, no illustrations, and some incidental mention of historical events.[8] In the same year Nathaniel Dwight issued a *Short but Comprehensive System of the Geography of the World*, and in 1821 William C. Woodbridge's *Rudiments of Geography* was published. The descriptive physical geography in each of these books was flavored with the new American consciousness. All went through several editions.

Prior to the decade from 1820 to 1830 the only attention that history received in the schools was in the form of incidental information pupils acquired as they learned to read English and Latin and as they studied geography.[9] Then the first history books began to appear. Davenport's *History of the United States* (1821) took its style from the earlier religious catechisms and cast its subject matter in the question-and-answer pattern, which was the most popular style of instruction at that time. Notable innovations were his inclusion of the Declaration of Independence, the federal Constitution, and a chronological history table, suggesting that the pattern of teaching history in the nineteenth century was chronological. The quick acceptance of American history as a proper school subject is attested by the fact that Samuel Goodrich's *A History of the United States* (1822) sold 150,000 copies within the first decade of its

---

[7] *Textbooks in Education*, p. 30.
[8] *Public Education*, p. 297.
[9] Rolla M. Tryon, *The Social Sciences as School Subjects* (New York: Charles Scribner's, 1935), p. 100. See also Cubberley, *Public Education*, p. 399.

publication.[10] Noah Webster's *History of the United States* (1832) introduced the study of the United States Constitution.

Since teachers of this period apparently closely followed the contents of these texts in their social-studies instruction, we can conclude that between colonial times and the early decades of the nineteenth century the pupils' social-studies experiences shifted from an almost exclusive concern with religious instruction to an equally strong emphasis on deeds of American heroes and incidents in the life of the new United States. Biographies, descriptions of wars, and partisan interpretations of political events became the subject matter for instruction in the new religion—Americanism.

However, it was the Civil War that gave the greatest impetus to the study of history as an independent subject. To reachieve the national political unity that had been so badly damaged by the war, many Northern cities added United States history as a required subject ". . . to emphasize American accomplishments, with the chief stress on the memorization of facts relating to our national heroes, wars, and political struggles."[11] The catechetical approach still persisted. The major goal was ". . . the development of patriotism and an enthusiasm for the Union."[12]

So it was that during the last third of the nineteenth century, history as a separate subject became firmly established in the last two grades of the elementary school. However, not until after 1900 was it generally found in the program of studies for the lower grades as well.[13]

The third social-science discipline to receive attention in the pre-progressive era was political science. For the most part, *civil government* (known today as *civics*) was studied only incidentally in geography or history classes, primarily in the form of questions about the Declaration of Independence and the Constitution. When offered as a separate course, civil government consisted of a structural study of local, state, and national governments. In the case of the latter, it meant a study of the three branches of government. The need to achieve national unity immediately after the Civil War caused educators to devote most of their civil-government instruction to the United States Constitution and the importance of the national government. After 1875, when fears that the Union would be split had been set somewhat at ease, civil-government classes began to treat broader issues as well.[14]

---

[10]Cubberley, *Public Education*, p. 399.

[11]Cubberley, *Public Education*, p. 399.

[12]Cubberley, *Public Education*, p. 399.

[13]*The Social Sciences*, pp. 131-132. See also I. James Quillen, "American History in the Upper Grades and Junior High School" in William H. Cartwright and Richard L. Watson, Jr., eds., *Interpreting and Teaching American History* (Washington, D. C.: National Council for the Social Studies 31st Yearbook, 1961), p. 345.

[14]Tryon, *The Social Sciences*, p. 275.

In summary, early colonial schools aimed to prepare children for membership in the church, so religious acculturation was the focus of the incidental social-studies instruction that children faced while learning to read and write. The American Revolutionary period introduced a secular religion—Americanism. Its adoption was urged by such statesmen as Abraham Lincoln, who, in a speech before the Young Men's Lyceum in Springfield, Illinois, on January 27, 1838, expressed this conviction:

> Let reverence for the laws, be breathed by every American mother, to the lisping babe that prattles on her lap—let it be taught in schools, in seminaries, and in colleges—let it be written in primers, spelling books, and in Almanacs;—let it be preached from the pulpit, proclaimed in legislative halls, and enforced in courts of justice. And, in short, let it become the *political religion* of the nation; and let the old and the young, the rich and the poor, the grave and the gay, of all sexes and tongues, and colors and conditions, sacrifice unceasingly upon its altars.

Finally, the Civil War made national unity of paramount importance because of the necessity for healing the country's wounds, and the elementary-school social-studies program was enlisted in the effort to achieve this unity.

We shall see in the following pages that the objective of Americanism as the principal aim of the social studies not only carried over into the twentieth century but also received increased emphasis whenever threats, either real or imagined, were felt within the nation.

The Progressive Era—1876-1957

The industrialization of America ushered in the progressive period. As Cremin has pointed out, progressive education ". . . began as part of a vast humanitarian effort to apply the promise of American life—the ideal of government by, of, and for the people—to the puzzling new urban-industrial civilization that came into being during the latter half of the nineteenth century."[15]

---

[15] Lawrence A. Cremin, *The Transformation of the School* (New York: Vintage Books, 1961), p. viii. Reprinted by permission of Alfred A. Knopf, Inc.

But how did progressive educators intend to improve people's lives? What did this humanitarian effort mean?

> First, it meant broadening the program and function of the school to include direct concern for health, vocation, and the quality of family and community life.
>
> Second, it meant applying in the classroom the pedagogical principles derived from new scientific research in psychology and the social sciences.
>
> Third, it meant tailoring instruction more and more to the different kinds and classes of children who were being brought within the purview of the school.
>
> Finally, Progressivism implied the radical faith that culture could be democratized without being vulgarized, the faith that everyone could share not only in the benefits of the new sciences but in the pursuit of the arts as well.[16]

In schools of the progressive era the social studies were expected to play an important part in turning these convictions into reality.

Curriculum development during the 80-year progressive period was marked by innovation and by debate between conservatives and several shades of progressives. For convenience of discussion, we can distinguish two general patterns of curricula that vied for dominance in the progressive era. One can be termed *multidisciplinary*, for it featured the teaching of social sciences as separate subjects. This was the pattern carried over from the nineteenth-century practice of teaching geography, history, and civil government as separate subjects from separate textbooks. During the progressive era several new departures for structuring multidisciplinary teaching were introduced. The second general pattern has been called *interdisciplinary*, for it attempted to integrate two or more of the social-science disciplines to form a single subject of classroom study. Throughout the period from 1876 to 1957 educators experimented with a variety of ways such integration or coordination might be accomplished.

In the following pages, rather than tracing social-studies developments in chronological sequence, we shall simply describe a number of the more striking proposals that arose and shall estimate the extent of their popularity.

Multidisciplinary Approaches

We noted that during the pre-progressive era history had a relatively late start, in comparison to geography, in influencing the curriculum. But

---

[16] Cremin, *The Transformation of the School,* pp. viii-ix.

during the progressive era history surged ahead to dominate the social-studies field. When legislatures prescribed courses of study in the social studies, American history was usually the subject of such prescriptions. The argument used to justify such emphasis was simply that the study of American history would make one a better citizen. In addition, in colleges the subject of history was far more prominent than such social sciences as anthropology or sociology, as there was much more material to write about in history than in the newer disciplines.

The curriculum experimentation within the multidisciplinary patterns focused mainly on which items of history and which ways of offering them to the learners would be most readily comprehended. We noted earlier that the dominant—probably the exclusive—way of organizing historical fare in the mid-nineteenth century had been to present events in their chronological sequence. The table of contents of a popular history text of the mid-1800s illustrates this pattern and points up the prominence accorded to military and political events. The volume is Charles A. Goodrich's *History of the United States*, 1857 edition:

> Period First, from the Discovery of America by Columbus, 1492, to the first permanent English settlement in America at Jamestown, Virginia, 1607.
> Period Second, from the settlement of Jamestown to the French and Indian Wars, 1756.
> Period Third, from the French and Indian Wars, 1756, to the commencement of the American Revolution, in the Battle of Lexington, 1775.
> Period Fourth, from the Battle of Lexington, 1775, to the Disbanding of the American Army at West Point, New York, 1783.
> Period Fifth, from the Disbanding of the Army, 1783, to the Inauguration of George Washington as President of the United States, under the Federal Constitution, 1789.
> Period Sixth, from the Inauguration of President Washington, 1789, to the Inauguration of John Adams, 1797.[17]

In like manner, each of the subsequent 10 chapters of Goodrich's text treated the term of a particular president. The final chapter ended with the inauguration of Franklin Pierce in 1853.

In the waning years of the nineteenth century, certain educators began to question the advisability of such a chronological approach to teaching history. However, in the 1890s the chronological method received strong backing from the American Herbartians. Their society was founded in 1892 by students who had returned from studying with the

---

[17]Tryon, *The Social Sciences*, pp. 432-433.

disciples of the German educational philosopher Johann F. Herbart (1776-1841) at Jena, Switzerland. The Herbartians quickly spread the idea through American teacher-training normal schools that the psychological and cultural development of children is enhanced by a chronological approach in teaching history. This culture-epoch theory held that the growing child relives intellectually the stages of development of cultures before his time, just as the unborn human fetus grows through stages that resemble the characteristics of organisms lower on the ladder of biological evolution. In effect, they believed, a chronological approach to history is the one that naturally fits the child's intellectual development.

But by 1910 other educators were seriously questioning the Herbartian rationale. These critics contended that:

1. Children from eight to thirteen years of age are unable to construct an orderly notion of temporal or logical relations.
2. The chronological approach assumes that the proper way to build up a knowledge of the past is through deduction rather than induction.
3. It is serviceable only to the trained historian as a structure about which to relate new information.
4. The recapitulation or culture epochs theory has no psychological basis in fact.[18]

These criticisms did not eliminate the chronological approach from the elementary social-studies curriculum, but they did open the way for alternative approaches to history, some of which were subsequently adopted in certain school systems in preference to the traditional design. Four of these proposals that eventually found their way into textbook patterns were (1) the reverse chronological approach, (2) the broadened-theme approach, (3) the biographical structure, and (4) the spiral or concentric-circles plan.

With the reverse chronological approach, instruction begins with a current event, and the class or textbook then moves backward in time to identify the causes behind the event. One argument in favor of this plan is that people are interested in present-day happenings, so learners' interest is more readily captured by beginning with familiar problems that concern them today rather than beginning with things remote in time and space. A strong advocate of this method of teaching history was the influential educational psychologist Edward L. Thorndike, who urged that history be made relevant to the pupils' experiences and interests.[19]

[18]Tryon, *The Social Sciences*, p. 436.
[19]Tryon, *The Social Sciences*, p. 446.

Some critics of the chronological approach did not wish to eliminate the basic structure. Rather, they suggested it place major emphasis on broader themes and topics. As a consequence of such emphasis, American history books would expand their concerns to include such matters as religion, literature, and commerce rather than focusing only on wars, politics, and personalities. Advocates of this plan often suggested that the teacher organize the materials himself and not depend on a single textbook. But the great breadth of topics available with such an approach was a challenge to the best prepared social-studies teachers and more than a challenge for the average ones. Consequently this wide-ranging intellectual-history approach was not adopted in nearly so many schools as its supporters would have liked.

Another alternative to chronological history was the biographical treatment. Grades 4 and 5 were deemed especially appropriate for this approach, since it was argued that 10- and 11-year-olds are natural hero worshippers, and if pupils would identify with the proper heroes, they would adopt proper ethics and become good citizens. The biographical structure was adopted with little question by national social-studies committees, textbook writers and publishers, and teachers. The typical biography furnished pupils a secure, romantic impression of history (mention of conflict and wrongdoing on the part of heroes was often washed out of such texts), and the biographical approach was not nearly so complex as several of the other curriculum patterns. It could be easily managed by authors and readily understood by readers.

The fourth alternative was the spiral, cycle, or concentric-circles plan. It was first advocated for the teaching of history and later was adopted for teaching other subjects. "In its practical application the idea means the teaching of the same body of material at different levels of instruction, adapting it, at each level, to the interests, capacities, and psychological development of those for whom it is intended."[20] Thus the American Revolution might be taught at grades 5, 8, and 11, with more complex factors and interpretations introduced at each higher grade level. We will see in our discussion of interdisciplinary curriculum designs that the spiral plan still has many advocates.

In the progressive era the subject of geography also underwent changes. The physical geography of the nineteenth century focused on descriptions of terrain, political boundaries, and the locations of cities and other concentrations of population. In the twentieth century, economic and cultural factors related to geography were emphasized. Ways of living in one region were compared with those of another. While some geography textbooks objectively described places and peoples, others offered fictionalized accounts of typical lives of children in diverse geographical

---

[20]Tryon, *The Social Sciences*, p. 447.

settings. The purpose of these tales was to encourage pupils to identify with the living patterns of agemates in other lands.

The subject of civil government became known as *civics* in the twentieth century, but it continued to be mainly a description of the structure of American government—national, state, and local. Although civics was a common subject in secondary schools, at the elementary level it was more often appended to history classes.

The progressive era, particularly after 1920, was marked by an expansion of methods and materials beyond the textbook. It is true that the text continued to serve as the core of history and geography study in most classrooms. However, teachers were urged, in their preservice education and through journals and curriculum workshops, to amplify textbook reading and recitation with a host of newer media and activities—bulletin-board displays, excursions, panel discussions, photographs and study prints, films, charts, slides, student-written reports, posters, murals, models of geographical sites and historical events, and student-made maps.

In concluding this discussion of multidisciplinary approaches during the progressive era, we can note that in most schools prior to World War I social studies centered chiefly around the study of history, featuring ". . . American Indians, holidays, and heroes in the primary grades; American history and its European origins in the middle grades; and American history, usually with some attention to American government, in the upper grades. Geography continued to have an importance in the middle and upper grades."[21]

Over the period between 1917 and 1957 the popularity of multidisciplinary patterns diminished markedly in the face of a great upsurge of interdisciplinary programs. However, many schools continued to offer history and geography as separate subjects, particularly in the upper elementary grades, with civics sometimes given as a separate subject for as long as a semester or a year. Textbooks continued to be the most accurate printed representations of what pupils were expected to learn in such programs.

Interdisciplinary Approaches

Many alternative structures for teaching social studies were proposed after World War I. These new departures were, in large measure, the result of educators' new convictions about the proper role of the elementary school in the child's life. John Dewey had been a philosophical guide for innovations in education for more than 20 years, stressing that ". . . the

---

[21]Wesley and Cartwright, *Interpreting and Teaching*, p. 17.

child is inherently an active being with impulses to communicate with others, to construct things, to investigate, and to create. These impulses should be recognized in the school, and opportunity given to the child to develop these impulses by engaging in such activities as language, manual and household arts, nature study, dramatics, art, and music. Hence, the origin of the 'activities' program."[22] The child was now seen as an active being seeking to understand the immediate world and to solve the problems met in his everyday life, not simply an empty vessel attending school in order to be filled up with historical, geographical, arithmetical, and scientific facts. Dewey and his followers saw education as problem solving, as the process of living a contemporary life, not simply a preparation for leading an adult life in the future. And since life's problems are not categorized into such subject-matter divisions as history, geography, art, health education, and mathematics, it seemed reasonable that school studies focusing on realistic problem solving should not be bound within subject-matter barriers. From such a line of thought as this, the interdisciplinary movement entitled *social studies* grew. As noted earlier, the National Education Association's social learnings section of the Commission on the Reorganization of Secondary Education (1916) was instrumental in legitimizing the term *social studies* as a replacement for the separate subjects of history, geography, and civics. The act of adopting this term demonstrated their conviction that a new interdisciplinary structure was needed.

The project approach to elementary social studies first achieved popularity in the 1920s. The method apparently originated in the teaching of agriculture. Rather than simply reading about agriculture, children faced the tasks of growing crops, canning fruit, raising farm animals, and the like. They learned facts and theories as needed to solve the problems met in carrying out the project. Soon the approach spread to other fields. In time, the term *activity curriculum* was substituted for *project* in many schools.

The growth of the activity approach was accompanied by the development of the *teaching unit* as an organizing device. The unit plan—a series of related daily activities or lesson plans—was devised to achieve a cluster of goals that could not be achieved during a single class period. In fact, a unit plan could extend over a period of several days, weeks, or months. The following terms came to be used interchangeably: unit of study, unit of work, experience unit, activity unit, and project.

The widespread growth of these interdisciplinary departures after 1920 was achieved, to a great extent, because the centers of power in

---

[22]R. Freeman Butts and Lawrence A. Cremin, *A History of Education in American Culture* (New York: Henry Holt, 1953), p. 345.

determining social-studies curricula had shifted. The advocates of history, who had dominated influential national commissions and had done most of the writing of textbooks, no longer wielded the influence they had enjoyed earlier. Leadership in curriculum revision decentralized so that curriculum plans were devised at state and local levels. A new set of specialists in *social studies* and in *curriculum* emerged to replace the historians and geographers. The new leaders were professors of education, curriculum directors in state departments of education and local school systems, and consultants and supervisors representing teacher-education institutions and the public schools.[23]

The new conception of interdisciplinary social studies placed far more responsibility for planning on the classroom teacher than had the textbook approach to history or geography. The guidelines for the teacher were typically in the form of a *resource unit*, meaning a series of general suggestions for goals and activities from which the teacher would select ones most suitable to his own situation. It was then his task to organize these activities into a coherent program of study for the class. Figure 1-1 illustrates the form in which a third-grade resource unit on boats was cast. It originated at Teachers College, Columbia University, the institution in which John Dewey spent his latter years and which was regarded as the mecca for the development of the new social studies of the 1920s and 1930s.

Besides the attempt to merge subject-matter disciplines, another strong influence, beginning in the middle of the progressive period, was a concern for suiting learning experiences to children's "natural" interests and their evolving levels of comprehension. With this goal in mind, curriculum developers structured elementary social studies on a pattern of social circles expanding outward from the child himself. Consequently, social learnings at the lower primary level focused on the child's most intimate environments—his home and his classroom. As he moved into the middle and upper grades, the scope broadened to the neighborhood, community, state, nation, hemisphere, and world. In addition to this spatial expansion, programs moved from the present to the past so that the child might compare his own society with those of other times.

State and district curriculum guidebooks were developed to direct teachers in developing units according to the expanding-environments design, and various publishers issued textbooks to match the plan. One of the most influential versions of this pattern was first devised by Paul R. Hanna at Teachers College, Columbia University, and was subsequently refined and updated throughout his years at Stanford University. Hanna's framework served as the basis for the Scott-Foresman social-studies

---

[23]Wesley and Cartwright, *Interpreting and Teaching*, p. 17.

textbook series, which continues to be one of the most popular today. Because of the significant role this pattern has played, we have dedicated Chapter 3 to an exposition of Hanna's expanding-environments design.

In summary, over more than three decades after World War I, the interdisciplinary departures from the earlier history-geography-civics tradition dominated elementary social-studies curricula. The period was marked by ". . . remarkable harmony among social studies curriculum theorists, teachers, supervisors of instruction, and publishers of text-books."[24] But the harmony was not to last.

The Post-Progressive Era: From 1957

On October 4, 1957, the Soviet Union launched the world's first man-made satellite, Sputnik I, much to the dismay of most Americans. In fear of being out-distanced technologically and culturally by the Russians, the United States government turned to its schools to find out what had apparently gone wrong with the nation's scientific progress and to learn how matters could be righted. The most immediate concern was with the "space race" and the physical science and technology on which it depended. But soon this attention to improving curricula had spread to the social sciences. The sense of urgency precipitated by Sputnik, combined with a growing concern among individual social scientists about social studies in the public schools, turned the 1960s into a decade of ferment for social-studies curriculum builders.

Two key concepts at the core of this ferment were those of *the structure of social-science disciplines* and *social-science inquiry*.

The term *structure*, in curriculum development in the 1960s, gained its widest popularity as a result of the writings of Jerome Bruner, professor of psychology at Harvard University. In his book *The Process of Education*, Bruner wrote that ". . . there is no reason to believe that any subject cannot be taught to any child at virtually any age in some form."[25] He further observed that "The task of teaching a subject to a child . . . is one of representing the structure of that subject in terms of the child's way of viewing things."[26]

---

[24]Paul R. Hanna and John R. Lee, "Generalizations from the Social Sciences," in John U. Michaelis, ed., *Social Studies in Elementary Schools* (Washington, D.C.: National Council for the Social Studies 32nd Yearbook, 1952), p. 70.
[25]Jerome S. Bruner, *The Process of Education* (Cambridge, Mass.: Harvard University Press), 1961, p. 47.
[26]Bruner, *The Process of Education*, p. 33.

A Unit of Study Related to BOATS Third Grade		Subject Matter Content Which Helped Solve the Problems

	Problems-Questions	Industrial Arts

Industrial Arts
   Construction of boats: Making pattern, shaping hull, making sail, making keel, casting weight for keel, making rack for boat, and testing boat.
   How boats developed from early times to the present day.
   The difficulty involved in building a toy boat so it will balance in water.
   Different kinds of sail boats.
   The need for a keel on a boat.
   Different methods of propelling a boat.
   Modern inventions in connection with the propulsion of boats.
   What makes boats float.
   Different uses of boats today.

History
   The Half-Moon directed interest to Hendrick Hudson and his ship.
   Historic ships: Santa Maria, Mayflower.
   Reference work, reading and discussions about:
      Vikings: What color and kinds of clothing did they wear? What did they eat? What kind of houses did they have? What were their boats like? Did Vikings have stores? How did Viking writing look? Story of Lief Ericson. The gods of the Vikings. Their beliefs.
      Phoenicians: Scenery, boats, people, trade, beliefs, clothing, cities, industries, etc.
      Egyptians: Scenery, country, boats, beliefs, tools, writing, etc. Story of the building of Solomon's Temple.
      Early Mediterranean peoples.

Geography
   Pictures of boat from newspaper which interested children in world geography.
   Geography related to countries studied.
      Norway: Country, climate, people and occupations.
      Phoenicia: Country, climate, people, trading routes, daily life of early people compared with that of today.
      Egypt: Country, climate, trading, etc.
   Map interest: Norway, showing ancient home of the Vikings.
      The Mediterranean countries, showing cities of Phoenicia and routes on which the King of Tyre sent materials for Solomon's Temple.
   Plasticene map of Mediterranean Sea and surrounding countries on which children sailed card-board models of early boats.
   Globe in frequent use to locate places mentioned.
   Outline world map, locating countries.
   Interest in determining distances (reading scales on map).
   How far is it from Norway to Phoenicia?
   How far is it from Norway to America?
   Building Lower Manhattan on floor with blocks to exhibit boats.
   Map was drawn on floor; buildings in New York City that helped most with sea travel.

Arithmetic
   Measuring for boat patterns and measurements in boat making.
   Figuring the number of board feet used by class in building boat racks.
   Arithmetic problems in connection with science experiment of water displacement and floating objects.
   What is a gram?
   What is a cubit?
   Dimensions of Solomon's Temple compared with dimensions of the Lincoln School.
   Children saw a cubit measure at the Museum.

Fine Arts
   Sketching and painting pictures of Half-Moon.
   Sketching and painting boat models.
   Drawing blackboard frieze showing history of boats.
   Ten easel pictures showing story of Lief Ericson.
   Cut paper pictures of boats.
   Painting Egyptian boats seen at Museum.
   Painting Viking pictures showing clothing.
   Painting modern boats.
   Making clay tablet.

Composition-Literature
   Stories written about the trip to see Half-Moon.
   Stories of other trips by individual children.
   Original poems about boats and the sea.
   Labels and invitations for boat exhibit.
   Written and oral reports about boats, Vikings, Phoenicia and Egypt.
   Stories for bulletin, room paper, council news, or absent class members, telling of class interest and study.

Reading
   Reference material pertaining to topics under discussion, found in school library or at home.
   Children's reading material: Lief and Thorkle, Viking Stories, Early sea people, Boat Book prepared by other Third Grade, material prepared by student teachers.

Science
   How can we tell if our boats will float and balance? Try out in delta table.
   Three experiments: Why do some objects float and why do some sink?
   How do people know how much to put into boat before it will sink?

Dramatization
   Play-Story of Lief Ericson, spontaneously prepared by class.

Music
   Old Gaelic Lullaby. Volga Boat Song. Sail Bonnie Boat.

Stimulation

In the spring of last year many of the boys of this group were interested in trains and other means of travel.

Many summer experiences with boats.

Wood in supply box cut in shapes suggestive of boats.

Bulletin prepared by the teacher.

Trip to see Half-Moon.

Trip to see boat models.

Problems-Questions

To construct boats that will look like a certain kind and with which children can play.

How do boats "go"?

Who first thought of making a sailboat?

How did people get the idea for different shapes for boats?

To know more about the people who traveled on the seas in early times.

To find out about the making of boats.

How many different kinds of boats do we have today and how is each kind used?

How did early people use their ships?

To find out about the different parts of a boat.

How do people know how much to put into a boat before it will sink?

FIGURE 1-1   An Interdisciplinary Resource Unit*

*Otis W. Caldwell, "The Lincoln Experimental School," The Foundations and Techniques of Curriculum—Construction, edited by Guy Montrose Whipple (Bloomington, Ill.: Public School Publishing Co., 1926), Vol. I, 26th Yearbook of the National Society for the Study of Education, pp. 281-282.

Probable Outcomes

Desirable Habits and Skills
- Better skill in sketching.
- Better skill in handling brush and paints.
- A beginning of the development of how to sew.
- Developing the habit of making a pattern before constructing an article.
- Developing skill in shaping wood by means of plane and spokeshave.
- Developing skill in using gouge and mallet.
- Developing skill in reading distances on map.
- Rapid growth in map drawing.
- Developing habit of reading the newspaper.
- Better skill in measuring.
- Ability to gather information on a certain subject and report to class.
- Increased ability in writing.

Attitudes and Appreciations

Economic:
- An appreciation of the use of weights and measures.
- What it means to construct a real boat that will float and balance properly.
- Appreciation of the change in the lives of the people caused by the discovery of iron and the use of sails.
- Appreciation of paper as a writing material.
- Appreciation of the modern inventions in connection with the propulsion of ships.

Social:
- What the early people contributed to the world.
- The number of people and industry it takes to supply materials for the construction of one building.
- Comparison of the ideas of fairness of the early people with the present day.

Recreational:
- Developing a joy in painting, sketching and drawing.
- Growing interest in reading books about historical peoples, inventions or boats.
- Playing with boats made.
- Interest in the construction of a toy boat.
- Interest in the construction of a real boat.
- The pleasure in making maps.
- The pleasure of playing with maps.

Aesthetic:
- Appreciation of the beauty in line and construction of boats.
- The adventure of the ship.

Information
- Knowledge of the development of the boat from raft to steamship.
- Who Hendrick Hudson was.
- General idea of historic ships.
- An interesting acquaintance with Vikings, Phoenicians, and Egyptians.
- General geographical knowledge of the world.
- What a cubit measure is.
- Knowledge of how to draw maps.
- Some idea of what makes objects float.
- Some idea of how to make boats balance in water.
- Some idea of how to construct a toy boat.
- How the early people made their clay tablets.
- How to make a clay tablet.
- The need for molds in casting metals.
- Some idea of how iron is made into different shapes.

Total Personality as Modified by the Foregoing Experiences

New Interests Leading Toward Further Activities

Interest in world geography and travel.

Maps and actual distances between given places.

The time it takes to get to certain places.

Interest in silk through answering the questions:

What kind of clothing did the Vikings wear?

How is velvet made?

Interest in what clay is: How it is prepared for our use and how it was prepared by early people for making clay tablets.

Interest in the Egyptian and Phoenician alphabet and how our alphabet was developed from it.

The materials the Egyptians used for writing.

Interest in metals.

Interest in weight of different metals through casting of lead for keels.

How metals are shaped.

Interest in the construction of modern buildings through reading about Solomon's Temple and comparing it with the construction of the Lincoln School.

Interest in other phases of transportation.

FIGURE 1-1   Continued

By *structure* Bruner meant that different academic disciplines are founded on particular ideas about the ways things are related to each other. For example, to illustrate the structural characteristics of mathematics, he explained that:

> Algebra is a way of arranging knowns and unknowns in equations so that the unknowns are made knowable. The three fundamentals involved in working with these equations are commutation, distribution, and association. Once a student grasps the ideas embodied by these three fundamentals, he is in a position to recognize wherein "new" equations to be solved are not new at all, but new variants on a familiar theme. Whether the student knows the formal names of these operations is less important for transfer than whether he is able to use them.[27]

Just as mathematics has structures that show how things are related, so have the social sciences—sociology, anthropology, economics, social psychology, and political science. And just as a "new mathematics" curriculum had been built around the structures of the discipline, so might a new social studies. Bruner's approach implied two steps in planning: "(1) the definition and description of the basic structure of a discipline by scholars in the field and (2) the formulation of tasks for the student which will lead him to discover (perhaps rediscover is a better term) and use this structure."[28] This second step implied that the pupil would not simply memorize structures but would be expected to seek them out for himself through the use of *inquiry* techniques, including techniques from the social-science disciplines about which he has been learning.

The ideas expounded by Bruner and other social scientists and educators might have exerted little influence on curriculum development had not the federal and state governments, along with private foundations and associations, furnished large sums of money for developing improved teaching materials. Publishers, interested in the new markets for textbooks that new departures in the social studies would open up, also contributed. The most influential effort, launched by the U.S. Office of Education in 1962, was Project Social Studies, which not only directly supported the development of materials at universities but indirectly stimulated innovation among private, state, and local agencies.

Two effects of this movement are particularly worth noting. First, the emphasis on structure of disciplines and on inquiry techniques forced a shift in the type of personnel concerned with curriculum revision. The

[27]Bruner, *The Process of Education*, pp. 7-8.
[28]Donald W. Oliver and James P. Shaver, *Teaching Public Issues in High School* (Boston: Houghton Mifflin, 1966), p. 229.

need to have subject-matter scholars identify the structure of their disciplines and their methods of inquiry legitimized the appointment of university social scientists to curriculum-development projects. It is true that educationists (professors of education, curriculum supervisors from school systems) were still active, but the proportion of their representation on curriculum committees was far smaller than it had been during the progressive era. As in the past, historians and geographers participated in textbook writing and the supervision of such writing. But now they were joined by scientists representing anthropology, economics, political science, social psychology, and sociology.

Second, the efforts to incorporate structure and inquiry into social-studies programs forced school systems and state departments of education to consider anew the basic purposes of elementary social studies. Those who had long advocated the teaching of American history and civics in order to promote good citizenship wondered whether a shift to inquiry and social-science structures was really wise. Would it not be best to have children develop a basic love for country and a loyalty to their nation's past before they start inquiring and questioning? Does not an inquiry attitude encourage doubt and social division rather than national unity? In response, some defenders of the social-science-structures approach said that learning social-science inquiry and learning to be a good citizen are two different matters having little or no connection. Social-science inquiry is an objective, intellectual pursuit like the techniques of mathematics and the physical sciences. It has nothing to do with a person's individual values and his loyalties to a state or nation. These people would have structures and inquiry represent the social-science study in schools, while training for loyal citizenship would be carried out by means of entirely different activities. Other defenders of the structures-and-inquiry approach believed that these very skills are the best route to good citizenship. In their view, the best citizen is one who can make accurate analyses of social phenomena and, on the basis of these analyses, act in wise ways. In some cases the citizen's analysis will cause him to support the status quo—that is, to conserve existing laws and systems of social intercourse. In other cases his analysis will cause him to support changes in present institutions and attitudes.

This debate continues today. The form of elementary social-studies programs in any community in the next decade or two will apparently be determined to a considerable extent by which forces in the community subscribe to which of the foregoing positions regarding good citizenship.

While advocates of structures and inquiry have been at work during the past decade or so, another segment of the educational community has also been operating to reinstate scholarly disciplines in the schools, but for rather different reasons. The purpose of these people has been to oust the "life adjustment" social studies of the progressive era in order to return to a multidisciplinary program rooted in the nineteenth-century history-geography-civics tradition. A florid spokesman for the return to the study of history has been Max Rafferty, superintendent of public instruction for California in the 1960's and 1970. In his book *Suffer, Little Children* he charged that:

> Ulysses and Penelope have been replaced by Dick and Jane in the textbooks of our schools. The quest for the Golden Fleece has been crowded out by the visit of Tom and Susan to the zoo. The deeds of the heroes before Troy are now passé, and the peregrinations of the local milkman as he wends his way through the stodgy streets and littered alleys of Blah City are deemed worthy of numberless pages in our primers. The sterile, stone-age culture of the Pueblo Indians looms large in our curriculum but the knightly Crusaders are ignored. . . . It is interesting . . . that modern education has deliberately debunked the hero to make room for the jerk.[29]

In his official capacity as the highest public-school official in California, Rafferty was able to alter the labeling of the state's curriculum offerings in the area of social phenomena. What had been known during the progressive era and into the late 1960s as social studies was changed back to history and geography. Rafferty's desire has been to provide heroes for today's children to emulate, models from the past on which to fashion future behavior. He has written that:

> "Education's first duty is to make possible the survival of our country. . . . A race of faceless, godless peasants from the steppes of Asia strives to reach across our bodies for the prize of world dominion. They are armed with all the sinister science which a psychopathic society can produce. To defeat their purpose will require more than our present brain power and our transient will. It will demand the massed wisdom and understanding of the great minds that have gone before us."[30]

Conclusion

We have now arrived at the end of our brief look at the evolution of elementary social-studies curricula in the United States from colonial days

---

[29]Max Rafferty, *Suffer, Little Children* (New York: The New American Library of World Literature, 1963), pp. 27-28. Copyright 1962 by The Devin-Adair Company. Reprinted by permission of the publisher.
[30]Rafferty, *Suffer, Little Children*, pp. ix–x.

to the present. With such an historical background in mind, we may find it easier to understand the foundations of the diverse curriculum patterns that are analyzed throughout the rest of this volume.

As a finale for the chapter, we close with a list of three dozen social-studies curriculum projects that have played a prominent part in education of the post-progressive era. The list is intended to serve two purposes. First, it illustrates the diversity of ideas and approaches that have emerged during the past decade or so. Second, it furnishes the names and addresses of project offices and of publishers so that you can obtain the curriculum materials for firsthand inspection.

Elementary Social Studies
Curriculum Projects of the Post-Progressive Era[31]

American Education Publications, Education Center, Columbus, Ohio 43216. Publisher of Harvard Project materials.

Anderson, Wallace. Intercultural Studies, University of Northern Iowa, Cedar Falls, Iowa 50613.

Arnoff, Melvin. The Development of First Grade Materials on "Families of Japan," 405 Education Building, Kent State University, Kent, Ohio 44201.

Bailey, Wilfred, and Marion J. Rice. Development of a Sequential Curriculum in Anthropology for Grades, College of Education and Department of Sociology and Anthropology, University of Georgia, Athens, Georgia 30601.

Becker, James M. International Affairs Education Center, Foreign Policy Association, 345 E. 46th St., New York, New York 10017 (Foreign Policy Association).

Berlak, Harold, and Timothy R. Tomlinson. Development of Elementary School Social Science Curriculum, Metropolitan St. Louis, Social Studies Center, Washington University, 303 MacMillan Hall, St. Louis, Missouri 63130.

Boston Children's Museum Social Studies Project. Materials available from Boston Children's Museum and American Science and Engineering, 20 Overland Street, Boston, Massachusetts 00215.

[31]This listing is the present writers' revision of an original compilation of projects by John U. Michaelis, subsequently updated by Frederick R. Smith and C. Benjamin Cox in *New Strategies and Curriculum in Social Studies* (Chicago: Rand McNally, 1969, pp. 181-186).

Brown, George I. University of California, Santa Barbara, Santa Barbara, Calif. 93106.

Brubaker, Dale L., and James B. Macdonald. University of North Carolina, Greensboro—University of Wisconsin, Milwaukee Social Studies Project, School of Education, Greensboro, North Carolina 27412.

Cawein, Paul E. Harvard-Newton Project in Business History and Economic Concepts, Newton Public Schools, Newton, Massachusetts 02159.

Collier, Malcom C. Anthropology Curriculum Study Project, 5632 S. Kimbark Av., Chicago, Illinois 60637.

Division of Education of the Bureau of Indian Affairs (Navajo Area) and College of Education at the University of New Mexico. University of New Mexico Project on the Social Studies in Navajo Indian Education, Albuquerque, New Mexico 87106.

Educational Research Council of Greater Cleveland. Materials available from Allyn and Bacon, Inc., 150 Tremont St., Boston, Massachusetts 02111.

Elementary School Economics Project. University of Chicago Industrial Relations Center, 1225 E. 60th St., Chicago, Illinois 60637.

Fox, Robert S., and Ronald Lippitt. Michigan Social Science Education Project, Center for Research on Utilization of Scientific Knowledge, University of Michigan, Ann Arbor, Michigan 48107.

Gibson, John S. The Development of Instructional Materials Dealing with Racial and Cultural Diversity in American Life, Lincoln-Filene Center for Citizenship and Public Affairs, Tufts College, Medford, Massachusetts 02155 (Ideology and World Affairs: Resource Unit). Boston: Houghton Mifflin, 1965.

Gill, Clark C. and William B. Conroy. Development of Guidelines and Resource Materials on Latin America, 403 Sutton Hall, University of Texas, Austin, Texas 78912.

Glens Falls City School District, 15 Quade St., Glens Falls, New York 12801.

Hennebry, Howard M., and K. L. Diem. Conservation Education Improvement Project, College of Education, University of Wyoming, Laramie, Wyoming 82070.

Lee, John. New Approaches to and Materials for a Sequential Curriculum on American Society, Social Studies Curriculum Study Center, Northwestern University, 1809 Chicago Av., Evanston, Illinois 60201.

Long, Harold M. Improving Teaching of World Affairs, Glens Falls Public Schools, Glens Falls, New York 12801 (National Council for the Social Studies) (Improving Teaching of World Affairs available from Council).

Maher, John E. Developmental Economic Education Program, Joint Council on Economic Education, 1212 Avenue of the Americas, New York, New York 10036.

Morison, Elting E. A Program of Curriculum Development in the Social Studies and Humanities, Educational Development Center, 15 Mifflin Place, Cambridge, Massachusetts 02138.

Morrissett, Irving. Social Science Education Consortium, Inc., 1424 N. 15th St., Boulder, Colorado 80304.

Rader, William D. Elementary School Economics Program, Industrial Relations Center, University of Chicago, 1225 E. 60th St., Chicago, Illinois 60637.

Rittschof, L. W. Wisconsin State Council on Economic Education, 517 Bolton Hall, University of Wisconsin-Milwaukee, Milwaukee, Wisconsin 53201.

Sanders, Norris M. Cooperative Curriculum Development Center, 1402 Manila St., Manitowoc, Wisconsin 54220.

Senesh, Lawrence. Elkhart, Indiana, Experiment in Economic Education Department of Economics, Purdue University, Lafayette, Indiana 47907 (The University, Elkhart Schools, and Carnegie) (Materials available from Science Research Associates).

Shaplin, Judson T. Development of a Model for the St. Louis Metropolitan Social Studies Center, Graduate Institute of Education, Washington University, St. Louis, Missouri 63130.

Toy, Henry Jr. Civic Education Project, American Heritage Foundation, 11 W. 42nd St., New York, New York 10036.

University of Chicago Industrial Relations Center, 1225 E. 60th St., Chicago, Illinois 60637.

Vadnais, Lawrence, and Gregory R. Annig. A Cultural Approach to the Study of History in Grades Seven and Eight, Mt. Greylock Regional High School, Green River Road, Williamstown, Massachusetts 02167.

Wallen, Norman. Development of a Comprehensive Curriculum Model for Social Studies, Grades, Including Procedures for Implementation, San Francisco State College, 1600 Holloway Ave., San Francisco, California 94132.

West, Edith. Preparation and Evaluation of Social Studies Curriculum Guides and Materials for Grades, College of Education, University of Minneapolis, Minneapolis, Minnesota 55455.

Wisconsin Education Association International Relations Committee, 119 Menoma Ave., Madison, Wisconsin 53700.

Zangrando, Robert L. Service Center for Teachers of History, American Historical Association, 400 A. Street, S.E., Washington, D.C. 20003 (Pamphlet series on various topics—62 in number).

2

Criteria for Comparing Programs

As indicated earlier, the purpose of this book is to describe a variety of curriculum patterns so that readers might better select or devise social-studies programs well suited to their own classrooms or school systems. To achieve this purpose, we have prepared six clusters of questions that we believe teachers and administrators should ask when analyzing curriculum proposals. These questions have determined the kinds of information we have included in the following chapters.

In Chapter 2 we describe the guide questions and explain why we consider each one important. We have labeled the six clusters: (1) value orientation, (2) scope and sequence, (3) methods and materials, (4) characteristics of learners and teachers, (5) evaluation procedures, and (6) conditions conducive to the adoption of a pattern. The examples cited throughout the chapter have been drawn from programs described in this book as well as from other sources.

Value Orientation

The first thing we would like to know about any curriculum proposal is what convictions or values it is supposed to promote. We can seek this information by posing two questions, one positive and the other negative.

First, *what values or beliefs does the plan feature or highlight?* Usually we can find the answer to this question within the rationale the authors of the program have written to introduce their plan. For example, the Franklin Social Sciences Program entitled *What Is Man?* and written by Lenz, Moss, and Hughes states in its opening pages that:

> The primary emphasis is on developing the skills of research necessary to investigate and understand the significant concepts of the social science disciplines including history, geography, political science, economics, anthropology, sociology, and social psychology.[1]

In contrast, the confluent-education proposal espoused by George I. Brown and his co-workers (described at length in Chapter 9) states:

> A goal we were striving for in our work was to help students become both *more free* and *more responsible.* We believed this could be done by increasing the student's sense of his own power to take responsibility for his behavior. Further, by providing experiences that made available ways to become free, followed by the actual experience of increasing freedom, we could help the student attain the personal satisfaction that is unique to feeling free. It was crucial that the two qualities, freedom and responsibility, be thought of as existing in an indivisible relationship.[2]

The second question is cast in a negative form, since what a new curriculum proposal stands for is sometimes reflected in what it is trying to replace in the schools. So the question becomes *what values or practices is the new plan a reaction against?* Again, we can usually find this information in the rationale with which the author prefaces his scheme. For instance, in explaining the background of the Harvard Social Studies Project, from which their jurisprudential approach to social problems developed (see Chapter 8), James P. Shaver and Donald W. Oliver wrote:

> Often social studies curricula provide the students no conceptual model for handling the important issues facing society.... Even when some such

---

[1] Margaret Johnstone Lenz, Penrod Moss, and Vivian M. Hughes, *What Is Man?: Problems for Research and Findings from Research* (Newport Beach, Calif.: Franklin Publications, 1969), Teachers Guide, Level C, p. 6. The Franklin Social Studies Program is not reviewed in detail in this volume since its general characteristics are in many ways similar to the plan described in Chapter 6.

[2] George Isaac Brown, *Human Teaching for Human Learning: An Introduction to Confluent Education* (New York: Viking, 1971), p. 228.

conceptual framework is part of the curriculum, the schemes of reflective thinking available to teachers . . . are based almost exclusively on scientific method . . . and/or propaganda analysis. . . . But neither is concerned directly with the value conflicts—such as that between equality and property rights in the current racial segregation controversy—which are at the heart of political controversy. . . .

Other factors adding impetus to . . . the Project . . . were the commonly reported dissatisfaction of students with social studies courses and the lack of observable effects on citizenship behavior of the present curriculum.[3]

Likewise, what is ostensibly wrong with present practices is the focus of an introductory statement for the Greater Cleveland Social Sciences Program. The statement is written by its director, Raymond English:

In teaching mathematics, we take it for granted that the student has acquired and is continuing to acquire a steadily growing body of knowledge. This assumption has never been made in the social sciences. Instead, courses are repetitious; the Pilgrims land each Thanksgiving; the Indians say "Ugh!" and "How!" in a pointless series of time-filling activities; false, sentimental versions of historical episodes are taught in early grades and then corrected in later grades. After such exposures, it is not surprising that students begin by despising social science and later make fools of themselves in social and political controversies.[4]

Thus we learn something of the values or beliefs a new social-studies plan is intended to emphasize either through what authors say their program stands for or through what it is a reaction against. Often, however, these introductory philosophical comments by program builders are of only limited aid in answering our queries because the terminology in which the writers have couched their remarks is subject to varied interpretations. For example, what is the nature of the *freedom* and *responsibility* that Brown mentions in his confluent-education approach? What kinds of *citizenship behavior* do Shaver and Oliver intend to influence? To answer these questions, it is necessary to inspect more precise descriptions of the curriculum designs. It is helpful to see lesson plans that are intended to carry these ideas into practice. It is even better to see the program in action in the classroom. When you observe the interaction of teacher and pupils and analyze their activities, you obtain a kind of operational definition of key concepts. (To furnish this kind of information about the

---

[3] James P. Shaver and Donald W. Oliver, "Teaching Students to Analyze Public Controversy: A Curriculum Project Report," *Social Education*, 28, No. 4 (April 1964), 191-194, 248.

[4] Raymond English, "Cleveland Says Good-by to Hit-or-Miss Methods," *Grade Teacher*, 84, No. 2 (October 1966), 116.

curriculum designs described in this volume, we have included in each chapter illustrative lesson plans or transcripts of classroom interaction between teacher and pupils.)

In summary, when we inspect a curriculum proposal, an initial factor we wish to investigate is the set of values or convictions the program features, so that we can estimate how well these values match our own.

Scope and Sequence

The second group of questions we pose relate (1) to the diversity of goals encompassed by the plan, called the *scope,* and (2) to the order in which pupils are expected to pursue the goals, called the *sequence*.

The Scope of the Plan

The most complete identification of the scope of a curriculum would involve detailing all the skills and items of information children are to face in the program. But listing these details in random order would prove confusing. The more practical approach is to identify an overall framework underlying the organization of the plan. From the vantage point of this framework, we can comprehend the scope and can then study the details as deeply as we choose. Our three purposes in analyzing the scope of a program are (1) to determine the curriculum builder's scheme for organizing the skills and information to be taught, (2) to understand the range of skills and knowledge encompassed by the scheme, and (3) to estimate how well the scheme and range match our own idea of what constitutes an effective elementary social-studies program. These three purposes direct us to the questions we shall ask about the scope of any curriculum proposal.

First, *what is the structure that determines which skills and knowledge the program is to include?* In most cases the authors of the plan explain their framework clearly. In other cases it is necessary for us to ferret out the organizational scheme ourselves.

When the curriculum plan takes the form of a textbook for pupils, the framework is typically reflected in the table of contents, sometimes augmented by introductory remarks in the preface. For example, a fourth-grade text entitled *Learning to Look at Our World* (Silver

Burdett Company)[5] is the first of a series of three for the inter-mediate grades. The preface states that the book involves a ". . . skillful blend of geography, history, economics, civics, sociology, and anthro-pology. . . ."[6] The volume introduces ". . . the pupil to the world setting in which his social education will take place, to the variety of peoples and ways of living that exist, and to the ideas of time, change, and sequence of events that he will need as his education progresses. In so doing, it develops skills in using maps, pictures, and other tools of the social studies."[7]

The impression derived from these prefatory remarks is that *Learning to Look at Our World* defines its scope from the viewpoint of geography. This impression is substantiated by an inspection of the table of contents, which lists 14 chapters, each centered on a geographical region or nation. At the end of each chapter is an "inter-unit" consisting of "pictures, maps, and test" which "aid in filling out the world picture and developing further the map- and picture-reading skills."[8] The table of contents is as follows:

This Is the Earth
1. LIVING IN THE UNITED STATES
    Dairy Farms and Fields of Wheat
    Living on a Ranch
    Growing Crops without Rain
    Living in Forest Lands
    Other Ways of Living
    Living in the City
    A Day in Winter
    Directions and Continents
2. LANDS OF THE MIDNIGHT SUN
    Alaska Has Changed
    The New Alaska
    The Arctic and the North Pole
    The Pacific Ocean
3. THE HAWAIIAN ISLANDS
    In Old Hawaii
    Today in Oahu
    South across the Equator

---

[5] From *Learning to Look at Our World*, by Kenneth S. Cooper, Clarence W. Sorensen, and Lewis Paul Todd. © 1969 by General Learning Corporation. Reprinted by permission of Silver Burdett Company.

[6] Cooper, Sorensen, and Todd, p. v.

[7] Cooper, Sorensen, and Todd, p. v.

[8] Cooper, Sorensen, and Todd, p. v.

12. WORKSHOPS IN BRITAIN
     Changing Ways of Working
     Giant Workshops Today
     The Atlantic Ocean
13. LIMA AND THE ANDES
     Rivers and the Desert
     The City of Lima
     A Highway for All America
     Land between Two Continents
14. WASHINGTON AND THE WORLD
     A Day in Washington
     How Ways of Living Changed
     Our Country and the World
     Maps of the World[9]

To discover the ways anthropological, sociological, and economic concepts are used in the program, it is necessary to inspect the book's reading material. Such inspection also reveals the specific scope of the map-interpretation concepts and skills that are included.

In sum, the scope of curriculum patterns that are in textbook form is discovered by analyzing the preface (or sometimes the introductory section of the accompanying teacher's manual), the table of contents, and—for the details of the scope—the reading matter itself.

Other curriculum patterns however, are not cast in the form of a textbook series. Instead, they are designs that use texts as only part of the materials for pursuing the goals. To learn the intended scope of such programs, it is usually best to analyze the documents that explain the basic rationale of the curriculum design. The documents may be a statewide or county curriculum guidebook or the booklet that describes the work of a particular curriculum-development project like those listed at the end of Chapter 1. To illustrate how such a document can reveal the scope of a plan, we shall turn to the proposed *Social Sciences Education Framework for California Public Schools* (kindergarten and Grades 1 through 12).[10] Analyzing this publication shows that the scope is more complex than that of the typical history, geography, civics, or expanding-environment program of the past, since it involves a greater diversity of intermeshed dimensions. The following excerpts from the framework may illustrate this point.

---

[9] Cooper, Sorenson, and Todd, pp. vi-viii.
[10] *Social Sciences Education Framework for California Public Schools* (Sacramento: Statewide Social Sciences Study Committee, 1968).

The California proposal is initially divided into three dimensions or facets of social phenomena: (1) modes and processes of inquiry—that is, investigative and planning skills, (2) social-science concepts that serve as tools of inquiry, and (3) social settings or topics, issues, themes, and problems in various times and places.[11] Although these three dimensions outline for us in a general way the realms encompassed by the program, we need to secure more details about each dimension in order to determine more precisely what the pattern includes and excludes. Thus we must next search for more precise definitions of the first dimension, the modes and processes of inquiry. The three modes are initially described in the following terms:

> The analytic, integrative, and policy modes are interrelated yet each has a central thrust that may be illustrated by considering three key questions related to inquiry in the social sciences and history.
> 1. Why do these phenomena behave as they do? This question is central in the analytic mode as attention is given to such phenomena as roles of individuals, urban functions, division of labor, uses of power and authority, conflict and other processes of interaction, productive resources, and decision making in political systems.
> 2. Who am I, or who are we, or who are they? This question is basic in the integrative mode as studies are made of particular individuals, groups, or events such as the student's own family, his school, the history of California, life in colonial America, living in Mexico, the life of a significant individual, and the origin and growth of Los Angeles.
> 3. What should I, or we, or they do next? This question arises in the policy mode in a variety of studies ranging from the making and carrying out of rules, evaluating the actions of individuals and groups, and finding ways to improve urban life to the making of decisions on economic and political problems, assessing proposals for aiding newly developing countries, and considering alternatives to various international problems.[12]

To understand more precisely what each mode entails, it is necessary to read descriptions of each of the subskills of which the mode is composed. For example, in the integrative mode pupils learn to *observe* social phenomena, *classify* them, *define* terms that describe their characteristics, *compare* them, *integrate* various observations to give overall cultural or historical meaning to a particular group of people or cluster of events, *draw inferences* that may be useful in other settings or for understanding other phenomena, and *communicate* the observations clearly to

---

[11] *Social Sciences Education Framework for California Public Schools*, p. 8.
[12] *Social Sciences Education Framework for California Public Schools*, p. 9.

others. The analytic mode includes the skills of observing, classifying, defining, inferring, and communicating as well as those of *drawing generalizations* and *contrasting characteristics* of phenomena. The policy mode focuses on taking action to solve problems. Its processes include *defining the problem, exploring the values* involved, *gathering pertinent data, proposing solutions, testing the solutions,* and *making a final decision.*[13]

The scope, in addition to including the foregoing skills, involves a series of concepts from history and the social sciences. Teachers are encouraged to have children derive their own concepts through use of the inquiry modes. Furthermore, the California program suggests some geographical or social settings in which these concepts might be applied. But unlike the prescriptive list of geographical settings in the table of contents of the fourth-grade text described earlier (*Learning to Look at Our World*), this program allows the classroom teacher some freedom in selecting the settings. In this sense, part of the scope is left up to the individual teacher or school. The linking of the three dimensions of the scope (inquiry processes, concepts, and settings) is illustrated by the following examples from material suggested for grades 5 and 6. The inquiry techniques of the left column are used for developing the concepts of the middle column as children study such settings as suggested in the third column, although other settings might be chosen that would teach the inquiry methods and concepts equally well (Table 2-1).

In summary, we recognize that the scope of our first illustrative curriculum (*Learning to Look at Our World*) is based upon a geographical-settings pattern with some historical, economic, anthropological, and political information included under the discussion of a setting. The proposed California program, on the other hand, is organized according to three intersecting dimensions: (1) inquiry modes and processes, (2) social-science concepts, and (3) geographical, historical, problem, or topic settings in which the processes and concepts are applied.

In contrast, the scope of some curriculum proposals, particularly in their early stages of development, is organized principally according to a viewpoint or methodology. For instance, Brown's confluent education (Chapter 9) focuses on a cluster of learning techniques. These techniques derive from sensitivity-training and Gestalt therapy practices that help pupils understand their own feelings and the feelings of others under a variety of conditions. So any learning experiences that aid the pupil in integrating intellect and feelings fall within the scope of Brown's curricular practices.

Many teachers do not restrict their social-studies offerings to a particular curriculum pattern whose scope is defined by such schemes as those above. Rather, they produce their own variety of activities by selecting

---

[13]*Social Sciences Education Framework for California Public Schools,* p. 7.

TABLE 2-1   Grades 5-6 Scope in the Proposed California Program

Grades 5-6; Mankind and Men: Interaction, Diversity, Individuality		
Modes and Processes of Inquiry	Illustrative Concepts	Illustrative Settings
1. What happens when different groups of men come in contact?		

Analytic
    Definition (behavioral)
    Contrastive analysis
    Generalization
Integrative
    Holistic integration
        (cultural)
Policy
    Valuing
	Interaction: coopera-
	    tion, conflict,
	    domination
	Stratification, class
	Values
	Value conflicts
	Geographic setting
		Spanish-Indian inter-
		    action, 16th century
		    Mexico
		English-Indian-African
		    interaction, 17th
		    century
		    Virginia

2. How have ethnic minority groups and individuals affected American development?		

Analytic
    As above
Integrative
    Holistic integration
        (historical,
        cultural)
	Migration, immigration
	Segregation, discrimina-
	    tion
	Cultural pluralism
	Ethnocentrism, racism
		The Irish in Boston
		The Chinese in
		    San Francisco
		Negroes and Mexican-
		    Americans in cities

3. How do different groups interact in the contemporary United States?		

Analytic
    As above
Integrative
    Comparison
    Holistic integration
        (cultural, historical)
	Spatial distribution,
	    association, interac-
	    tion
	Decision making and
	    law
		Selected cases of group
		    interaction
		The student's community

4. How do groups interact in different cultures?		

Analytic
    Observation
    Classification
    Behavioral definition
    Contrastive analysis
    Generalization
Policy
    Valuing
	Race: biological, social
	Culture, cultural
	    diversity
	Class, caste
	Racism, ethnocentrism
	    and related
	    psychological
	    processes
		Brazil
		India
		Other societies

TABLE 2-1   (Continued)

Grades 5-6: Mankind and Men: Interaction, Diversity, Individuality		
Modes and Processes of Inquiry	Illustrative Concepts	Illustrative Settings
5. How is any man like no other man?		
Integrative	Individuality,	Periclean Athens
Observation	individualism	An African culture
Classification	World view: myth,	Late medieval western
Definition (refined)	religion, ideology	Europe
Holistic integration	Creative expression	Confucian China
(cultural, historical)	Media of expression	Mexico
	Expression of values	

elements from diverse sources. To learn the rationale that defines the scope of their programs, it is usually necessary to ask them why they have included certain activities. Sometimes their answers reflect a consistent scheme. In other cases, either their plan seems helter-skelter or they are unable to rationalize why some of the activities have been pursued. For instance, one teacher explained, "I have the children bring current events from the newspaper each week, because I think they should know the main happenings of the day. I've done Mexico for years and got tired of it, so this year we're doing Japan. This past week we talked quite a bit about the truck drivers' strike since the kids were interested in why the principal had to bring the lunch milk in his car. We've been reading this book on American heroes because we have enough copies for everyone in the class."

So much for the organizational scheme for the scope of the curriculum. The second question we wish to ask is *what range of skills, information, or attitudes is encompassed by the pattern?* In other words, what things are included and what things are excluded from the plan?

In the case of the program that uses a textbook or a series of texts as its core, this question is readily answered by inspecting the contents of the text and the accompanying teacher's manual. Sometimes the contents of the textbook represent the entire range of items included in the scope. In other cases, the text contents are the essential core, which is to be supplemented by other suggested activities, areas of study, or books. A fairly clear impression of the range of geographical settings covered in *Learning to Look at Our World* is provided by the contents quoted earlier. However, in the proposed California framework, only the scope of inquiry processes is suggested in any very complete way by the book that describes the program from kindergarten through grade 12. The concepts and settings specified in the plan are labeled "illustrative" so that teachers can recognize that the definition of scope in these two domains is open-ended. Teachers are expected to go beyond the illustrative concepts and settings on their own initiative. It is expected that the range of concepts and settings will be broader than that specified in the guidebook.

The range is even more open-ended for those programs that define their scope more by a teaching methodology than by geographical or historical settings or a particular set of concepts. For example, since the principal scheme for determining the scope of Oliver's jurisprudential framework is a teaching-learning pattern adapted from courtroom procedures, any variety of public social issue can be drawn into the range of study (Chapter 8).

For individual teachers' eclectic programs, it should be apparent that an understanding of the range of skills, information, and attitudes that are included must be gained either from interviewing the teacher or from observing the program in action throughout the year.

Once we have answered these first two questions about the scope of a curriculum design (the questions concerning the organizing *scheme* and the *range* of items included), we are ready to ask a third: *How well do the scheme and range match my own idea of what constitutes an effective elementary social-studies program?*

This question obviously assumes that you already have in mind an idea of what a suitable social-studies program should cover. Your idea serves as the scale against which you measure new curriculum proposals. What you currently have in mind may be either a precise set of criteria or only a vague feeling for what is good social studies. If your criteria are already precise, your task is merely one of lining them up against the organizational scheme and range of the new curriculum proposal you are analyzing. If your criteria are as yet ill-defined, you are likely interested in seeing what kinds of standards various authors of curricula propose so that you can adopt those ideas that appear most convincing. In such an event, your reading the various rationales offered by the advocates of the curriculum patterns reviewed in this present volume may help you formulate more concretely the standards of scope to which you can willingly subscribe.

Sequence

Just as we asked three questions about scope, so we can pose a trio of similar ones about sequence: (1) *What is the sequence of skills or topics proposed in the curriculum design?* (2) *Upon what rationale is the sequence founded?* (3) *How well does this sequence match my own idea of the order in which the skills or information should be offered?*

The *proposed order* mentioned in the first question is easily identi-fied in curricula that center around a textbook or series of texts. You simply inspect the order in which the books are arranged and the chapter sequence within each book. For example, the five books in the Laidlaw Social Science Program for kindergarten through grade 3 are in the follow-ing sequence: *People and Their Needs* (kindergarten and readiness), *People at Home* (Grade 1, Level 1), *Families and Social Needs* (Grade 1, Level 2), *Communities and Social Needs* (Grade 2), and *Regions and Social Needs* (Grade 3). The eight units that compose the Grade 1, Level 2 book are titled Families in Our Country, Where Families Live, Maps and Globes, Families in Other Lands, Houses in Other Lands, Schools in Our Country, Schools in Other Lands, and Our Country.[14]

Likewise, state or county or city curriculum guidebooks describe their programs in a sequential pattern. The kindergarten-through-grade-12 order of studies in the California proposal is listed as follows:

Grades K-2	Mankind: Man's Distinctive Characteristics
Grades 3-4	Man and Land: Cultural and Geographic Relationships
Grades 5-6	Mankind and Men: Interaction, Diversity, Individuality
Grades 7-9	Systems: Economic and Political; Urban Environment
Grades 10-11	Historical Integration: Relation of Past and Present
Grade 12A	Decision Making: Deciding Social Policy in the United States
Grade 12B	Capstone Courses: A Variety of Offerings[15]

The suggested order of activities in the California scheme for a given grade level is illustrated in Table 2-1, page 38.

Like state and county guidebooks, the materials issued by such newer curriculum projects as those listed at the close of Chapter 1 usually include a recommended sequence of studies or sometimes alternative sequences. Many of the project directors have come to recognize that if their proposals require that teachers and school systems deviate markedly from existing practices, only a small number of schools will adopt the new departure. So by operating according to a rule of thumb regarding innova-tion (the greater the change that a new plan requires of teachers, the less likely they will adopt the plan, and vice versa), the project personnel have often tried to suit the pattern of their proposals to the existing sequence of studies. For instance, the 20-day unit entitled *Concept of Culture* devised by the Anthropology Curriculum Project (Chapter 11) for first

---

[14] Frederick M. King, Dorothy Kendall Bracken, and Margaret S. Sloan, *Families and Social Needs* (River Forest, Ill.: Laidlaw Brothers, 1968), p. 3.
[15] *Social Sciences Education Framework for California Public Schools*, p. 29.

grade is designed to treat topics met in traditional first-grade social studies and is arranged so that it may be inserted into the year's studies without disrupting a sequential program that may compose the overall curriculum for the grade. The lesson topics include:

Pre-test
Introduction—How We Study People
Economics—Houses
Economics—Material Culture (Furnishings and Tools)
Economics—Earning a Living
Social Organization—Household
Social Organization—Community (Living Together in Groups)
Religion
Summary and Review
Post-test[16]

In a similar manner, Oliver and Shaver arranged their seventh-grade experimental program in a sequence that dovetailed with the traditional study of American history, geography, current events, and vocational guidance—topics that were already established as the core of the curriculum[17] (Chapter 8).

The foregoing descriptions of sequence relate to printed curricula. However, the sequence of a curriculum in practice is often quite a different matter and does not represent such a logical order. For a variety of reasons, teachers deviate from the printed sequence. They skip topics, merge others, alter the order of items, and insert topics of their own. For example, textbooks may not arrive on time, so the teacher may spend the first few weeks on current events. If a visitor from another country is available, the teacher may invite the guest to speak to the class on a day that is convenient for the visitor though not in logical order as far as the curriculum is concerned. If some of the pupils have not mastered earlier map-reading skills, the teacher may devote a week to reviewing the skills. Hence, in order to know the actual sequence of studies in a given classroom, it is not enough to know the general curriculum design for that grade level. It is necessary also to talk with the teacher.

Our second question about the order of topics is *upon what rationale is the sequence founded?* In some instances the authors of a curriculum

---

[16] *Teacher's Guide, Concept of Culture* (Athens, Ga.: Anthropology Curriculum Project, 1965), p. 4.

[17] Donald W. Oliver and James P. Shaver, *Teaching Public Issues in the High School* (Boston: Houghton Mifflin, 1966), p. 254.

design specifically describe the logic of their sequence. In others it is necessary to infer the foundation from the proposed pattern.

An example of a specified rationale is the explanation Hanna has offered for his expanding-communities sequence:

> The sequence of themes or emphases is drawn from the fact that each of us lives within a system or set of expanding communities that starts with the oldest, smallest, and most crucial community—the family placed in the center of the concentric circles—and progresses outward in ever widening bands through the child's neighborhood community; the child's local communities of city, county, and/or metropolis; the state community; the regions-of-states community; and the national community. . . .
>
> The rationale for each of the expanded bands of the system is found in the necessity and the desire of the lesser communities to join other similar lesser communities in forming a larger community to provide through united effort means of carrying on basic human activities not possible within the resources of each of the lesser communities working in isolation. One can understand each of these interlocking communities better by studying the system. . . .
>
> All the interlocking social science disciplines are seen as part of the seamless web that we experience in living in family or state or nation.[18]

In like manner, the *Man in Action Series* (Prentice-Hall) of textbooks moves from the familiar to the less familiar in a progression of ". . . family, neighborhood, community, state, national, and international experiences."[19] However, rather than placing these expanding circles at different grade levels, the authors of the series ". . . take the position that this progression should occur frequently within the individual elementary grade level. . . . Lessons should make use of experiences drawn from the child's own social and cultural environment in the first stages of the development of any concept. When the concept is familiar to the student, it should be applied in the examination of less familiar content, including a study of foreign cultures."[20]

Furthermore, the *Man in Action Series* has drawn upon the theoretical work of Piaget for setting the sequence of instruction.

> The Swiss psychologist, Jean Piaget, has identified a series of mental processes which children use in their interactions with their environment. These

---

[18]Paul R. Hanna, "Revising the Social Studies: What is Needed? *Social Education*, 27, No. 4, (April 1963), p. 192. Reprinted with permission of the National Council for the Social Studies and Paul R. Hanna.

[19]Vincent Presno and Carol Presno, *Man in Action Series: People and Their Actions in Social Roles, Teachers Edition* (Englewood Cliffs, N.J.: Prentice-Hall, 1967), p. T8.

[20]Presno and Presno, *People and Their Actions in Social Roles,* pp. T8-T9.

processes are general in nature and are applicable to the solution of a great variety of problems.

Piaget suggests that there are several levels of intellectual development. Each level has its own characteristics. In each of these stages, the child acquires new mental skills which help him function more efficiently. For example, children in the sensory motor stage have difficulty classifying according to attributes but will group objects by spatial proximity. Children at the concrete stage are ready to develop the ability to classify objectives according to attributes. . . .

One of the major objectives of the *Man in Action Series* is to help students acquire the mental processes that are prerequisites for the formal stage (which follows the sensory-motor and concrete stages) of mental development. Lessons are organized to place the student in the position where he must apply the mental processes to the solution of problems. Social science concepts, methods, and data become the vehicles by which the student reaches higher order mental skills.

The mental processes to be employed are called for in a sequence that is consistent with the developmental ability of children.[21]

The logic of the sequence illustrated earlier in the chapter by the table of contents of a textbook—*Learning to Look at Our World*—has been described by the authors of the program:

From typical and more or less familiar places and ways of living in the United States, the pupil is led to less familiar places and ways of living. The places chosen for study demonstrate general geographic concepts, such as the effect of distance from the equator on climate. At the same time, the societies chosen for study are at first relatively simple in organization and historical background. As the pupil's accumulated experiences permit him to understand more complex ideas, more complex societies are studied.[22]

An examination of the table of contents reveals a further aspect of the logic behind the sequence. The units in the book represent a general geographic progression around the world, as if the pupils were taking a global trip moving west from San Francisco and ending in Washington, D.C.

As noted earlier, authors of programs sometimes do not state the rationale behind the suggested sequence. The reader must infer the logic of the program from the order of its topics. The unspecified rationale is

---

[21]Presno and Presno, *People and Their Actions in Social Roles,* p. T9.

[22]From *Learning to Look at Our World,* by Kenneth S. Cooper, Clarence W. Sorenson, and Lewis Paul Todd. © 1969 by General Learning Corporation. Reprinted by permission of Silver Burdett Company.

illustrated by the tables of contents of two collections of biographies intended for use in the middle and upper elementary grades. The first of these volumes is *Trail Blazers of American History*. It offers 25 biographies in chronological order under a series of unit titles that, in some cases, are only slightly different from each other:

Unit One: Finding a New World (1. Christopher Columbus 2. Henry Hudson 3. Robert de La Salle)

Unit Two: Making Homes in a New World (4. Captain John Smith 5. William Bradford 6. William Penn)

Unit Three: Making a New Nation (7. Paul Revere 8. Benjamin Franklin 9. George Washington)

Unit Four: Making Homes in a Wilderness (10. Daniel Boone 11. Father Serra 12. Sam Houston 13. Marcus and Narcissa Whitman)

Unit Five: Leading People in a Time of Trouble (14. Abraham Lincoln 15. Robert E. Lee)

Unit Six: Making a Better Life (16. Horace Mann 17. Clara Barton 18. Jane Addams 19. George Washington Carver)

Unit Seven: Inventing Ways to Improve Daily Living (20. Cyrus Hall McCormick 21. Alexander Graham Bell 22. Thomas Alva Edison)

Unit Eight: Traveling Faster (23. Grenville Dodge 24. Henry Ford 25. The Wright Brothers)[23]

The volume titled *American Biographies* adopts five overall units reflecting several areas of prime concern in modern-day social life in America, then offers within each unit a series of biographies that represent, in a rough way, several consecutive eras in United States history. The book includes a larger number of modern biographies than does the *Trail Blazers* volume.

Unit 1: Law and Government (Thomas Jefferson, John Marshall, Abraham Lincoln, Franklin Roosevelt, Earl Warren)

Unit 2: Civil Rights (Roger Williams, Frederick Douglass, Susan B. Anthony, Walter White, Martin Luther King Jr., Thurgood Marshall)

Unit 3: Rise of Industry and Labor (Samuel Slater, Eli Whitney, Henry Ford, Samuel Gompers, A. Philip Randolph)

Unit 4: Growth of Cities (Benjamin Franklin, Jacob Riis, Luis Muñoz Marín, Robert Weaver)

Unit 5: Education, Arts, and Science (Horace Mann, Winslow Homer, Mark Twain, Langston Hughes, Marian Anderson, Enrico Fermi)[24]

---

[23]Miriam E. Mason and William H. Cartwright, *Trial Blazers of American History* (Boston: Ginn and Co., 1961), pp. 5-6.
[24]Eva Knox Witte, *American Biographies* (New York: Holt, Rinehart, and Winston, 1968), pp. 5-6.

Why the authors of *American Biographies* placed the units in the foregoing sequence is not explicitly stated. But the reason the names within a unit appear in this particular order is evidently to form a kind of chronological progression of people who became known for contributions within a given field.

In most classrooms, teachers follow the basic sequence of topics proposed by the curriculum guidebook or by the textbook series. Some, however, alter the suggested order, either because they disagree with the author's logic or because local conditions render some other order of topics more feasible. For example, when Black History Week is approaching, a teacher might prefer to have children read all the biographies of Negroes in the *American Biographies* text, leaving the other biographies until another time. Or a teacher who feels that children gain a better historical sense by moving from the present into the past might have his class read the chapters of *Trail Blazers of American History* in reverse order. So again, if we are to learn the logic that dictates the sequence of a social-studies program in a given classroom, we must talk with the individual teacher as well as inspect the written guidebook or text she may follow.

The third question we posed was *how well does this sequence match our own idea of the order in which skills and information should be offered?* As in the case of the scope of the curriculum, we have at least two options in arriving at an answer to this query. We may have clearly in mind a rationale that we think is the most appropriate one on which to found a sequence, and we compare various curriculum patterns to this standard. Or, if our convictions about what rationale is best are not yet completely formed, we can analyze a variety of rationales and accept the one that appears most convincing.

Materials and Methods

As used throughout this book, the term *materials* means the paraphernalia of the teaching-learning process—books, magazine articles, blackboards, charts, tapes and tape recorders, films, television broadcasts, and the like. *Methods* refers to the instructional procedures, or what the teacher and pupils do. Methods often involve the use of materials.

Obtaining Materials

The instructional materials that are either recommended or implied by one curriculum proposal often differ from those of other proposals in their variety, specificity, and expense.

An example of a program using little variety of materials is the jurisprudential approach (Chapter 8), which depends entirely on cases of social conflict, usually summaries of issues that have appeared before supreme courts. At a moderate level of variety is the instructional program recommended in the teacher's manual accompanying the *American Biographies* text.[25] In addition to the textbook itself, the suggested materials include supplementary books from which excerpts are read by either the teacher or the pupils (Benjamin Franklin's *Autobiography* and *Poor Richard's Almanac*), newspapers that the pupils themselves write, postage stamps bearing pictures of the person they are reading about, photographs or drawings of the biographee, and copies of songs of his times (union songs from Samuel Gompers' day). At the great-variety end of the scale are such school-system curriculum guidebooks as the Rochester (Minn.) Public Schools Course of Study at the fifth-grade level. It recommends the use of numbers of maps (political, land-use, rainfall), kits of pictures (*Pioneers West to the Mississippi, New Orleans*), filmstrips (*Indians of the Plains, History of Transportation*), motion pictures, (*Louisiana Purchase, Life in the Mountains*), text and reference books (*America's Frontier, History of a Free People*), phonograph records (*The Santa Fe Trail, Sam Houston—the Tallest Texan*), and such pupil-created materials as drawings of historical events, maps of pioneer trails and settlements, models of ships, short biographies of pioneer heroes, and a time chart of inventions.[26]

In appraising a curriculum design we need to recognize that a wide variety of materials is not necessarily a virtue. Rather, the degree of variety should be appropriate to the kinds of objectives in the program. It is hard to imagine how Oliver's jurisprudential approach could profitably use many different types of materials, for by its very nature it focuses only on cases that pupils debate. On the other hand, the Rochester schools' fifth-grade program focusing on the exploration of the American West would appear to profit from a wide range of materials. So the amount of variety that best suits a program depends upon the program goals and, to some degree, the maturity level of the pupils.

Programs differ not only in the range but also in the specificity of the teaching materials. Perhaps the best way to compare programs on this specificity-generality dimension is to define four points along a specific-general scale and cite examples of curriculum proposals that represent each of these points. We shall begin at the very specific end of the scale.

Point 1: All basic materials in the plan have been furnished to the teacher. He need not obtain or create any other materials. An example of such a highly specific plan is the Holt Urban Social Studies series, which

---

[25] Witte, *American Biographies*, pp. TG 29-30.
[26] *A Course of Study in Social Studies (Grade 5)* (Rochester, Minn.: Rochester Public Schools, 1964), pp. 72-96.

focuses on ethnic relations in an inner-city setting. In addition to textbooks for the pupils, the program furnishes correlated filmstrips, phonograph recordings, and "Picture-Study Pad" workbooks.[27]   A teacher's guidebook accompanying each textbook suggests related activities, but all the essential materials are furnished in the basic program package.

Point 2: Some detailed materials are furnished with the program, and others are described but not furnished. An illustration of this level of specificity is Rand McNally's kit of study prints, which are intended to stimulate children to draw astute inferences from observing pairs of photographs. The kits in the series are entitled *Interaction of Man and Man, Interaction of Man and His Environment, Interaction of Man and His Resources*, and *Interaction of Man and His Past*. This 80-picture program, designed for primary grades, centers on the study prints but includes recommendations for supplementary materials that the teacher is expected to obtain or create himself, such as snapshots and magazine illustrations, specified supplementary books (*Children's Games from Many Lands* and *Songs of Many Nations*), pupils' drawings, models, and children's stories.[28]

Point 3: No materials are furnished with the program, but specific directions are given for creating the materials or obtaining them. Many city and county curriculum guidebooks are of this sort. For instance, the Bucks County (Penna.) *Sample Units for New Emphases in Elementary Social Studies* guidebook includes such recommendations as the following:

> A large book called "Now We Go to School" could be developed as a class project. Here in the book, kept on a large easel or stand, might be:
>
> —Children's drawings of their homes and families (labeled by teacher)
>
> —A map of the community with homes indicated, and routes followed to school
>
> —A classroom map and school plan
>
> —List of school workers visited or who've visited the class
>
> —Rules the class has made for living together
>
> —Pictures children draw and stories they dictate
>
> —Records of class birthdays and family size
>
> —Records of special events and holidays
>
> —Pictures of food we eat and clothing we wear[29]

---

[27] Peter Buckley, *Audio-Visual Kit for William, Andy and Ramon and Five Friends at School* (New York: Holt, Rinehart and Winston, 1967). See also the teachers guides for *Living as Neighbors* (1967) and *Five Friends at School* (1966) from Holt, Rinehart and Winston.

[28] Jack B. Spatafora and Patricia Finegan, *Teachers Manual, Interaction of Man and Man* (Chicago: Rand McNally, 1969).

[29] *Sample Units for New Emphases in Elementary Social Studies, Book 1 for K-3.* (Doylestown, Pa.: Bucks County Office of Education, 1963), p. 36.

In addition, the films, filmstrips, and museum exhibits recommended in the Bucks County guidebook are available in the county's audio-visual library, so that teachers have practical ways to obtain the items they wish to use.

Point 4: Neither the actual teaching materials nor specific directions are furnished with the curriculum design, but general descriptions of desirable materials are given. This level of specificity is often found in professional education books that propose a new tack in teaching social studies. For instance, the volume by Clements, Fielder, and Tabachnick entitled *Social Study: Inquiry in Elementary Classrooms* offers many suggestions of the following type:

> The study of history involves the scrutiny of documents; the reading of journals, letters, and epics; and the examination of the arguments and ideas that men have proposed regarding the affairs of Then and There. In this activity, students may explore their skill at inquiry and experience a measure of human contact with other times and cultures. . . .
>
> A teacher of historical inquiry must know his sources. The nearest large library contains scholarly journals, standard source books, collections of letters, records, legal contracts, and the works of the great writers of antiquity; and the teacher should become familiar with them. . . .
>
> Bills, advertisements, contracts, journals, notebooks, and letters are useful contemporary records that survive from both ancient and modern cultures. . . .
>
> Newspapers . . . memoirs and autobiographies are often useful . . . documents.
>
> Census data, financial records, and other statistical information are available for Western European countries. . . .
>
> Laws and regulations are another source of data regarding Then and There. . . .
>
> Pamphlets, editorials, and speeches are useful sources of political and social opinions. The *Communist Manifesto* is one famous and provocative illustration of this sort of writing.[30]

To illustrate how such materials can be used once the teacher has obtained them, the authors of *Social Study: Inquiry in Elementary Classrooms* provide a broad range of examples of what might be learned by perusal of specific documents. However, the problem of determining how and where to secure the recommended materials is still the teacher's, since he has not been furnished them by the authors of the program.

Let us now consider the advantages and disadvantages of these several levels of specificity of instructional materials. The most specific

---

[30] H. Millard Clements, William R. Fielder, and B. Robert Tabachnick, *Social Study: Inquiry in Elementary Classrooms* (Indianapolis: Bobbs-Merrill, 1966), pp. 241, 244-248. Reprinted by permission.

level—with all necessary materials provided for the class in completed form—obviously is a great convenience for the teacher. He need not use his time, thought, and energy to search out or produce books, pamphlets, films, maps, and models himself. The fact that the materials are all at hand ready to use heightens the likelihood that he will employ them. A second advantage is that teaching paraphernalia issued by a publisher, local department of education, or national curriculum project are designed precisely to fit the particular program. The study prints illustrate the exact points made in the textbook, the phonograph recordings are correlated with the scenes in the filmstrips, and the workbook activities are designed to furnish practice in applying the concepts of the text. A third advantage is that prepared materials usually have been tried out in a variety of classrooms before being cast in their final form. Since they have been tested in use, teachers often feel confident that such published materials will suit their own grade level better than something they themselves might create.

On the other hand, instructional materials at the very specific end of the scale may also involve disadvantages. First, if they are reading materials, such as textbooks or workbooks, they may not suit the ability levels of the children in the particular classroom. A single textbook adopted for use by every pupil in a fifth-grade class will typically be too easy for some and too difficult for others, since the range of reading ability among a roomful of fifth graders usually extends from about grade 2 through grade 9 or 10. Second, materials associated with a nationally published curriculum plan are usually not well adapted to local conditions. The scenes pictured in textbooks, the social problems posed in case studies, and the factors that influence the solutions to such problems are not precisely the ones found locally. So it is necessary for the teacher and pupils—or at least the local school system's curriculum supervisors—to furnish materials that focus on conditions of the community. A third disadvantage of specific materials furnished with a curriculum plan is that children miss the opportunity for increasing their skills that they frequently gain from going through the process of making their own materials. For example, their skills of collecting information and organizing it into a written report are enhanced when they themselves develop a pamphlet on "How Our Town Got Its Name" or "Problems of the Postal Service." Their understanding of maps is furthered as they themselves draw maps showing the chief industrial centers and farm products of their state. They learn both history and dramatic skills when they write a radio script about "Lincoln at Gettysburg" and tape-record the play. The final disadvantage is that commercially prepared curriculum packages, with their array of visual and auditory materials, are frequently more expensive than the school's budget will allow. In fact, the cost of materials is often the primary influence behind a school administration's unwillingness to adopt a new curriculum pattern. When the school board makes a heavy investment in textbooks and accompanying paraphernalia, it is reluctant to discard these materials until they have become well worn from years of use.

In summary, when you analyze the teaching materials of a curriculum proposal, it is useful to determine how well they fit your own school's needs in terms of the variety of recommended materials, the specificity of the recommendation, and the cost.

Teaching-Learning Methods

Methods or procedures are the processes pupils and teachers go through in trying to achieve the learning goals. Just as curriculum plans differ in the variety and specificity of their proposed teaching materials, so they differ in the variety and specificity of their suggested methods. They also vary in their assumptions about the talents and interests of pupils and teachers. In this section we consider the factors of variety and specificity. In the following one we focus on the assumed characteristics of learners and teachers.

But before illustrating methods from different programs, we should mention three reasons the issue of method types is significant in appraising curriculum patterns.

First, some methods are more efficient than others in accurately communicating skills and concepts to the learners. For instance, when children engage in creating and interpreting maps they typically gain a better understanding of the location of different geographical features than when the teacher merely describes these features verbally. Likewise the time relationships among historical events are understood more adequately when pupils create or fill in time-line charts. They more readily comprehend the relationships among value judgments of participants in social conflicts when they must defend a position in a social controversy than when such problems are only described to them.[31] Consequently we would expect an assessor of curriculum designs to analyze the variety of methods proposed in order to estimate how directly and accurately they communicate to pupils the kinds of skills and knowledge on which the program focuses.

Second, some programs have stronger potential than others because they provide alternative methods for reaching the same goals. Pupils who

---

[31] For two curriculum designs that engage pupils in analyzing and adopting value positions, see: Donald W. Oliver and James P. Shaver, *Teaching Public Issues in the High School* (Boston: Houghton Mifflin, 1966); Louis E. Raths, Merrill Harmin, and Sidney B. Simon, *Values and Teaching* (Columbus, Ohio: Charles E. Merrill, 1966).

do not learn readily by one method may still be able to attain the goals by means of another. A child who does not read well enough to comprehend the elements of the Bill of Rights may be able to derive an understanding of them from a filmstrip and accompanying recording or from a class discussion. So in appraising several curriculum patterns, we wish to ask whether they suggest alternative methods for different pupils to achieve the objectives.

Third, if methods are to be most effective, they should motivate children—that is, interest pupils in working diligently toward the learning goals. Therefore, in judging curriculum proposals we will wish to estimate how adequately the suggested learning activities will stimulate pupils to pursue the goals enthusiastically.

With these three criteria in mind, let us now illustrate the varieties of recommended methods in three programs. At the little-diversity end of the scale is the jurisprudential teaching of public issues (Chapter 8). The authors of this variety of instruction propose two general approaches to methods: the historical-crises approach and the problem-topic approach.[32] They propose a general strategy for teaching the analysis of political controversy, which is to be used within either of these systems of organizing the curriculum. The strategy consists of eight major steps or intellectual operations through which the teacher's assignments and question-and-answer procedures are to guide the pupils. Although the authors do not contend that this is the only method to use in pursuing the learning goals, it is the approach they describe in most detail.

In Raths' curriculum proposal, which, like the jurisprudential method, focuses on helping pupils clarify their values, the authors recommend a greater diversity of classroom procedures. The basic method is titled "the clarifying response" and refers to ways teachers can reply to pupil remarks so as to encourage pupils to investigate the values that underlie their opinions and actions. The second method with its allied teaching material is called "the value sheet," which "in its simplest form consists of a provocative statement and a series of questions duplicated on a sheet of paper and distributed to class members. The purpose . . . is to raise an issue that the teacher thinks may have value implications for students. And the purpose of the questions is to carry each student through the value clarifying process with that issue."[33] Other instructional methods recommended include the value-clarifying discussion, role playing, the contrived incident, and zigzag lesson (begins with an unusual, teasing question), the devil's advocate (the teacher adopts an unpopular value stance), the value continuum, thought sheets (pupils hand in thoughts important to them), weekly reaction sheets, open-ended questions, time diaries, autobiographical

---

[32] Oliver and Shaver, *Teaching Public Issues in the High School*, pp. 126-133, 138-159.
[33] Raths, Harmin, and Simon, *Values and Teaching*, pp. 51, 83.

questionnaires, the public interview, the decision-making interview, voting, student reports, and action projects.[34]

Even further along the scale of diversity of methods are the activities suggested for a unit on industrialization of the United States, included in the fifth-grade course of study of the Rochester (Minn.) Public Schools. The following sample illustrates the range of methods proposed:

Make sectional maps of the farming, shipping, and fishing areas of the north.

Discuss early ship-building in New England.

List the products raised on the farms.

Make a water mill.

Make cloth by using a carder, spinning machine, and loom.

Show and discuss filmstrip 1413: *New Frontier, New Democracy, and Industry.*

Show motion picture: *Life in a Fishing Village.*

Read in *Our Country's Story* pages 106-114.

Show pictures of early tools manufactured, such as: brooms, hoes, spoons, bowls.

Read from Ralph Linton, *The Study of Man*, "100% American."

Make a time chart of inventions.

Draw maps showing centers of manufacturing.

Discuss labor laws of the early period compared to those of today.

Display set of classroom pictures: *Coming of the Machine.*

Collect samples of grain.

Build a model southern plantation on the sand table.

Make a mural showing slaves working in the cotton fields.

Make a booklet which includes information on types of farms in the south.[35]

In sum, curriculum proposals vary in the diversity of methods they recommend. In comparing proposals, it is useful to review the variety of suggested methods in order to estimate how accurately they might communicate the skills and knowledge implied in the teaching objectives and how adequately they would enable children of varied talents and interests to pursue the goals.

Just as a specificity-generality scale can be conceived for comparing teaching materials, so a similar scale can be devised for comparing methods. Here we shall distinguish three orientation points along the scale. We would define them as follows, beginning with the most specific end of the line.

---

[34] Raths, Harmin, and Simon, *Values and Teaching*, pp. 112, 162.
[35] Adapted from *A Course of Study in Social Studies (Grade 5)*, pp. 92-99.

Point 1:   Each step of each lesson is spelled out for the teacher. The clearest examples of this level of specificity are the teacher's manuals that accompany many textbook series. These programs are designed to be as far as possible "teacher proof." The hope is that nearly any teacher, simply by following the directions, can enable the pupils to attain the goals, despite any individual differences in background and talent that teachers might display. Table 2-2, taken from a second-grade teacher's guidebook, illustrates this kind of suggested procedure in using the material on pages 110-111 in the pupils' textbook.

Point 2:   Each step of a general methodology is described and illustrated, but it is the teacher's responsibility to adjust this methodology to the particular topics the class studies. This degree of specificity is frequently found in curriculum proposals that have at their core a methodology rather than a sequence of concepts to be learned. Such specificity is found in Oliver's jurisprudential approach (Chapter 8) as well as in the Raths-Harmin-Simon technique of studying values.[36] Following is an example of a series of teaching steps recommended for the use of role playing or sociodrama with a class. In its original version, the set of 11 steps is presented with illustrations of each step followed by suggested sociodrama story situations that teachers may use outright or adapt. However, to conserve space, we list below only the steps without the illustrative material:

In conducting a sociodrama, the teacher can:

1. Explain the role-playing technique to the class in simple terms.
2. Select a problem situation that is of interest and importance to the pupils.
3. Tell enough of the story situation to set the scene.
4. Select pupils to act out the situation.
5. Define the problem and the role of each pupil.
6. Define the audience's role.
7. Suggest the actors' first remarks so they will know how to begin.
8. Sometimes modify the drama in a way which necessitates the actors' facing some of the consequences of their decisions.
9. When necessary, step in to reemphasize the audience and participant roles or to aid the actors in taking the next step.
10. Stop the drama at any point that seems desirable.
11. Open a general discussion and, as a result of student comments, perhaps allow other pupils to work through the problem situation in a different manner.[37]

---

[36]Raths, Harmin, and Simon, *Values and Teaching*, pp. 51-162.
[37]Adapted from R. Murray Thomas, *Social Differences in the Classroom* (New York: David McKay, 1965), pp. 157-162.

TABLE 2-2   A Second-Grade Teacher's Guidebook *

Concepts

1. Many people in warm lands live in villages.
2. Villages must provide places where people can get jobs.
3. Villages must provide facilities to help people meet their needs for recreation, food, and schools.

Recommended Procedure

Getting Started *Have the children observe the picture at the top of page 110. Ask, "What is the man shown in the picture doing?" (He is throwing a net into the ocean.) Then ask, "Why is this a good way to catch fish?" (The net can trap many fish at one time.) Have the children use this picture and their knowledge of Hawaii to think of other ways the man shown could get food. (He could farm. He could pick fruit from the palm trees shown in the picture.) In discussing the picture, refer to the accompanying annotations. Point out, or have the children discover, that the houses shown in the picture and the fish net could be made of materials readily available to the Hawaiians.*
Developing the Lesson *Have the children study the paragraph to the right of the top picture on page 110 to learn (1) the name of an animal often raised by Hawaiian villagers, (pig) and (2) what plant they often grow. (taro [ta′ro])*

Ask the children to study the remaining paragraph of text material on page 110 to learn (1) what part of the taro plant the Hawaiians eat, (root) (2) how taro is prepared, (It is cooked, then pounded into a paste.) and (3) what prepared taro is called. (poi)

Point out that changes are taking place very rapidly in Hawaii. With better transportation facilities, more and more stores and shopping centers are being built in small villages. As a consequence, fewer and fewer people are depending upon poi. Have the children read page 111 aloud and then discuss answers to the questions asked in this text material. Use their answers to these questions to stress the fact that Hawaiian children live much as the children in our other states do.
Concluding the Lesson *Have the children answer the concluding question on page 111. Then ask, "Why might you enjoy living in a small Hawaiian community?"*
Going Further *Some of the children might like to make a list of the Hawaiian words they have learned in this section. They could then find other Hawaiian words in an encyclopedia or a book about Hawaii and teach these words to the other children.*

Evaluation

Ask the children, "In what ways is life in Hawaiian villages similar to your life? How is it different?"

Evaluation, Section 1

Ask the children to tell how the climate of Hawaii has influenced such things as (1) why people move to Hawaii, (2) the jobs done by Hawaiians, and (3) why people like to visit Hawaii. The responses given by the children will help you to evaluate their depth of understanding of concepts presented in this section.

Frederick M. King, Dorothy Kendall Bracken, and Margaret A. Sloan, Communities and Social Needs, Teachers' Edition *(River Forest, Ill.: Laidlaw Brothers, 1968), p. T73.*

Point 3: A general method is suggested, but the steps for carrying it through are not described. Frequently state, county, or city curriculum guidebooks propose methods in this form. Sometimes teacher's guidebooks that accompany texts include such general suggestions. For instance, the following ideas are taken from recommendations for teaching units at the fourth grade level in Madison, Wisconsin, schools:

> Construct models of weapons used for hunting and protection by different groups of people.
>
> Describe an imaginary trip in a desert sandstorm.
>
> Write about excitement and danger in mountain regions.
>
> Discuss how mountains and valleys have helped make Switzerland and other mountain areas famous.
>
> Find out how climate, land, and other factors affect the kinds of foods produced in different parts of the world.
>
> Dramatize a Mexican market place.[38]

Once you identify the predominant level of specificity of methods suggested in a curriculum plan, you then face the task of deciding which level is best for the school system or the classroom you have in mind. To arrive at a sensible decision, you need to know something of the abilities of teachers who would be expected to use the program. Teachers who are somewhat inexperienced or who lack the boldness or ingenuity to attempt new instructional tactics will usually profit most by highly specific descriptions of methods, such as the lesson plans in teacher's manuals that accompany textbooks. These manuals usually propose specific steps for introducing the lesson, specific questions with which to initiate discussions, and specific assignments for children to carry out through reading. In contrast, teachers who have had successful experiences with many methods do not need to have the steps laid out for them, unless a very novel procedure—like jurisprudential teaching, "the clarifying response," or sensitivity training—is being proposed. The experienced, ingenious instructor needs only the general suggestion of a method. He can figure out for himself the steps that will be best suited to his own group of pupils and classroom facilities.

Frequently a social-studies program furnishes each of these levels of specificity because it includes (1) a state, county, or city course of study that provides the basic objectives, scope, sequence, and general suggestions for methods, (2) reference books for teachers that illustrate steps in

---

[38]*Education for Human Relations—Intergroup Understanding, Kindergarten—Grade 6* (Madison, Wis.: Department of Curriculum Development, Madison Public Schools, 1964), p. 107.

exemplary teaching procedures, like inquiry techniques and sociodrama, and (3) textbooks and accompanying teacher's manuals that match the course of study. In such instances, the teachers have at hand both specific and general descriptions of methods, so they can choose for themselves the level that suits their individual talents and background experiences. The question of individualizing a program brings us to our next topic: assumptions that different curriculum planners make about the nature of pupils and teachers.

Characteristics of Learners and Teachers

Throughout this chapter we have periodically implied three questions that we need to ask when appraising curricula. At this juncture we may profitably pose these questions outright and illustrate what to look for in printed curricula in order to answer them: (1) What does the curriculum plan assume about pupils' characteristics? (2) What does it assume about teacher characteristics? (3) How accurately do these assumptions match the characteristics of the pupils and teachers that I have in mind as I evaluate this curriculum pattern?

Sometimes the assumptions are explicitly stated. Often they are not stated, possibly because the authors of the plan have not been aware that they held such beliefs. In the following paragraphs we shall identify several of the more common of these premises and shall illustrate them with examples from various curriculum plans.

Assumptions about Pupils

Many curriculum proposals of past years have apparently been founded on the belief that all children at a given grade level are alike in reading skill, writing and speaking ability, experiential background, and interests. But everyday experience, as well as hundreds of psychological and sociological studies, has proven how false this assumption is.

In a typical school system the reading skills of children at a given grade level will range over twice the number of grades as that grade's number. For instance, at the second-grade level, children's reading ability will spread over at least four grades. The least adequate second graders read no better than beginning first graders, and the most apt read as well as average fourth graders. Likewise, in a fifth grade the children's reading skills will range over at least 10 grades, the least adequate pupils reading only as well as an average first grader and the most adequate as well as an average tenth or eleventh grader. Of course, the range of reading skills in a specific classroom may not be so great, especially if the school assigns pupils to classrooms according to their apparent reading abilities. But even if such ability grouping is practiced, there will be a spread of several grades represented among the pupils, particularly in the upper-elementary classes. Obviously, then, a typical textbook, suited to the ability of the average child in the class, will be too difficult for some of his classmates and will fail to challenge the advanced skills of others.

Not only do children vary in their capacity to absorb written information, but their skills of verbal expression—writing and speaking—also vary significantly. After a fourth-grade class visits a supermarket, one child may write a fluent report of what he has observed, using complete sentences and an apt selection of vocabulary to convey a logical stream of ideas. In contrast, a classmate may write only a few words, misspelled and disorganized, and thus he fails to communicate what he apparently experienced on the excursion. Though most children express themselves far better in speech than in writing, the oral abilities found at a particular grade level also range from the nearly incoherent to the highly lucid.

In recent years the attention focused on economically or culturally disadvantaged children has emphasized the vast differences that can exist in the experiential backgrounds of American elementary-school pupils of the same age level. A child growing up in the impacted tenement district of a major industrial city brings to school a far different set of mental images than one who grows up in an upper-class suburban neighborhood. The child raised in a sharecropper's shack comes to school with a different storehouse of impressions than the one raised in a middle-class home in a small city. So pupils from the tenement or sharecropper's shack have been dubbed "culturally deprived" because their background experiences have not prepared them well for succeeding in the traditional American school.

Critics of the term "culturally deprived" have pointed out that these socially disadvantaged pupils are not devoid of cultural learnings. Indeed, their backgrounds of experiences have often been quite rich. But the problem is that the traditional school curriculum is founded on cultural expectations that are more often within the realm of middle- and upper-socioeconomic-class families than of lower-class groups. One effort to right this imbalance of background experiences has been the "head start" programs for pre-kindergarten children of lower-socioeconomic-class or bi-cultural backgrounds. In these programs children are furnished opportunities to learn many of the things that children from middle- and upper-class homes normally meet in family and neighborhood life. A further equalizer of experiences has been television. Since the great majority of American homes have television sets, children today share more vicarious experiences prior to entering elementary school than they ever did in the past. Furthermore, in the field of elementary social studies, curriculum developers have endeavored to create materials and programs better adjusted to the experiential backgrounds of children from various American subcultures. The curriculum approach analyzed in Chapter 10 represents one such pattern designed for use with inner-city pupils.

Anyone who spends time with children recognizes that they do not all have the same interests. A social-studies unit on People of the Pacific may capture the attention of some fourth graders but may leave others unmoved. Whereas one child may eagerly participate in a Christmas play, another may refuse to take part under any circumstances. Apparently such differences in pupil interests are the result of a combination of factors whose nature is still somewhat unclear to psychologists and educators. It seems that at least part of a child's incentive to learn comes from unsolved problems he is facing in his own life. Thus, a girl who yearns for companions may enthusiastically read a story about a child her age who learned how to make friends. Or the girl may attempt to compensate for her friendless state by learning a hobby like playing the piano or caring for pets. In other cases successful performance at an activity stimulates a pupil to continued pursuit of that same learning. A boy who is praised for his role in a panel discussion may seek further opportunities to take part in discussions and debates and, in order to perform well again, may read widely on the topics to be discussed. Often children are willing to pursue the school's intellectual tasks simply from a desire for adult or peer approval, not because of any inherent interest in the subject at hand. For such approval, pupils memorize the names of the American presidents, the products of the state, the capital cities of the nation, and "the six causes" of the Civil War. Still a different sort of motivation is that vaguely understood quality *curiosity*. Children are often enticed to learn by something that is novel or puzzling to them. But whatever the combination of reasons behind pupils' willingness to learn, it is clear that the social-studies topic or activity or incentive that motivates one child will not necessarily motivate his classmates.

Formulators of curriculum designs have given varied degrees of attention to these matters of children's differences in communication skills, experiential background, and interests. A few samples from representative curricula will illustrate this point.

An example of a textbook program that seems to consider children at a given grade level to be very much alike is the Singer social-studies series.[39]   At least the teacher's manual suggests few if any ways to differentiate instruction according to differences in children's communication skills and interests. The children's textbooks do, however, pose questions intended to stimulate the readers to compare the contents of the stories in

---

[39]C. W. Hunnicutt and Jean D. Grambs, *Teacher's Manual for Your Community and Mine* (Syracuse, N.Y.: L. W. Singer Co., 1966).

the book with similar experiences in their own lives, thus encouraging children to establish a connection between their own backgrounds and the contents of the book. In addition, the teacher's manual recommends activities that enable the pupils to apply the concepts from the book to their own lives. To the authors' credit is the fact that the texts are written in simple vocabulary and syntax, so that the material in each book is suited to the reading level of most children in the grade for which the book is intended. But to challenge the better readers, the teacher would have to recommend other, more advanced books, some of which are listed in the teacher's manual.

Considerably more difficult from the standpoint of reading level for the age group using it is the American history text by Ver Steeg, *The Story of Our Country*. But the numerous, high-quality illustrations would aid the pupil who does not read well to acquire concepts through picture and map study. In this case the teacher's manual gives some attention to possible pupil differences in interest and skill by including for each chapter a list of "additional activities for individuals and groups." However, it is up to the classroom teacher to determine which activities would be suited to which kinds of learners. For instance, here are typical suggestions that accompany Chapter 13: The Nation Formed a New Government.

1. Explain in other words each of these sentences and tell to what situations each one refers.
   a. The fate of the new nation was hanging by a thread.
   b. Washington felt that his first duty was to his country.
   c. Hamilton believed that the "new" government should pay the debts of the "old" government.
2. Read about the way a President was elected in Washington's time. Compare that way to the one used today. Share this information with the class. . . .
3. Hold a constitutional convention to write a brief constitution for the class.
4. Find out the number of times that the Constitution has been changed and what the changes, or amendments, were. When was the latest change made?[40]

In evaluating the foregoing types of activities, you may wonder whether all of them are not designed for the more able fifth grader. They

---

[40] Brenda Pfaehler and Clarence L. Ver Steeg, *Teacher's Edition, The Story of Our Country* (New York: Harper & Row, 1965), p. 72.

perhaps do not represent a range of difficulty levels that might accommodate the communication skills and interests of all the children—gifted, average, and less capable.

In contrast, an increasing number of textbook writers are designating activities for different levels of learners. For instance, in the teacher's guide prepared by Brock and Wilkin for the Scott, Foresman series, there are separate activities listed for average learners, more mature learners, and less mature learners. Typical of these suggestions are the following ones. They are selected from a variety of ideas accompanying Unit 5, which discusses "Why Are City Governments Needed?" and "How Are Metropolitan Communities Governed?" The children's textbook, entitled *Metropolitan Studies*, is intended for third graders.

> *Average Learners*: Have pupils help prepare a political science chart for local governments to be placed on a bulletin board. Head the chart "Government." Divide the chart into three main sections: town or city, county, and metropolitan. Divide each main section into two parts, one headed "Structure" and the other headed "Function."
>
> Use the chart for discussing structures and functions of the different kinds of government. Under "Structure" and "Function" enter some details for each kind of government. This will help the children who do not readily understand the structural and functional similarities and differences of various kinds of local governments. . . .
>
> Have pupils get some maps of their own county or metropolitan area. Have them list the villages, towns, and cities in the county or metropolitan area to get an idea of some of the different governments that exist in their area. . . .
>
> *More Mature Learners*: Have pupils dramatize a radio or television interview between a mayor or a city councilman and a radio or television news reporter. Have pupils pretend there is a community problem and the interview is being held to see what the mayor or councilman feels should be done to solve it. . . .
>
> *Less Mature Learners*: Have pupils ask some people in their neighborhoods what some of their local community problems are and what they think should be done about them. Have the pupils report their findings to the class.[41]

If indeed the authors have accurately estimated the difficulty level of various activities, their suggestions would appear to be a time-saver for classroom teachers who wish to differentiate assignments according to the abilities and interests of pupils in the classroom.

So far in our discussion of individual differences we have mentioned only those curriculum designs that appear in the form of a textbook or a

---

[41]Paul R. Hanna et al., *Investigating Man's World, Metropolitan Studies, Teacher's Edition.* Copyright © 1970 by Scott, Foresman and Company, Glenview, Illinois 60025. Philippines Copyright © 1970 by Scott, Foresman and Company. All rights reserved.

series of texts. Curricula published in the form of county or city courses of study also vary in the degree to which they provide for diverse pupil abilities and interests. Most of these guidebooks suggest a variety of activities for each unit in the program but do not designate which of them might best suit the needs of different kinds of pupils. The decision about which children might profit most from which activity is usually left entirely to the teacher.

In summary, curriculum proposals vary in the degree to which they accommodate for individual differences among pupils. Some plans provide a single route for pursuing the learning goals. Others suggest alternative routes, or at least they list options for supplementing the basic activity of textbook reading, but they do not designate which alternative might be most appropriate for which kind of child. Still other plans provide alternative or supplementary activities as well as suggestions about the types of children each activity might best suit.

Assumptions about Teachers

Many of the assumptions that authors of curriculum proposals make about teachers have already been implied in earlier sections of this chapter. There are authors who assume that the typical teacher lacks the time or wisdom to determine the scope, sequence, and content of daily lessons. Therefore, they provide not only the sequence of materials needed in the program—like textbooks, workbooks, and filmstrips—but also the specific questions that the pupils might be asked throughout the lesson and the activities that might supplement the reading and discussion sessions. Curricula in the form of county or city courses of study typically are founded on the belief that teachers know the steps that compose such teaching methods as class discussion or the use of a film or the production of a drama. Therefore, the course-of-study booklet confines its attention to outlining the sequence of teaching units, their goals, general methods, and the specific materials that can be used for pursuing the goals (textbook passages, supplementary books, films, recordings, charts, realia). As noted in the foregoing paragraphs, some curriculum designs assume that the classroom teacher needs aid in developing activities that suit the program to different levels of pupil ability and interest. Other designs leave all such decisions up to the teacher.

Consequently, as you compare social-studies patterns, you may wish to decide which of them appear to be founded on the same assumptions that you hold about the teachers who would be expected to implement the programs in the classroom.

Evaluation Procedures

In the process of education, the operation through which you answer the question "How well did the learners achieve the goals?" is termed *evaluation, assessment,* or *appraisal*. For purposes of comparing social-studies curriculum plans, three aspects of evaluation worth noting are those of (1) specificity of appraisal techniques, (2) suitability of appraisal devices to pupils' levels of maturity, and (3) appropriateness of techniques to the goals. We shall cast each of these in the form of a question and illustrate the way they appear in various curriculum designs.

How specifically does the curriculum proposal describe evaluation procedures? Some published plans direct no attention to appraisal. They fail to discuss this aspect of teaching either out of neglect or on the assumption that the evaluation procedures are self-evident. A clear example of such a plan is the conservation-education course of study and textbook series devised by the Conservation Curriculum Improvement Project of the South Carolina Department of Education.[42] Although the teacher's guidebook gives extensive attention to instructional methods, it says nothing about evaluation as such.

Other curriculum schemes suggest appraisal devices, but do so in very general terms, such as "give a test over the following concepts" or "observe children's responses to questions asked in class." In these instances it becomes the classroom teacher's responsibility to formulate the questions and to decide when a pupil's remark during a discussion reflects an adequate command of the subject.

A further step toward specificity is the provision of questions, either in the teacher's guidebook or in the pupil's text, that can be used as the stimuli for class discussion or as items on an essay test. When used for discussion, the questions enable the teacher to combine instruction with evaluation. The questions simultaneously provide the teacher with evidence about how well pupils are achieving the goals and stimulate children to think through an issue. As an illustration, we can inspect questions proposed in the teacher's manual for the elementary-school text entitled *People and Their Actions in Social Roles*. The social-science concept the pupils are expected to grasp is: "Social systems establish different roles to perform necessary functions." The concept is to be applied in an analysis of the problems faced by modern cities. The pupils are asked to inspect a picture in

---

[42]Matthew J. Brennan, ed., *People and Their Environment: Teachers' Curriculum Guide to Conservation Education* (Chicago: J. G. Ferguson, 1969).

their textbook showing a city street clogged with traffic. Smoke pours from a factory smokestack, buildings are in need of repair, and trash is spilled in a nearby yard. The teacher's manual recommends that pupils be asked these questions:

1. What does the word *problem* mean?
2. What problems do you think the people in this city might have? Tell why you think these may be problems.
3. What tasks do you think must be done to solve some of the problems?
4. What roles or jobs are used in your city to help solve some of these problems? Example: traffic commissioner, policemen.
5. What actions would you expect of the people who will perform the necessary roles?
6. What would happen if there was not a role of traffic commissioner, sanitation worker, doctor, or teacher?
7. Can you think of some roles that are needed to solve some of the problems of the following groups: the army, the United States of America?[43]

The foregoing pattern of furnishing discussion questions is the most popular of the provisions for evaluation in published curriculum proposals, both in curriculum plans that take the form of textbooks and in those issued as city or county courses of study.

Another step toward specificity of appraisal devices is the "check-up test" or "chapter review" that is printed either in the pupils' textbook or in the accompanying teacher's guidebook. Sometimes the test questions require a short written or oral explanation. In other cases they require multiple-choice, fill-in, matching, or true-false responses. The answers to the questions are typically printed in the teacher's manual, so the teacher need not take the entire responsibility for deciding what composes an adequate answer, as he must when only discussion questions are suggested. Typical of such end-of-the-unit test items are the following excerpts from the third-grade textbook *Regions and Social Needs*:

Social Science Facts

1. Where could you go to see deserts?
2. Where could you go to see canyons in a desert?
3. What is adobe?
4. What materials besides adobe do desert families use for their homes?

---

[43]Presno and Presno, *People and Their Actions in Social Roles*, p. 18.

Social Science Ideas

1. How do you explain why deserts form where they do?
2. How do canyons form in desert lands?
3. How do you explain why many desert families live as nomads?

Test 1:   Social Science Words

On your paper write the word to use in each _____ . Choose from these words.

oasis	canyons	cactus	tent	Gobi
yurt	nomad	irrigation	tribe	Sahara

1. Running water forms   as it flows across rocks.
2. An _____ is a place in a desert that has a source of water.
3. A _____ moves from place to place to graze his animals.
4. Mongols build a _____ out of poles and felt.

Test 2: Facts and Ideas

1. Which of these might a desert family be most likely to use for making a home?
   a. skins   b. fur   c. steel   d. adobe
2. Which of these help desert families make a living?
   a. date palms   b. goats   c. steel   d. camels
3. Which of these sentences are true?
   a. Deserts have more than ten inches of rain a year.
   b. Deserts often form at places where winds rise to cross mountains.
   c. Desert nomads always live in tribes.[44]

So it is that on a scale of generality-specificity of evaluation suggestions, curriculum proposals range from *no suggestions at all* at one end of the line to the other extreme of *specific test questions and their answers.* Most classroom teachers probably prefer the latter option, for it gives them the opportunity of either using the ready-made items or rejecting them in favor of their own creations.

Now to the second question. *How appropriate are the suggested appraisal techniques for the ability levels of the pupils?* A basic principle emphasized by experts in the field of evaluation is that the form of an

---

[44] Frederick M. King, Dorothy Kendall Bracken, and Margaret S. Sloan, *Regions and Social Needs, Teachers' Edition* (River Forest, Ill.: Laidlaw Brothers, 1968), pp. 74-75.

appraisal device should not be a barrier to discovering what the pupil has learned. In classroom practice this principle is often violated. The wording of test questions or the requirement that the answers be cast in a particular form can prevent a child from displaying what he actually knows about social studies. The child who is not a skilled reader may not comprehend what a question is asking, so he does not know how to respond even though he understands the social-studies facts or concepts being measured by the question. Some children, even when they understand what is being asked, cannot respond adequately because their skill in written composition is not equal to the requirement that they prepare their answer in essay form. When such objective-type items as multiple-choice, completion, matching, or true-false are used, children may give incorrect answers because they are unfamiliar with the type of item rather than because they have not achieved the learning goal.

Consequently, when you judge the suitability of the evaluation portion of a curriculum proposal, it is useful to estimate how well the suggested techniques are adjusted to the communication skills of the children. This judgment is made difficult by the fact that the range of skills represented among children in a given classroom is often rather broad. Thus the essay-type item that might be appropriate for one of the more apt pupils will be inappropriate for his less mature classmates. In such cases the appraisal techniques recommended in the curriculum plan may be adopted directly for use with the average or advanced children, but the teacher or the schoolwide curriculum committee may need to devise other appraisal approaches for children who do not read or write or speak so fluently. To some degree the published curriculum plans that specify different learning activities for children of different maturity levels provide for these variations in pupils' skills, since the activities serve both as teaching methods and as means of evaluating what children have learned.

Our third question is: *How closely do the recommended evaluation techniques match the learning objectives?* Or, phrased another way, how appropriate are the appraisal items to the stated goals? In order to judge this factor, we first need a clear statement of the learning goals for the lesson or unit. Then we must match the suggested evaluation procedures with the goal, assuming that the closer the match the better the tie between the objective and its assessment.

Some evaluation plans are clearer than others in their statement of objectives. For example, the following three objectives have been drawn from three different curriculum plans:

To develop in the student an appreciation of the family.[45]

---

[45] Project Development Committee, *Recommended Program, Family Life Education, Grades Kindergarten through Twelve* (Pleasant Hill, Calif.: Educational Planning Center, Department of Education, Contra Costa County, 1967), p. 13.

Raw materials are important to the success of industry in a nation.[46]

The learner will be able to state in his own words one or more ways to study man.[47]

These examples differ in their focus. The first emphasizes teacher intention (To develop . . .). The second is simply a statement of a concept that the children are to grasp. The third focuses on what type of pupil behavior will demonstrate that the child has reached the learning goal. Authorities in the field of evaluation generally agree that the third form—objectives in terms of pupil behavior—is the most efficient way in which to cast goals. They contend that the purpose of education is to alter the learner's patterns of thinking and acting. If you are to appraise what changes have occurred in someone else's thought or action, you must do so on the basis of behavior you observe—speech, writing, or other physical acts. Therefore, goals stated in terms of desired student behavior are the most practical guides to evaluation procedures.

The three sample objectives also vary in their degree of specificity. The first is very vague. In fact, the term *appreciation* is so poorly defined and is interpreted in so many different ways by educators that it is an extremely inadequate guide for determining either teaching methods or evaluation procedures. Does appreciation mean the same as *enjoyment* or *liking?* Is the child supposed to like the idea of family in general or to enjoy his own family? Or does appreciation mean "recognizing the social role of . . . ."? Is it enough if the child can describe the functions of the family in various societies? Or does appreciate mean both enjoy and recognize and, perhaps, attempt to defend? How can you evaluate children's progress toward such an objective when its meaning is so vague?

The second objective, the one concerning raw materials, is far more specific than the first. It defines with greater precision the domain of knowledge in which we should evaluate. The third appears even more specific in that it enables us to recognize more readily the limits within which a pupil's response should fall if he is judged to have achieved the learning goal. In effect, appraisal is rendered easier and more precise when objectives are more specific and are cast in terms of expected student behavior. (For an interesting, brief guide to stating objectives in this manner, see Robert F. Mager, *Preparing Instructional Objectives*. Belmont, Calif.: Fearon, 1962.)

As noted earlier, considering the form of the learning goal is only half the task of judging item appropriateness. The other half consists of estimating how closely the recommended evaluation procedure corresponds to the objective. To illustrate this process, we can consider the

---

[46]*A Course of Study in Social Studies (Grade 5)*, p. 46.
[47]Lenz, Moss, and Hughes, *What Is Man*, p. 24.

appraisal suggestions for the third of the foregoing objectives (". . . one or more ways to study man") as given in the teacher's manual of the Franklin Social Sciences Program for this particular lesson. The manual includes two evaluation options:

> Given a picture depicting six diverse examples of man and questions regarding procedures used to learn about man, the learner will state in his own words one or more ways to study man.
> Given a sheet of newsprint folded in four, learners may draw pictures to show ways man studies man and why he needs many different ways to study man.[48]

The first of these alternatives appears to be the more direct measure of the stated goal. However, for the less verbal child who has some drawing ability, the second would seem appropriate. In each case the stated goal and appraisal methods are closely related, so we would conclude that the evaluation items are appropriate to the objectives.

In the curriculum plan from which the second of our illustrative goals was drawn, no evaluation technique was recommended for the objective we listed, so we cannot say anything about item appropriateness. We are in hardly any better position with the "appreciation of the family" goal, since the course of study containing that objective gives no specific guidance for appraisal techniques that might be used. Rather, this course of study simply appends to the end of the unit the recommendation that evaluation consist of "group discussion, individual conferences, observations, written work (picture books, illustrations, teacher)."[49] What this final suggestion—*teacher*—is intended to mean is not made clear. In effect, for this first-grade family-life education unit, both the goals and the evaluation suggestions are too vague to enable us to estimate how well they match.

A particularly difficult task faced by the curriculum builder who specified his evaluation suggestions is to create test items or rating devices that measure pupils' true comprehension of a generalization or concept rather than simply the rote memorization of facts in a textbook or from a teacher's lecture-discussion. That is, in order to insure that pupils have grasped a generalization, the testing situation should represent an application of the generalization to situations other than those used as examples in the text or lecture. We can illustrate this point by citing some generalizations and concepts that are the goals of a chapter from a popular

---

[48] Lenz, Moss, and Hughes, *What Is Man*, p. 28.
[49] Project Development Committee, *Recommended Program*, p.14.

fourth-grade textbook whose table of contents was listed earlier in our discussion. Three of the "generalizations expected" and "concepts emphasized" are:

> Geographic phenomena such as topography, vegetation, and climate can be charted on maps and globes by symbols and scales.
>
> The distribution and use of natural resources affect where man lives and how he lives, particularly how he earns a living.
>
> *Irrigation* is a system of canals, rivers, or pipelines that artificially provides crops with the proper amount of water at the proper season. Irrigation increases production, reduces the chance of crop failure, and enables men to live prosperously in a region where rainfall is sparse.[50]

In analyzing the recommended true-false test items apparently designed to measure pupils' comprehension of such ideas as the foregoing, we note that some of the items would indeed require understanding of the concept or generalization, whereas others could be answered from rote memory, for they are almost direct restatements of phrases in the pupils' textbooks. Here are two examples of true-false items that require comprehension of a general principle, since the items cast the concept in a somewhat different form than that of the textbook:

> Orange trees would grow well in Minnesota.
>
> Farmers who use irrigation can get water even when it does not rain.[51]

Here are examples of two items that depend on direct memorization of textbook statements that appear in the same section of the textbook as the foregoing quoted passage. That is, they do not require the application of a generalization to a new setting:

> Our largest city is New York.
>
> Fishermen need compasses and maps to keep from getting lost at sea.[52]

So we may conclude that if the goal of this social-studies program were to help children comprehend and apply generalizations and concepts

---

[50] From *Learning to Look at Our World*, by Kenneth S. Cooper, Clarence W. Sorenson, and Lewis Paul Todd. © 1969 by General Learning Corporation. Reprinted by permission of Silver Burdett Company.

[51] Cooper, Sorenson, and Todd, p. 335.

[52] Cooper, Sorenson, and Todd, p. 335.

rather than learn specific facts, then the first two items would be appropriate and the last two would not. But if the program aims to teach both generalizations and specific facts, then all four of the items might be considered suitable. (We might note in passing that true-false items are usually not the most suitable type of test question, since they are too susceptible to guessing and misinterpretation. The foregoing questions on irrigation, compasses, and New York would likely be improved if cast in a multiple-choice or matching form.)

To close our discussion of evaluation aspects of curriculum designs, we may note that when teachers themselves devise appraisal techniques, they often do not select the varieties of appraisal that are best suited to the learning goals. For instance, in a third-grade unit on People in Groups, one of the principal aims was to help children improve their skills of social interaction by permitting others to voice opinions on controversial topics during group discussions rather than attempting to stifle opposing views. The teacher taught a lesson in which a variety of illustrations of group meetings were presented and discussed by the class. At the close of the period, the teacher evaluated the pupils' achievement of the goal by asking the class: "Do you think every child working in a group should have a chance to give his ideas?" In response, the pupils chorused "Yes," and the teacher went on to the next topic, apparently satisfied that the learning goal had been reached. However, the weaknesses of this form of appraisal are obvious. The children's verbal response may have no relation to their behavior. Consequently, the evaluation technique was inappropriate. A more suitable method of appraisal would be to have the children conduct small-group meetings. During the discussion sessions the teacher or a pupil-observer for each group would note the extent to which different children encouraged or allowed other group members to voice their opinions on controversial topics.

Conditions Affecting Curriculum Adoptions

This final section of the chapter is directed especially to readers who have not yet tried to introduce new curriculum patterns into classrooms. People already experienced in curriculum development recognize that finding or creating a new plan is usually far easier than getting it into practice. However, neophytes in this field are often surprised and frustrated when they discover what complex manipulations are needed to implement a new proposal. As a forewarning of the problems that can be encountered, we shall describe five general factors that influence the likelihood that an existing curriculum pattern can be altered in favor of a new one. You may find that keeping these factors in mind while you analyze a curriculum proposal will enable you to estimate more accurately your chances of effecting its adoption in some school or classroom that interests you.

The following discussion centers around five beliefs we hold about the curriculum-change process. We shall state these as postulates or rules of thumb. They are proposed not as a definitive list of factors but as some of the more important dimensions that warrant consideration when plans are laid to introduce curriculum changes.

Postulate 1: The more time, effort, emotional tension, and money required of people who must implement the curriculum change, the less likely the change is to be effected.

This initial postulate is founded partially on the conviction that it is more comfortable in general for us to continue doing things our present way than to learn new ways. Changing our techniques of teaching demands time we might use for other activities. The typical elementary-school teacher is expected to be expert in a variety of fields—reading, writing, arithmetic and the new mathematics, art, music, science, health education, and social studies. It takes time and energy enough simply to keep up with daily instructional tasks in these areas, much less devote hours to creating or learning new ways of teaching social studies. Teachers seem generally more willing to adopt a *packaged* social-studies curriculum plan (textbooks, filmstrips, workbooks for pupils, a suggested set of lesson plans in a teacher's manual) than to adopt a general outline or viewpoint whose details they must fill in by themselves. This is because the packaged program requires less time, effort, and emotional tension than the one the teacher must create.

Another obvious deterrent to curriculum change is the financial outlay required. Teachers are reluctant to spend their own funds for books, filmstrips, and curriculum guides. School boards are also hesitant to spend the taxpayers' money unless the promised results of the new plan are substantially greater than the results of present practices. So the greater the cost, the greater the reluctance.

Changing the curriculum not only requires unwelcome expenditures of time and thought for many classroom teachers and administrators, it also means taking some risk. If a teacher has depended in the past on textbook reading and recitation, he runs the risk of failing before the class if he now attempts the courtroom-confrontation technique that Oliver's jurisprudential approach involves. If a teacher has never conducted spontaneous dramatics or role playing, he risks classroom chaos by attempting sociodrama as a means of clarifying elements of ethnic conflict. So the greater the risk, the greater the reluctance to adopt a given methodology.

In sum, curriculum proposals that involve slight alterations of present practices and expenditures are relatively easy to accomplish. When major changes in teaching methods and materials are proposed, they are not likely to be accomplished unless the positive forces described below under Postulates 3 and 4 are particularly strong.

Postulate 2: The more people involved in the curriculum change, the more difficult it is to accomplish the change.

The reasons for this proposition are apparent. Innovation within a single classroom requires only that a particular teacher alter his practices. But when an entire school or school system attempts curriculum revision, scores of teachers and administrators who have various talents and attitudes must be influenced, and the efforts of all must be coordinated. The strategies successful for effecting change in one classroom may not be successful in another. Recognizing these facts, some school districts begin curriculum change in a few classrooms or in a pilot-project school rather than throughout the district. After changes have been satisfactorily carried out in a limited number of classes, other sectors of the school system are included in the curriculum changes.

Postulate 3: The greater the dissatisfaction with present conditions and the greater the promised rewards for adopting the new departure, the more likely a new curriculum proposal will be adopted.

In Postulate 1 we suggested that teachers, administrators, and school-board members generally prefer not to change. They feel more comfortable doing things in the customary ways. But they tend to prefer familiar patterns only when they are relatively well satisfied with the product of their efforts. As they become unhappy with children's social behavior or social-science knowledge, they seek to find better ways to teach. Thus, dissatisfaction helps overcome the inertia of the status quo.

It is useful to think of dissatisfaction as relative rather than absolute. The amount of dissatisfaction with the present curriculum that a teacher feels can change from one time to another. In other words, when we speak of *relative dissatisfaction* we mean the amount of discrepancy between what the individual perceives the present situation to be and what he believes might or should be possible. We propose that the greater the gap between the person's perception of the current curriculum and his perception of what should or could be accomplished, the greater the effort he is willing to expend to change conditions. If this proposition is true, then an important step toward implementing curriculum innovation is to make teachers and administrators increasingly unhappy with existing practices. This fomenting of discontent is one of the chief functions of the introductory statement or rationale that typically prefaces a new curriculum plan. The author points out what he believes is wrong with current curricula and assures the reader that what he is about to propose is far better.

But the leverage necessary to move teachers and administrators to action is not exerted merely through promises of better social-studies outcomes than presently are obtained. Often promises of subsidiary rewards or punishments are as important, or even more so, in effecting changes in social-studies practices. A school principal may offer a variety of incentives—either implied or forthrightly presented—for stimulating teachers to alter their methods and materials. Such incentives include free time to plan, opportunities for in-service education, credit toward salary increases, a better chance of obtaining tenure, recognition at faculty meetings, opportunities to display the curriculum-development work before visiting parents and educators, articles printed in the school newsletter or town newspaper, and the like. For failing to participate in curriculum innovation, the teacher may incur such sanctions as direct criticism from the principal and from colleagues, reduced opportunities for promotion and salary increases, and reduced funds for teaching materials.

Just as the school principal can either stimulate or retard curriculum innovation by his use of rewards and punishments, so the superintendent of schools can influence the amount of interest and energy the individual principals direct toward curriculum proposals that the superintendent and his staff would like to promote. Similar influences are wielded at the county, state, and national levels. During the 1960s, large amounts of federal money were paid to colleges and to school districts that were willing to engage in curriculum development of specified varieties. In the area of social studies, projects aimed at solving racial and inner-city problems were particularly encouraged.

In addition to stimulating dissatisfaction with present social-studies practices and offering extrinsic rewards for social-studies innovation, people who wish to institute new curricula are also assisted or obstructed by the degree of success experienced by curriculum workers (teachers, supervisors, administrators) as their project continues. If the workers' initial efforts yield satisfying results, they are stimulated to greater efforts and can overcome more demanding problems. If their initial attempts bring less success than they had hoped, they often are unwilling to carry on with much enthusiasm. Consequently, whatever can be done to help curriculum personnel set realistic subgoals and progress smoothly toward them is a positive step toward effecting more ambitious innovations.

Postulate 4: Extensive curriculum revision cannot be expected unless people in the upper levels of the school's power hierarchy enthusiastically support it.

Although this appears to be a truism, the fact that it is ignored in practice suggests that it is worth mentioning here. Individual teachers sometimes create new social-studies approaches, which they subsequently attempt to share with their colleagues. However, without the approval and backing of the principal or grade supervisor or curriculum coordinator, they usually are unable to influence the practices of many other teachers. Many innovative practices require substantial funding for textbooks, atlases, reference books, field trips, and the like. Such funding requires the efforts of administrators who make decisions about the budget. Free time for curriculum planning also requires the authorization of administrators. Hence, the "grade roots" approach to curriculum innovation, which finds teachers on their own initiative proposing new patterns, has proven to be quite limited in its overall effectiveness. At an early stage in a curriculum project, it is necessary for the administrators who control funds, rewards and punishments, the allocation of school time, and school facilities to be enthusiastically supportive of the work.

Postulate 5: The curriculum becomes revised in name only if classroom teachers are not prepared with the skills and materials they need to carry out the specific steps of the new methodology and if no evaluation is made of their progress.

This proposition is the converse of Postulate 4. In school systems that ostensibly have adopted "social-science inquiry" or "group process" as part of their social-studies program, the teaching that goes on in many classrooms does not resemble what the authors of these approaches had in mind. This discrepancy between the publicized program and actual practice occurs because teachers are unable to carry out the required methodology with any degree of skill and confidence. Either they lack proper training or they lack the requisite personality characteristics. Therefore, the school must institute a suitable in-service training program to insure that teachers command the skills required to bring the new plan into reality. Otherwise, each teacher is on his own to dig out as best he might the instructional techniques described in the teacher's manual, if indeed such a manual exists.

Visits to classrooms will show that it is not uncommon for a school superintendent or principal to adopt a new social-studies pattern and purchase the materials designed for its implementation—books, study prints, maps, charts, filmstrips, recordings—but fail to provide the training and incentives teachers need to put the pattern into practice. Social studies as the children experience it may differ little from its form under the former program, since the teacher's methods are unaltered. So in order to learn whether a given curriculum plan is in effect in a school, it is not enough to talk with the principal or curriculum coordinator. It is necessary as well to see how the plan appears in practice in the individual classrooms.

These, then, are the five postulates that we shall refer to periodically in the following chapters as we comment on the likelihood that a particular proposal might be adopted in various kinds of schools.

Conclusion

In this chapter we have developed a series of criteria or questions we believe are important for the analysis of social-studies curricula. These criteria form the framework for subsequent chapters of the book. As we inspect the curriculum plan on which each chapter of Parts Two and Three focuses, we shall attempt to answer these queries:

Value Orientation

What values or beliefs does the plan feature?

What values or practices is the plan a reaction against?

Scope and Sequence

What is the structure that determines which skills and knowledge the program is to include?

What range of skills, information, or attitudes is encompassed by the pattern?

What is the sequence of skills or topics proposed in the design?

Upon what rationale is the sequence founded?

Materials and Methods

What variety of materials are recommended?

How specifically are materials described, and what materials are furnished?

What variety of methods are recommended?

How well do the methods apparently communicate concepts and skills to children?

How well do the methods accommodate for children's learning differences?

How likely is it that the methods will motivate children to work toward the goals?

How specifically are the teaching methods described?

Characteristics of Learners and Teachers

What does the curriculum plan assume about pupils' characteristics?

What does the plan assume about teachers?

Evaluation Procedures

How specifically does the proposal describe evaluation procedures?

How appropriate are the suggested appraisal techniques for the ability level of the pupils?

How closely do the recommended evaluation techniques match the learning objectives?

As far as possible we have the authors of the curriculum patterns that appear in the following chapters give in their own words the answers to these questions.

Two

Complete Social-Studies Programs

The term *complete program,* as we use it in Part Two, means a curriculum designed to provide the pupils an entire set of social learnings over a school year or, in most cases, over a sequence of years. In contrast, the term *partial program,* as used in Part Three, means a curriculum plan intended to furnish only a portion of the children's social learnings.

The number of complete programs available in the United States today runs into the thousands. Such programs appear in various forms—as textbook series, as special curriculum-project materials, and as state, county, or city courses of study. In addition, some complete programs are unique to a single school or to a single classroom. With so many curriculum designs from which to choose, we have found the task of selecting five representative ones for Part Two to be quite demanding. To guide our choice, we used the following criteria.

In order to warrant inclusion in Part Two:

1. The curriculum materials should be readily available to educators who would like to inspect them firsthand. The application of this first criterion greatly reduced the number of curriculum designs under consideration. Most county, city, and single-school courses of study are printed in quantities sufficient only for local use, so they are not readily available to educators outside the local area.

2. The pattern should be a representative one. That is, it should display characteristics typical of a number of other modern curriculum designs.
3. The pattern should not closely resemble another of the illustrative programs included in Part Two. In other words, we have attempted to avoid duplicating representative curriculum patterns. Therefore, everyone's favorite social-studies program will not be found in the following chapters. However, a program that resembles the favorite is probably included.

The first pattern selected through use of the foregoing criteria is Paul R. Hanna's Expanding-Communities plan (Chapter 3). It is illustrative of a textbook-centered program that began in the progressive era of the 1930s and has subsequently been revised to incorporate newer theory and methodology in the field of social-studies teaching.

The second is Paul F. Brandwein's *Social Sciences: Concepts and Values* (Chapter 4), which represents a textbook-centered plan that evolved in the late 1960s to focus on a balanced study of social-science disciplines and a concern with the values that underlie social behavior.

The third is Hilda Taba's "teaching strategies" (Chapter 5). Her program illustrates a plan devised cooperatively by personnel in a county and professors from a nearby college. Like many state, county, and city social-studies designs, it is not organized around a particular textbook series but uses a variety of reading materials. The most distinctive characteristic of Taba's plan is the system of carefully structured instructional strategies that teachers are expected to employ.

The fourth is a modern version of the traditional history-geography program (Chapter 6), which uses as its core a chronological-history textbook and a geography textbook.

The fifth pattern in Part Two represents those programs that focus on a single discipline, then draw in other social sciences as they relate to the central discipline (Chapter 7). The plan we chose to illustrate this type is Lawrence Senesh's curriculum entitled *Our Working World.* It emphasizes economics but also gives some attention to history, political science, social psychology, sociology, and anthropology as these fields bear on economic behavior.

Each of these five curricula is described in terms of the set of analytical elements introduced in Chapter 2.

3

Hanna's Expanding Communities

In the early 1930s Columbia University's Teachers College was still the energizing force behind the progressive-education movement. Key members of the faculty, like John Dewey and William Kilpatrick, continued to emphasize the desirability of understanding children so that schooling might be suited to their growth and thought patterns. Harold Rugg, George Counts, and John Childs continued to stress the importance of studying society so that children might learn to play significant roles in improving their world.

It was in this atmosphere of progressive fervor that Paul R. Hanna earned M.A. and Ph.D. degrees and joined the Teachers College staff as a specialist in social studies. In 1935 he transferred to Stanford University where, over the next 35 years, he developed a multidisciplinary, expanding-environments curriculum, which has determined the nature of the Scott, Foresman and Company textbook series in the social sciences.

Over the last two decades or more the general structure of the Hanna program has remained essentially the same. But as new theory and practice have been proposed for improving the teaching of social studies, Hanna and his colleagues have altered their texts and teacher's manuals to accommodate for innovations.

Hanna's plan is properly labeled a complete program, for it attempts to provide for nearly all of the child's social understandings and skills throughout the elementary grades and into the secondary school.

The Goals of the Program

In its most recent version, the Scott, Foresman textbook series is titled *Investigating Man's World.* It is ". . .designed to help elementary school children develop systematic ways of thinking about and studying the world in which they live. It is a social studies program to generate patterns of thought and analysis that children can use in a lifetime of work, leisure, and citizenship."[1]

Scope and Sequence

The line of reasoning that determined the kinds of studies and their order in this program was explained several years ago by Hanna in an article in the journal *Social Education:*

> The sequence of themes or emphases is drawn from the fact that each of us lives within a system or set of expanding communities that starts with the oldest, smallest, and most crucial community—the family placed in the center of the concentric circles—and progresses outward in ever widening bands through the child's neighborhood community; the child's local communities of city, county and/or metropolis; the state community; the regions-of-states community; and the national community. This set of communities—family to nation—is a highly interdependent system: e.g. the problems and possible solutions of the family group are always colored by the larger communities of which the family is the smallest but core group. Even the national community reaches inward through all of the intervening bands of lesser communities to influence the life of the family group.
>
> The rationale for each of the expanded bands of the system is found in the necessity and the desire of the lesser communities to join other similar lesser communities in forming a larger community to provide through united effort means of carrying on basic human activities not possible within the resources of each of the lesser communities working in isolation. One can understand each of these interlocking communities better by studying the system: ultimately the American family can only be understood within the cultural complex that we know as the national personality; or the state community can be seen much better if one knows the composite characteristics of the family

---

[1] Paul R. Hanna, Clyde F. Kohn, John R. Lee, and Clarence L. Ver Steeg, *Investigating Man's World, Metropolitan Studies, Teacher's Edition* (Glenview, Ill.: Scott, Foresman, 1970), p. 3.

communities and of the local communities that have come together to form the particular state community under study. [See Figure 3-1.]

Suggested grade assignment of emphases. The logic of the expanding-communities-of-men design suggests that each larger component community be studied *in sequence* by the child. In the first grade, the child might start his study of the system with emphases on his own family and his own school. As he studies each of these communities, he learns what phases of life are properly the concern of himself as a member of these small intimate groups. He also learns that families need to join families to provide, through neighborhood apparatuses, fire protection, food and clothing, schools, etc. Consequently, the child moves naturally to the third emphasis in the sequential structure—the neighborhood community which exists to provide services not available to families or to the school in isolation.

This particular social studies design may assign the study of the neighborhood to the second grade. However, the grade assignment of the community to be emphasized is relatively unimportant; following *the sequence* from the lesser community to the next larger is the governing principle here.

The sequence typically followed in schools adopting this structure is as follows.

Grade	Emphasis
One	1. The child's family community
	2. The child's school
Two	3. The child's neighborhood community
Three	4. The child's local communities: country, city, county, metropolis
Four	5. The child's state community
	6. The child's region-of-states community
Five	7. The U. S. national community

The grid of basic human activities (social science disciplines). Over this set of expanding communities of men, we now lay a grid of clusters of human activities. [See Figure 3-2.] Universally, men in groups have in the past, do now, and no doubt will continue to carry on basic human activities, here catalogued under nine headings: protecting and conserving life and resources; producing, exchanging, and consuming goods and services; transporting goods and people; communicating facts, ideas, and feelings; providing education; providing recreation; organizing and governing; expressing aesthetic and spiritual impulses; and creating new tools, technics, and institutions. Note the similarity of the names given these clusters and the names used to designate social science disciplines: "producing, exchanging, and consuming" might as well be labeled *economics;* "organizing and governing" could be replaced by the term *political science.*

The point to stress here is that the grid of basic human activities (essentially the regrouping of the content of the social science disciplines) is laid over each of the expanding communities of men: the child studies the ways men in groups carry out the several basic human activities in each community. While it is to be expected that the class, in studying its state, may focus first on one cluster of

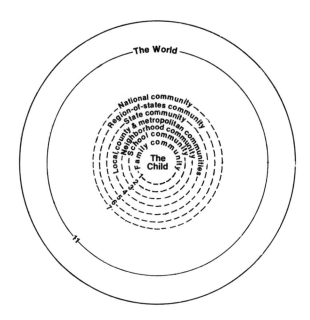

FIGURE 3-1   Expanding Communities of Men

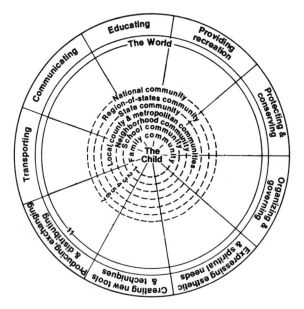

FIGURE 3-2   Categories of Basic Human Activities Overlaid on Expanding Communities

activities and then another, this structure encourages the holistic approach to the community being studied. All the interlocking social science disciplines are seen as part of the seamless web that we experience in living in family or state or nation.

The place of geography and history. Another dimension of this proposed structure for the social studies program is of great significance. Each of these expanding communities has both (1) a spatial dimension that we know as geography, and (2) a time dimension that we know as history. The child who studies his national community in grade five, for instance, must know the geographic arena within which the national life is rooted. The physical location of the United States national community must definitely be known; the arrangement of physical and cultural features cannot be neglected or the study of our nation will not take into account place-to-place differences or similarities. Likewise our nation cannot be known and appreciated unless the history of its origins, its values, its periods of struggle, and its successes are background against which we assess the present and chart the future. But in this proposed framework of the social studies program for the first five grades, geography and history are not offered in separate courses, but contribute their content and processes to the expanding communities of men as each community in turn is studied to discover how it carries on the basic human activities to supplement the work of the lesser communities.

Possible emphases beyond the United States national community. But our suggested design for the elementary school social studies is, to this point in our statement, incomplete. We have yet to complete our particular logic of expanding communities of men beyond the national community. Modern science and technology made obsolete the once defensible notion that the nation is the ultimate boundary of the system of expanding communities of men. We know today that nations cannot exist as islands: some multinational values, institutions, laws, and customs are even now appearing, while others wait for the birth time when men shall find it desirable and possible to welcome larger-than-national communities.

What we face today is a new set of *emerging* communities of nations that are increasingly important to the survival of the lesser national communities. These larger-than-national communities can be identified and assigned sequentially to school grades in some such pattern as this: [See Figure 3-3.]

Emphasis

8.   U.S. and Inter-American Community
9.   U.S. and Atlantic Community
10. U.S. and Pacific Community
11. U.S. and World Community

There is logic to support a reversal of Emphases 8 and 9 on the grounds that the Atlantic Community is of greater significance to us.

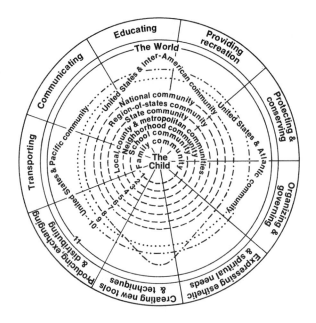

FIGURE 3-3   A Social Studies Curriculum Design

Let it be re-stressed that the sequential order of the emphases is more important than the assigning of the study of a given community to a particular grade. One school district or state might telescope and assign both the national and the Inter-American communities to grade five; the Atlantic, the Pacific, and the world communities to grade six. Or another district might stretch the design through grade seven, or grade eight, or even grade nine, depending upon the decisions to be made in the remaining grades of the secondary school.

Several strategies of this design should be noted here. When the child moves beyond his national community, he is now focusing on the need for multi-national solutions. The social studies program need not take each and every one of the more than 20 nations in the emerging Inter-American community for detailed study. The child should begin to observe the nearly half-billion people living on the American continents, working together through multinational action to create private and public solutions to their common problems. The U.S.-Canadian joint efforts could be studied realistically. The Alliance for Progress could be examined as one possible approach to the concern all of us have for economic, social, and political development of our neighbors to the south. Attention would be given to the nature of power and international policy as well as to cultural comparisons. The history we have in common in the Americas of ten thousand years of Indian culture, 300 years of European colonization, and 100 years of struggle for freedom and independence is probably of greater use to our youth than a detailed study of the history of any single neighbor nation. The design calls for the larger and more universal pictures of emerging multinational communities.

Another strategy of this social studies design should be explained here. The pupil is not encouraged to jump about aimlessly from community to community or from culture to culture. He does not, in this structure, make the difficult and often meaningless leap from an emphasis in grade two on the study of his neighborhood and other U.S. neighborhoods to a comparative study of Japanese neighborhoods that are part of a totally different cultural pattern. Such cultural contrast and comparison has its place in the total design. But is it not more appropriately assigned to Emphasis 10, the U.S. and Pacific community? A neighborhood community in Japan clearly reflects its national community which in turn reflects the cultures of the Orient. Is it not a preferable sequence to move systematically through the expanding communities from family through nation; then, having gained considerable knowledge of the several closely interrelated communities of which an American child is a citizen, is he not ready to compare and contrast meaningfully those faraway lesser communities that are a part of a very different national and world-regional culture?

We do not intend by this design-control to preclude that exciting content which emerges from the living current scene and invites side excursions into places and times not strictly related to the community assigned to a particular grade. Such enriching experiences make life varied and challenging. But the teacher has the obligation to prevent these side interests from displacing the main theme as set out in whatever design on which the district or state has agreed.[2]

Materials and Methods

The most essential materials for conducting the Scott, Foresman program are the texts for children and the accompanying teacher's guidebooks. Kindergarten children's material is in the form of study prints. Above that level the texts consist of reading matter profusely illustrated with colored photographs, charts, graphs, and maps.

Although the pupil's books contain the core of ideas and skills to be taught, they are not viewed by their authors as substitutes for the classroom teacher. Nor are they conceived to be the only suitable materials for implementing the expanding-environments plan. The teacher

[2] Paul R. Hanna, "Revising the Social Studies: What Is Needed?" *Social Education,* 27, No. 4 (April 1963), 192-195. Reprinted with permission of the National Council for the Social Studies and Paul R. Hanna.

is expected to fill out the program with a variety of learning activities, both those recommended in the accompanying guidebooks and ones of his own creation. The guidebooks not only suggest how the texts might be used, but they also list trade books and films that can be used to illustrate the social-science concepts and generalizations on which the program centers. In effect, the child is expected to spend only a minor portion of his social-studies time reading the text.

The relationship between the children's texts and the suggested instructional methods is perhaps best clarified through examples drawn from two of the textbooks and their allied teacher's guide materials. As the illustrative segments from the first-grade and fourth-grade texts will indicate, the writing style changes from the primary to the intermediate grades. For instance, in the first-grade book entitled *Family Studies,* the authors have developed a sequence of concepts through pictures and brief narratives about fictional families. In contrast, the fourth-grade text, *Regional Studies,* is composed of questions and direct factual descriptions.

Hanna's earlier opinion about the desirability of holding to a strict expanding-environments pattern in the primary grades has been altered slightly in the latest edition of the text series. Whereas in the early 1960s he had suggested that his curriculum pattern did not encourage the pupil to jump ". . .from community to community or from culture to culture," the first-grade text in its most recent version directs children's attention to their own families, then gives some recognition to families in foreign cultures by means of questions at the end of several units and through a closing unit on Mexican families. Likewise, the second-grade book entitled *Local Studies* places initial emphasis on American communities but subsequently dedicates a full unit to a study of France and accords two pages each to Brazil, Tanzania, Norway, Turkey, India, and Australia.

Now we will illustrate the presentation pattern in the first-grade text. The following passage covers four pages from unit six on *rules,* a unit designed to introduce several political-science concepts. A picture on the opening page shows a classroom of children. The teacher is talking to a boy who is standing and selecting a book from a table.

"Sit down, Tom," Miss King said. "You know the rule. You must stay in your chair when others are working. Sit down and go back to work."

Tom said, "May I tell you something?"

"Yes," said Miss King, "what is it?"

Tom said, "I don't think the rule is fair."

"Why don't you think it's fair?" said Miss King.

Tom said, "I did my work. Now I'd like to look at a book. I don't want to just sit. The rule about staying in your chair isn't fair to me."

"Tom is right," said the children. "We don't want to just sit after we do our work."

"Well," said Miss King, "maybe you are right. What can we do about the rule?"

"We can make a new rule," said a girl.

A boy said, "We can make a rule that is fair. We can vote. That's how people make rules."

All right," said Miss King. "We will vote on a new rule. What rule do you think would be fair to all of us?"

After thinking, the children said, "When I have no work to do, I can get a book to read. I must not make noise when other children are working."[3]

On the page following the end of this dialogue, a picture of the classroom shows the teacher totaling the pupils' votes on the chalkboard. The text poses the following questions for children to answer about the dialogue and the accompanying picture:

> What are the children and Miss King doing?
> Do you think the boys and girls will vote to have a new rule?
> If the children vote for a new rule, who will follow it?
> Will the children who voted "no" have to follow the rule?
> Will all the children have to follow it?[4]

To see the kinds of suggestions the textbook authors offer to the teacher for using this reading passage effectively, we can turn to the teacher's edition of the text. The teacher's guide explains that the passage is designed to teach children the following values or understandings:

> A democratic group permits its members to disagree over goals and directions, to discuss rules, and to vote on some rules affecting themselves.
>
> Disagreements must be worked out democratically by the persons who are involved in obeying and enforcing the rules.
>
> Rules and laws made by a group reflect the group's value system.[5]

In addition to explaining the central understandings that children are expected to gain from the reading material, the teacher's

---

[3]Paul R. Hanna, Clyde F. Kohn, John R. Lee, and Clarence L. Ver Steeg, *Investigating Man's World, Family Studies, Teacher's Edition* (Glenview, Ill.: Scott, Foresman, 1970), pp. 112-114 (children's text section). Copyright © 1970 by Scott, Foresman and Company.

[4]Hanna, Kohn, Lee, and Ver Steeg, *Family Studies*, p. 115.

[5]Hanna, Kohn, Lee, and Ver Steeg, *Family Studies*, pp. 112-114.

guide recommends the following kinds of questions for stimulating class discussion:

> What is probably happening in the picture?
>
> Is it sometimes good to change rules? Why? Can a new rule turn out to be a bad rule?
>
> Can you think of some rules you would like to change or to make? Why? What procedure would be necessary?
>
> What kind of school rules might children help make? (some regarding the playground, games, and care of materials, and some regarding the classroom)
>
> What goes along with making rules? (the responsibility for following the rules)[6]

At the end of each unit that focuses on seeing family and school groups from the perspective of a particular social-science discipline, the teacher's guidebook proposes a series of activities from which the teacher is to select or adapt ones suited to the children in his class. For example, the list of activities for the unit on rules is as follows:

Activities

Average Learners

Have pupils. . .

1. . . . suggest the reasons for the rules at your school relating to the drinking fountain and walking in the halls. Write the rules on a large chart and have groups of children draw pictures showing the correct behavior in both places.

2. . . . dramatize meeting new children in their neighborhood. Stimulate their thinking by asking, "What would you say? How could you help new children play the games that are popular in your neighborhood?"

3. . . . divide into groups. Guide each group in establishing three rules for playing an ABC Block game. Then have one child from each group transfer to another group and proceed to play the block game by the rules established in his group.

4. . . . dramatize a family problem of rule breaking, such as children not coming home promptly from school, or not being quiet in the

---

[6] Hanna, Kohn, and Ver Steeg, *Family Studies,* (teacher's guide section), p. 72.

morning if they wish to get up and play before breakfast. The situation should cover the incidents resulting from the rule breaking, and the working out of a solution to the problem.

5. . . . practice using tools properly. If tools such as a saw, a hammer, a screwdriver, etc., are not available in your classroom, try to acquire these from the custodian or a carpenter.

6. . . . dramatize ways that they help to clean up at home, such as sweeping the floor, picking up toys and putting them away, washing dishes, hanging up clothing, and the like.

7. . . . role play a classroom situation in which they participate in making decisions about rules that are good for a particular school.

8. . . . analyze the classroom rules. If they decide some need to be changed, guide them in following the democratic procedure of rule making.

9. . . . become aware of how to act and what to do when something unexpected might happen. It might be an accident or an embarrassing situation such as spilling something, falling over something, losing something, or bumping into someone.

More Mature Learners

Have pupils . . .

1. . . . use their imagination in thinking of situations that could develop in their neighborhoods if there were no family rules, school rules, or neighborhood rules. Let class decide on three or four they think will be the best to show on a mural. Assign pupils to draw specific things. After drawings have been colored and cut out, help pupils to arrange them in the proper place on the mural.

2. . . . ask their parents to help them do some research at home on the origin of certain rules or customs such as why a man, when accompanying a lady, walks on the outside of the street, why people are fined for throwing trash out of the car, why men and boys take off their hats when entering a home, why a more or less definite time is set for children to go to bed. Reserve a special time for the pupils to report their findings in class.

3. . . . invite another class to visit the classroom to discuss rules. This should help them to understand that some rules in classrooms are general everywhere and necessary for all groups; others are very similar to those they have helped to establish in their room.

4. . . . compose a humorous story from a topic such as The Home with No Rules, The Neighborhood with Too Many Rules, The Town Named Rules, The School with the Big Rules, and the like.

Less Mature Learners

Have pupils . . .

1. . . . discuss things requiring rules that could be included in a mural showing children playing in the school's neighborhood. After each pupil has named what he would like to make for the mural, have pupils make, color, and cut

out their drawings so that they can be arranged and pasted on a large background.

2. ... discuss the rule they like best in their home and the reason they think the rule is very good. Pass out sheets of paper so the pupils can make drawings showing themselves relating to the rule in some way. Let pupils copy caption, "Our Favorite Rule," from the chalkboard.

3. ... dictate an invitation to the principal to visit the class and discuss groups of school rules and how they came about. He may include rules general in all schools; those that are particular with the children's school; those for all the people at the school, and those for only the children.[7]

The previous passage gives us an idea of the Scott, Foresman approach at the first-grade level. Let us now turn to the fourth-grade text and the allied teacher's guidebook to see how the authors' tack changes at the intermediate grade levels.

As the teacher's edition of *Regional Studies* explains, this volume:

... is primarily a methods book designed to develop in pupils the skills of social scientists. Throughout the text many different states and regions of states are used as prototypes or as case studies to show the pupils how to investigate man's world. Once the methods of investigation have been presented, pupils are given the opportunity to apply them in an investigation of their own state, regions of states, and foreign regions.

Regional Studies is divided into three parts, each part dealing with a different kind of region. In *Part One*, the study focuses on states. In *Part Two*, the study centers on uniform regions of states—states grouped for study because they have one or more characteristics in common. In *Part Three*, the study concentrates on functional regions of states—states that have cooperated to solve common problems or to achieve common goals.

Within each part, the pupils examine the region under study from the points of view of seven social studies disciplines—anthropology, economics, history, human geography, physical geography, political science, and sociology. Each discipline is a unit of study and provides one method for investigating a region. To gain a full understanding of the region, it must be examined from the points of view of all seven disciplines.[8]

So in contrast to interdisciplinary textbooks, which attempt to merge various social-science approaches into a single narrative to furnish a

---

[7] Hanna, Kohn, and Ver Steeg, *Family Studies* (teacher's guide section), pp. 74-75.

[8] Paul R. Hanna, Clyde F. Kohn, and Clarence L. Ver Steeg, *Investigating Man's World, Regional Studies, Teacher's Edition* (Glenview, Ill.: Scott, Foresman, 1970), p. T-7. Copyright © 1970 by Scott, Foresman and Company.

study of a society, the Scott, Foresman books are multidisciplinary in their distinct separation of the seven social-science disciplines.

As noted above, each of the three major parts of the fourth-grade textbook is separated into units. The opening page of each unit of Part One provides a glossary of terms specific to the discipline on which the unit is focused. As an example, the glossary for the economics unit is reproduced in Figure 3-4. Following the glossary, the authors have prepared several pages explaining concepts of the particular discipline, and questions are posed for class discussion or for pupils to answer individually. This pattern of explaining concepts and posing questions is illustrated for the anthropology unit (see Figure 3-5). Some units also include pages dedicated to the practice of skills, such as map interpretation or the use of a dictionary. Finally, each unit closes with a page of questions and suggested activities intended to give the pupil experience in "thinking" and "investigating" like a social scientist. To illustrate this element, we have reproduced in Figure 3-6 the material from the end of the history unit.

At the intermediate grade levels the teacher's guidebook also suggests activities the pupils can carry out as follow-up experiences to their textbook reading. However, in contrast to the first-grade teacher's manual, the guidebook at the fourth-grade level first suggests general class activities that all pupils will follow, then a few additional items intended for average, more mature, and less mature learners. In some instances these suggestions are quite specific; they tell the teacher precisely what to do. In others, the recommendations are rather general and depend for their success on the teacher's own initiative.

FIGURE 3-4   *Glossary of Economics Terms from "Regional Studies"* *

Hanna, Kohn, and Ver Steeg, Regional Studies, *p. 86.*

budget A plan for the way income is to be spent in a given period of time. States, schools, businesses, families, and individuals use budgets.

buying power The amount of goods and services that a person can buy.

capital Buildings, machines, materials, and money needed to produce goods and services.

consumer A person or a group that uses goods and services.

debt Something owed to a person or group. Debt is usually in the form of money.

demand The amount of goods or services that people want.

economics The study of how people produce and use goods and services to meet their needs and the needs of others.

expenditure Money spent.

factors of production Labor, capital, natural resources, and technology are factors needed to produce goods.

goods Materials that are produced to meet people's needs and wants.

income Money that comes in. States receive income from taxes. People receive income for doing work.

income tax A government tax on a person's income.

labor force People who work to produce goods and services.

medium of exchange Anything used in exchange for goods and services. Money is usually the medium of exchange.

money Coins and paper money used by a government as a medium of exchange and as a standard of value.

natural resources All of the land and raw materials that are needed to produce goods and services.

price The amount of money for which a good or service can be bought or sold.

producer A person or group that makes goods and services.

public welfare Money provided by the government to those who are in need of help.

sales tax Tax put on goods at the time they are sold.

services Work that is done by people to care for the needs of others.

specialization Doing one kind of work. Individuals may specialize in their work. Doctors, policemen, teachers, and factory workers specialize in the work that they do. States may specialize in certain goods and services.

standard of value The worth of money in terms of goods and services. The dollar is used as the standard of value in all of the states.

supply The amount of a good or service that is for sale.

technology The tools and the "know-how" men have for producing goods and services.

FIGURE 3-5   Presentation of Facts in "Regional Studies" *

Hanna, Kohn, and Ver Steeg, Regional Studies, *p. 55.*

Races of Man

Do the major races of man live in your state?

Are there smaller racial groups in your state?

Anthropologists study people who lived long ago. They also study people who live today. To study people of today, anthropologists place all people who have some similar *physical features* into the same group. Some anthropologists say that there are three major groups of *man*. These groups are named by their skin color: black, or the Negroid group; white, or the Caucasoid group; and yellow, or the Mongoloid group. Each of these groups is a *race* of *man*. Each of these *races* is made up of many smaller racial groups. Members of each major *race* and many of the smaller racial groups are found in every state.

To learn what is meant by the word *race*, study the facts below. To learn about the major *races* of *man* study the facts and pictures on the next page.

Understanding Race

Does *race* mean *language?*

People of many races may speak the same language. You speak the English language, but you do not belong to the English race. There is no English race. You may speak the Spanish language, but you do not belong to the Spanish race. There is no Spanish race. People of any *race* may speak English, Spanish, or any other *language*. Race does not mean *language*.

Does *race* mean *nationality?*

People of many races may be the same nationality. Your nationality is American. You live in the United States of America. Some Americans have white skin. Some Americans have black skin. Some Americans have yellow skin. All Americans are the same nationality, but all Americans are not the same *race*. *Race* does not mean *nationality*.

What does *race* mean?

Now that you know some of the things that race does not mean, it will be easier to learn what race does mean. A *race* is a group of people who have some similar *physical features*. Some of these features are passed on to their children.

What sort of features do children receive, or inherit, from their parents? Color of skin, color of eyes, color of hair, shape of the nose, shape of the head, and shape of the body are some of the *physical features* that children often receive from their parents.

Have you ever been told that you have eyes like your mother? Have you ever been told that you are tall like your father? Perhaps someone has said, "You have your grandmother's hair," or "Your nose is like your grandfather's." Now you know some of the things that *race* does mean.

FIGURE 3-6   *Activities from the End of a Unit in "Regional Studies"**

Hanna, Kohn, and Ver Steeg, Regional Studies, p. 184.

Unit Activities: Working as a historian

Thinking as a historian

1. Make a time line of your life from the date of your birth to the present time.

There have been too many events in your life to include them all on your time line, so you must choose the most important ones. Of the following list of events, pick out those you think would be important enough to put on a time line: your birth; the time you fell down and skinned your knee; your first day of school; a day you were late to school; a vacation trip; the birth of a brother or sister. Your own time line will include events like those you picked from the list and will not be exactly like any other person's time line.

Investigating as a historian

1. Look at the time line you made for your state's history. Pick out one of the events you listed, and write a report on it. Do research in a library.
2. Pick out another of the events and draw a poster advertising it. Look at the poster on page 143 to see the way posters used to be written. Write your poster in this old-fashioned way.
3. Pretend you are one of the earliest settlers in your state. Your state wants to attract more settlers to come to your state and help develop it. Write a letter back home to England, France, Spain, or wherever your state's early settlers came from. Tell the person to whom you are writing about the new state. Tell about your state's natural resources, its natural setting, and the bill of rights in your state's constitution that protects your freedom. Write the best letter you can, so the person receiving it will want to move to your state.

Examining a foreign state: Katanga,
Congo Republic, Africa

The Congo Republic in Central Africa produces about one tenth of all the world's copper. Most of this copper comes from an area in the province of Katanga. Here is one of the richest areas of copper in the world.

The copper was discovered in Katanga in 1892. Unlike the discovery of gold in California and the rush that followed it, the discovery of copper was not followed by a rush of large numbers of people to the area.

The copper was located in a part of the Congo that was difficult to reach at that time. Before mining could be undertaken, railroads had to be built. Refineries had to be built to remove the copper from the ore. Many other things had to be done before the copper ore became a natural resource of Katanga. Do you think that copper has affected the history of the province of Katanga?

The following excerpts illustrate something of the variety of suggested activities for units on political science, human geography, sociology, and history.

Political Science:

Class Activities:

1. Write a class letter to the Council of State Governments, 1313 East Sixtieth Street, Chicago, Ill. 60637. Ask for a list of the governors of the 50 states and their political parties. On an outline map of the states, color in one color all of the states having Democratic governors. Use another color for all the states having Republican governors. Make a map key to explain what the colors stand for.

    Compare your map with the map on page 264. Is the political party that is in office in your state now the same party that has had predominant political leadership in your state in the past? Are there any political regions of states on your map? Is your state now in a Democratic or Republican region?

2. To learn more about how your state functions as part of a political region, write a class letter to your governor. Find out if he has had a formal or informal conference with the governors of other states in the region to discuss common political problems. Ask what has come about as a result of such meetings. Ask your governor if dates have been set for another such meeting.

Average Learners:

1. If you live in a Democratic political region of states, does it mean that everyone in your region is a Democrat? If you live in a Republican region of states, does it mean that everyone in your region is a Republican? Write a paragraph explaining what it does mean.

More Mature Learners:

1. Write a paragraph explaining why you think it is, or is not, a good thing that there are two major political parties in the political region of states in which you live.

2. Bring newspaper and magazine articles about political activity to class. Discuss the effects of the political action mentioned in the articles on the citizens of the political region in which your state is located.

Less Mature Learners:

1. Bring pictures and headlines from newspapers telling about political leaders in your political region of states. Discuss what these political leaders are doing for the citizens of these states.[9]

Human Geography:

Class Activities:

1. Play a game of "Identify the Farming Region." Place the following items on eight desks in your classroom: desk 1—a few kernels of corn and pictures or models of livestock; desk 2—a few vegetables and pieces of fruit, or cans of the same; desk 3—cotton fabric and a piece of sterilized cotton; desk 4— empty cartons of butter, cheese, and milk; desk 5—an assortment of food products and animal pictures or models; desk 6—a few grains of wheat, barley, and other grains; or flour and cereals; desk 7—pictures or models of cattle and some blades of grass; desk 8—vegetables or other food products and a container of water.

   Have the pupils examine the items on the desks. Using the map key on page 274 to help them remember all of the different farming regions, ask the pupils to write down the number of each desk and the name of the region it represents. Correct the papers in class. Ask the pupils which desk or desks have products on them that represent the kind of farming done in their own state.

2. Divide the class into groups representing the kinds of farming shown on the map key on page 274. Ask each group to discuss the following questions and make a report to the class. Why does the region specialize in a particular product? How will the farmers dispose of their surplus? What would happen if no surplus were produced for one year because the crop yield was poor or the livestock became diseased? How would this affect the farmers? How would it affect the markets?

3. Ask the pupils to find the strip city nearest the place where they live by using the map on page 280. Have them do research to find out why this area developed into a strip city. What cities and towns are part of this strip city? Do any transportation facilities help link the cities together?

---

[9] Hanna, Kohn, and Ver Steeg, *Regional Studies,* p. T-67.

Average Learners:

1. Investigate the commercial agricultural region of which your state is a part. Where is the market for the chief agricultural product of the region? What goods and services do people need from other regions? What services do the cities in the region provide?

More Mature Learners:

1. Select a commercial agricultural product such as wheat or corn. Find as many manufactured products as you can that contain some form of this crop. You will find many such products by reading the labels on food cans and packages.

Less Mature Learners:

1. Find pictures of corn, wheat, dairy, manufactured products, and others. Paste the pictures on a large outline map of the United States in the regions in which they are produced.[10]

Sociology:

Class Activities:

1. Using the table on page 240, make a bar graph of the expected 1975 population of the nine census divisions. Arrange the divisions in order of their size, so that the longest bar will be at the top of your page and the shortest bar at the bottom. Which census division has the largest population? Which has the smallest population? Where does your census division rank? Look at the map of the census divisions on page 239. Is the census division with the most people also largest in size of area? Do you think that population size depends entirely on size of area?

Average Learners:

1. Write a paper in which you discuss the problem of rapid population growth. Suppose, for example, that the population of your census division doubles in the next ten years. Discuss some of the problems that might arise as a result of such rapid growth in population.

---

[10]Hanna, Kohn, and Ver Steeg, *Regional Studies,* p. T-71.

2. Look in the *Sociology Facts,* pages 377-381, to find the population figures for the states in your census division. Rank the states in order of population. Which of the other states in this group are most like yours in size of population? Why do you think the states with the largest populations have attracted the most people?

More Mature Learners:

1. Write a paper in which you discuss why you think it is helpful for the United States Bureau of the Census to estimate what the population of the 50 states will be many years in the future. Which people in your state and adjoining states will need to know in advance how many people will be living there in the next ten or twenty years?
2. On an outline map of the 50 states, show the census division in which your state is located. Look in an atlas to find the largest city in terms of population in each state in your division. Mark the locations of the cities on the map. Find out what has attracted people to move to each of these urban centers.

Less Mature Learners:

1. Many people move from small towns to large urban centers in your state. Many other people move from the central part of the urban centers to the suburban areas. Write a paper discussing reasons for people moving to and from the urban centers.
2. On an outline map of the 50 states, label and color the states in your census division.[11]

History:

Class Activities:

1. Do research about songs sung by early settlers in your state. Tell what they reveal about the way of life in early times.
2. Make a mural of major events in your state's history. On an outline map of your state, show where these events took place.
3. Divide the class into two groups, one to be delegates to the first constitutional convention, the other delegates to a new convention. Compare and contrast their trips to the capital. Emphasize the changes that have taken place in your state in the time between the conventions.

---

[11] Hanna, Kohn, and Ver Steeg, *Regional Studies,* p. T-59.

4. Write a class letter to your secretary of state for information about your state seal. Ask about the meaning of the symbols on the seal. Find out who designed the seal and when it was adopted as the official seal of your state. Ask for a copy of the seal in color which you can display on the class bulletin board.

5. Do research to find out how natural factors have affected the history of your state. How have natural factors affected the location of highways? Industries? Population distribution?

Average Learners:

1. Write a report on why your state chose its particular bird and flower.

More Mature Learners:

1. Compare the last revision or the current proposals for revision of your state's constitution with its first constitution. What economic, social, and political factors may have brought about these changes?

Less Mature Learners:

1. Study the words in the official or unofficial song of your state. When was it written? What does the song tell you about your state?[12]

In summary, the methodology of Hanna's expanding-communities approach begins with the study of textbooks and then extends to a variety of other activities that are frequently differentiated according to the learning maturity of the different children in the class.

Characteristics of Learners and Teachers

One of the most prominent innovations among the drawings of people that illustrate Scott, Foresman's most recent version of the text

---

[12] Hanna, Kohn, and Ver Steeg, *Regional Studies*, p. T-41.

series is the frequent inclusion of racial groups other than whites. Americans of African, Oriental, and Indian ancestry are shown in many occupational roles at many levels of the social class structure. This racial diversity, which is also being featured in many other new textbook series, apparently reflects the awakening of publishers to the fact that school children are racially varied and profit from being able to identify with those of their own color in the texts. Many of the drawings that illustrate social-studies concepts show racially integrated groups—a school team including whites, browns, and blacks or an office in which Americans of African, Oriental, and European ancestry hold desk jobs of apparently equal responsibility and prestige.

One of the most basic of the assumptions about children that underlie the expanding-communities pattern is that young pupils are most interested in, and are best able to comprehend, those things that are close at hand. Only when they have understood the immediate environment are they properly prepared to view the next of the expanding circles of communities.

A further assumption, reflected in the suggested learning activities, is that children within a given classroom vary in their ability to comprehend social-studies concepts and to use these concepts in explaining their world. Therefore, experiences are recommended for three levels of learning maturity.

An assumption about teachers that the Hanna design makes is that the classroom instructor is capable of adjusting the basic pattern to fit a variety of children and teaching styles. As the fourth-grade teacher's manual points out:

> Flexibility of use of the many component parts is one of the outstanding characteristics of *Regional Studies.* The units in *Part One* introduce the seven disciplines and the basic concepts that are used throughout the book. These units may be studied in any order that is most suitable to the class situation . . . [and] in as much depth as is appropriate to the varying abilities of the pupils. . . . Many pupils will complete all of the units in *Part Two* and *Part Three*, whereas a few pupils may complete the study of only some units in each of these parts. . . .
>
> Some concepts may be understood in one lesson, while others may require several lessons, depending upon the social studies background of the class.[13]

The Hanna plan further assumes that teachers are well prepared to conduct class discussion and direct such activities as the construction of a

---

[13] Hanna, Kohn, and Ver Steeg, *Regional Studies,* p. T-9.

mural or the organization of an excursion. General ideas for class activities are offered in the teacher's guidebooks, but the steps for carrying these out so that they represent true social-science inquiry are usually not specified. Although sequences of questions for discussion are presented, the rationale underlying the sequence is not explained.

Evaluation Procedures

The guidebooks accompanying the textbooks do not focus attention on the evaluation phase of teaching. Perhaps the authors have assumed that the techniques for assessment are so obvious that they do not warrant direct discussion. The apparent evaluation devices are the questions children are to answer and the activities they carry out. Unlike some textbook manuals, the Scott, Foresman series does not furnish objective-type test items.

Conditions Affecting Adoption of the Plan

During the progressive-education era in the United States, most school systems established elementary social-studies programs that followed the expanding-communities design. Therefore, the present-day scope and sequence of the Hanna plan is compatible with an overall social-studies pattern already familiar in most school districts. Adopting the Hanna plan would require no great deviation from the past.

On the other hand, the concentration on separate social-science disciplines is a development of the 1960s and thus represents something of an innovation, one that older teachers might find strange and uncomfortable. But this emphasis does place the latest version of the Scott, Foresman approach in line with the newer social studies, and therefore the series should appeal to school personnel who want to keep their program up-to-date.

From the viewpoint of finances, the adoption of this program requires a considerable expenditure of funds for textbooks and for the supplementary trade books and filmstrips needed to carry out the plan in its most complete form. Administrators who have already purchased a different social-studies textbook series in recent years are likely to be reluctant to support an overall transfer to the Scott, Foresman series, particularly since the program is designed as an entire kindergarten-through-grade-6 plan. Buying books for only one grade level would not suffice unless the school began at the kindergarten level and added one set of books each year as the children moved up from one grade to the next. However, it is doubtful that the school's sixth-grade teachers would want to wait six years to adopt the new approach simply out of consideration for the textbook costs involved.

Conclusion

In summary, the Hanna expanding-communities approach illustrates a curriculum pattern that originated during the progressive era and that has recently been updated to incorporate innovations in the field of elementary social-studies theory and practice. The program is organized around a series of textbooks for children, augmented by teacher's guidebooks that suggest an array of learning activities to accompany the textbook reading. Hanna and his associates have attempted to aid teachers in suiting the curriculum to individual pupil abilities by differentiating between learning activities appropriate for slower learners and those recommended for average and advanced pupils. The task of determining what evaluation procedures to use with the program is left mostly to the classroom teacher's own initiative.

4

The Social Sciences: Concepts and Values

Not only have several of the established textbook series—such as Hanna's—been revised to incorporate ideas gained from recent social-studies developments, but new series have been created with the newer curriculum ideas as their core.

We have chosen to illustrate one sector of these modern departures by describing a series entitled *The Social Sciences: Concepts and Values.* The concepts-and-values program was developed under the direction of Paul F. Brandwein, president of the Center for the Study of Instruction and an adjunct professor at the University of Pittsburgh. The text materials are published by Harcourt Brace Jovanovich, the company that has financed the Center.

Although the first textbooks in this social-studies series were not published until 1970, Brandwein should not be considered a newcomer to the field of elementary curriculum. His work in social studies was preceded by several successful years of producing text materials for the teaching of physical and biological sciences.[1] The conceptual approach that he recommended for the teaching of science

---

[1] Paul F. Brandwein, *Substance, Structure, and Style in Science,* revised edition (New York: Harcourt Brace Jovanovich, 1968).

has obviously influenced the design that he recommends for the effective teaching of social sciences in kindergarten through grade 9.

The Program's Rationale

The personal convictions that determined the key features of this curriculum pattern were voiced by Brandwein in his Abbott Memorial Lecture at Colorado College in 1967. He first expressed his belief that two key outcomes should be produced by children's social learnings in a democratic society—responsible consent and responsible dissent.

> *There is a discipline of responsible consent.*
> Its aim is to interpose evidence, reason, and judgment between desire and action.[2] Its techniques are the methods of intelligence. Its structure consists of concepts and values; its body of content, of the knowledge, skills, and attitudes coming from man's long search for the good life and for correct action.
> *There is, conversely, a discipline of responsible dissent.*
> Its aim is, again, between impulse and action to interpose evidence, reason, and judgment. Its techniques are, again, the methods of intelligence. Its structure, too, consists of the concepts and values deriving from human interaction, and the great repertoire of its body of content comes from the interactions of citizens in their quest for an effective society, one that resolves conflict and confers peace and prosperity.
> A discipline of responsible consent and the human ends it serves can be realized through appeal to rational and mature judgment. It is basic to responsible action. . . .
> The social sciences play a fundamental role in life and living. The tactics and strategy of teaching the social sciences lead the teacher to create situations by means of which students explore human behavior and human society in order to develop orderly explanations of human action and to test effectively these orderly explanations through the variety of ways that are part of the methods of the social scientist. . . .[3]

In effect, the Brandwein curriculum leads pupils to seek to discover concepts and to test them, with *concepts in the social sciences* defined as

---

[2] Brandwein writes that "I am haunted by the thought that this is John Dewey's phrase (or one very much like it), which I may have fixed in memory at one of his lectures or through my reading." Paul F. Brandwein, *Toward a Discipline of Responsible Consent* (New York: Harcourt Brace Jovanovich, 1969), p. 1. Copyright ©1969 by Harcourt Brace Jovanovich, Inc. and reprinted with their permission.
[3] Brandwein, *Toward a Discipline of Responsible Consent*, pp. 1, 3.

"orderly explanations of human action as it relates to people, objects, and events."[4] This curriculum is also designed to help children seek and test values, with *values* meaning people's beliefs about which things in life are good and which are bad, which are desirable and which are undesirable, which are proper and which are improper.

Viewed another way, Brandwein's *concepts* and *values* theme is a reaction against what he considers undesirable teaching and inadequate curriculum structures of the past. First, he sides with those other critics of educational practice who believe that teaching children concepts is far superior to teaching them facts.

> Concepts have stability. New nations may develop as "new data," but the concept of "nation" remains. Within a child's schooling in the past generation, Africa exploded into nationhood. It can be argued that the "old facts" about Africa that were taught the child are no longer tenable, and no longer can serve the child, but the concept of nationhood was, and is, tenable and still serves the child in his attempts to understand his culture and to live successfully in it. Postulate a child entering the first grade and being subjected for the next twelve years to a "fact"-oriented, topic-centered course of social studies. At the current rate of generation of knowledge, perhaps little that he learned will be "true" as "fact" at the time of his leaving high school. His "school life" would, in a sense, have been "wasted." Postulate another child, one taking part in a curriculum based on concepts. Time, new data, and attendant processes, which secure the dynamic operations that are part of concept-seeking, feed the concepts. Twelve years later, the data will have changed. China may no longer be Communist, or may be fascist; the satellite states of Russia may all be democratic, or part of Russia may be so inclined; the United States may have fifty-four states, the Constitution yet another amendment; the wheat, corn, rice, and oat crops may be even larger; a new technology may be burgeoning and we may no longer be interested in "outer space" but in "inner space." Nevertheless, "nation," "scarcity," "man," "interaction," "norms," "values," "family," "interdependence," "community," "environment," "time," "rules," "law," "role" will be conceptually his, with a host of viable subject matter to feed them. He can use these concepts to explain the new nations, the new cycles, the new behavior he meets.
>
> Concepts in the social sciences are maps of the social universe. They remain relevant to life and living; hence they are stable intellectual currency.[5]

A second objection to past and present social-studies teaching that is implied in Brandwein's program relates to values. Brandwein's comments suggest that he is critical of two kinds of teachers—those who impose their

---

[4] Brandwein, *Toward a Discipline of Responsible Consent*, p. 5.
[5] Brandwein, *Toward a Discipline of Responsible Consent*, pp. 10-11.

own *substantive* values on children and those who fail to face the issue of conflicting values and thus convey the idea that there is no significant difference among values.

To understand the way values are treated in the Brandwein design, it is necessary to recognize the distinctions he draws among three types of values: behavioral, procedural, and substantive. He follows Edwin Fenton's belief that "teachers have the right to teach the first two; the third, they do not."[6] In explaining the distinction he draws among these three varieties, Brandwein has written:

> . . . children should give others in class the right to be heard; they should keep the classroom clean; they must not disrupt class. These are the decent routines of the classroom; they are *behavioral values*. So is adherence to the laws enacted by properly constituted lawmaking bodies. . . .
>
> Even as in science students need to accept the data developed and tested empirically as a result of experimentation, and as in mathematics they accept rationale and deduction, so, too, in the social sciences, evidence must be respected. Evidence, reason, and judgment—rather than prejudice—are *procedural values*.
>
> But substantive values, Fenton argues, are another matter. Among examples of such values, he cites: "Money is more important than anything else" and "If the individual wants one course of action and society another, then the individual ought to do as society dictates."[7] He contends—if we read him aright—that teachers should *not* teach the substantive values "as a set of truth," but should, where appropriate, teach *about* them by raising the issues so that each child can examine them in terms of the canons of critical thinking.[8]

The pursuit of concepts and values, in Brandwein's view, requires "the technique of inquiry" that he prefers to call *the methods of intelligence*—"the methods that pervade the sciences, and the humanities as well." His curriculum design is intended to furnish pupils practice in using these methods "for seeking and testing effective reality."[9]

Finally, the author sees the teacher of social studies not only as a guide to the rational analysis of concepts and values through use of the methods of intelligence, but also

> . . . in the ministry of mercy. The teacher heals; if the classroom does not heal, it has no teacher, only an instructor. An instructor is only as large as his

---

[6] Brandwein, *Toward a Discipline of Responsible Consent*, p. 6.

[7] Edwin Fenton, *Teaching the New Social Sciences in Secondary Schools: An Inductive Approach* (New York: Holt, Rinehart & Winston, 1966), p. 43.

[8] Brandwein, *Toward a Discipline of Responsible Consent*, pp. 6-7.

[9] Brandwein, *Toward a Discipline of Responsible Consent*, p. 7.

subject; the teacher is as large as life. If the proper study of mankind is man, then it is proper to use for it the tools of the teacher—and these include compassion and mercy. Children do not always choose their parents well, or their heredity, or their environment, or their proper moment in history. Thus, above all, a teacher heals.[10]

Scope and Sequence

The Brandwein textbooks and accompanying teacher's manuals for kindergarten through grade 6 were published in 1970. Materials for the junior high were scheduled for completion in 1972, with a senior-high program planned for later publication based on research into the social-science needs of grades 10 through 12. In the following discussion we are concerned only with the scope and sequence from kindergarten through grade 6.

Brandwein sees the curriculum as the school's attempt to "reduce the randomness" of children's experiences by offering a structure that helps children order and interpret experience. This structure is reflected in the chart of scope and sequence in Figure 4-1. To read the chart, you will find it useful to note first the items up the left margin and those across the bottom. The left margin focuses on values or responsibilities, labeled *behavioral themes*. The bottom margin focuses on *cognitive schemes* or concept seeking. The numbered levels ascending from the lower to the upper portions of the chart represent grades of the elementary school. The body of the chart, within the heavy black lines, shows how the cognitive schemes of the bottom margin intersect with the value-seeking or behavioral themes of the left margin to produce what children will study (the concepts) at each grade level. In other words, to find what is recommended for first graders, you look across the row labeled *Level 1.* To find the development of concepts in geography from one grade to the next throughout the elementary school, you look up column C, which rises above *Cognitive Scheme C*. Or, to see how concepts from the discipline of economics are developed grade after grade, read the items on the six levels above the *Cognitive Scheme D* column.

Unlike some of the newer curriculum schemes that attempt to organize their material in a multidisciplinary pattern that matches precisely the social-science disciplines in higher education, the five cognitive schemes of the Brandwein design are only general approximations of the

---

[10]Brandwein, *Toward a Discipline of Responsible Consent,* p. 7.

Level 6. Responsibility for man and his environment—through development of systems of behavior	6. Biological and cultural inheritance result in variation in the people of the earth.	6. Social systems are shaped by the values of interacting groups.	6. Political organization alters the map.	6. Economic systems are shaped by the values of the culture.	6. Political systems are developed, changed, or maintained through the interaction of individuals and governments.
Level 5. Responsibility for man and his environment—through cultural patterns of behavior	5. The interaction of biological and cultural inheritance results in the adaptation of man to his environment.	5. Cultures in varying environments have similar components.	5. Man modifies the environment in order to utilize his resources and increase them.	5. The patterns of buying and selling depend upon choices people make.	5. Regional and national governments co-operate.
Level 4. Responsibility for man and his environment—through adaptive patterns of behavior	4. Man inherits and learns patterns of behavior.	4. Man learns social behavior from groups with which he interacts.	4. Man utilizes his environment to secure basic needs.	4. Man interacts to utilize available resources.	4. Man's peaceful interaction depends on social controls.
Level 3. Responsibility for man and his environment—through adaptive behavior of the larger group	3. Community groups adapt to the environment.	3. The characteristics of a community are the result of interactions between individuals and other groups in a specific environment.	3. Communities develop different modes of adaptation to different environments.	3. The culture of the community determines the use of resources.	3. Community groups are governed through leadership and authority.
Level 2. Responsibility for man and his environment—through adaptive behavior of the basic group	2. Members of the family group are alike because of heredity and environment.	2. The family group teaches the child the social behavior of his culture.	2. Family groups throughout the world live in different environments.	2. Family groups utilize resources to satisfy their needs.	2. Members of family groups are governed by rules and law.

FIGURE 4-1   A Conceptual Schemes Approach to the Social Sciences*

Level 1. Responsibility for man and his environment—through adaptive behavior of the individual within the group	1. Individuals resemble each other.	1. Individuals learn from each other.	1. Individuals live in different environments on the earth.	1. Individuals use the resources available to them.	1. The behavior of individuals is governed by commonly accepted rules.
Behavioral Themes (Based on Value-seeking)					
Cognitive Schemes (Based on Concept-seeking)	COGNITIVE SCHEME A Man is the product of heredity and environment.	COGNITIVE SCHEME B Human behavior is shaped by the social environment.	COGNITIVE SCHEME C The geographic features of the earth affect man's behavior.	COGNITIVE SCHEME D Economic behavior depends upon the utilization of resources.	COGNITIVE SCHEME E Governments resolve conflicts and make interaction easier among people.

*Paul F. Brandwein et al., Principles and Practices in the Teaching of the Social Sciences: Concepts and Values, Blue—Level 1 (New York: Harcourt Brace Jovanovich, 1970), pp. T-20, T-21. Copyright © 1970 by Harcourt Brace Jovanovich, Inc. and reprinted with their permission.

disciplines. In other words, his pattern does not separate anthropology, social psychology, history, and sociology as distinct entities. Rather, it uses concepts and facts from each of these fields as they seem appropriate for Cognitive Scheme B (Human behavior is shaped by the social environment). On the other hand, certain of the cognitive schemes draw most of their concepts from a single field. This tendency is particularly true of Schemes C (geography), D (economics), and E (political science and government), which depend only in a minor degree upon neighboring disciplines.

The chart in Figure 4-1 offers only a gross idea of the overall structure and the key concepts that are pursued. To understand the supporting concepts that become the subgoals for lessons within each cell of the chart, it is necessary to read the explication of each column as presented in the teacher's manuals that accompany the Brandwein textbooks for pupils. As an illustration we have reproduced in Figure 4-2 a more detailed version of the column above Cognitive Scheme B. This shows which instructional units at each grade level are designed to carry children toward a comprehension of the ideas related to the concept-statement "Human behavior is shaped by the social environment."

So far in our inspection of the scope-and-sequence chart, we have centered attention on the columns—that is, on the concepts to be taught. How, then, do the behavior themes (value seeking) intersect with these concepts at each grade level? Brandwein has explained it in this manner:

> Proceeding in a sequential and hierarchal patterning of curriculum from Level 1 to Level 6, one can observe that pervasive through the fabric of the cognitive levels are the values that condition our behavior. And in analyzing the variety of behavior, to determine the value of each in adapting to the environment, children employ activities rooted in analysis and synthesis. Thus, in Cognitive Scheme E, the child in Levels 1 and 2 learns to understand and value "rules" as developed by his group. His parents dictate what is "good" and what is "bad"—clean hands, clean dress, being on time, using acceptable language, playing at appropriate times and in appropriate places. The values of class and family and peer group are behavioral values.
>
> Later, through the uses of history (colonial history and the history of the early pioneers), the child contrasts the lives of his forebears with his own. Through contrastive analysis of the life of a Puritan family, or an Eskimo family, or an African family with his own, he comes to know that values have changed. . . .
>
> On a more complex level, within the web of the cognitive, the child begins to understand that "Human desires are greater than the resources available to meet the expressed needs." He begins to understand the need for *choice*. And with the understanding of the crucial play of choice within our economic system, values become critical. . . . And . . . slowly he apprehends and comprehends the meaning of the values that are an essential part of the systems of democracy and representative government of which he is a part. At last he begins to read "We hold these truths to be self-evident" as "We hold these values to be self-evident. . . ."

Level 6.

Responsibility for man and his environment— through development of systems of behavior.

Unit Three

A Probe into Social Systems

Social systems are shaped by the values of interacting groups.

Unit Two

The City as Center

Social systems are shaped by the values of interacting groups.

Emphasis on Sociology and Cultural Anthropology:

The city as a center. Children gain insight into the development of the city as man changes from food-gatherer and hunter to food-grower. Children trace the transition of village to city, focus on the nature of the attraction of the city and the richness of city life. As population increases, the problems of the city multiply and thus there is focus on the technics which enable man to create a good life for all. More than 70 percent of Americans live in cities now, hence the relevance of more individual insight into the concepts of social control as related to environment as synthesized within the concept-statement (given at the left).

Emphasis on Sociology:

The effect of the interaction and inter-dependence of individuals and groups on our social system. Children view how values influence behavior, how social controls serve as regulators of human behavior. Children synthesize the social system of which they are members. They analyze norms and values, roles, and norms of behavior, roles of leadership and "followship," as well as a variety of roles within groups. Children begin to understand the nature of conflicting values and conflicting roles; they gain insight into status and social mobility. The children search, in short, into the data which give meaning to the concept of social control and social system as synthesized in the concept-statement (at the left).

Level 5.

Responsibility for man and his environment— through cultural patterns of behavior.

Emphasis on Cultural Anthropology:

Components and forms of culture. Children analyze a variety of cultures in various geographic environments (Hopi, Kpelle, Eskimo) and compare and contrast

FIGURE 4-2   Content within Cognitive Scheme B: Human Behavior
Is Shaped by the Social Environment

Unit Two	*their special cultural forms within the cultural components. Clearly, although the forms vary, cultural components are shared by all. Children come to recognize that people create and change cultural forms. Children investigate the richness of cultural forms in a variety of selected cultures and compare and contrast these cultures with their own. They gain further insight into the concept of socialization in relation to the environment as they come to see the relevance of the concept-statement (at the left).*
A View of Cultures *Cultures in varying environments have similar components.*	
Level 4. *Responsibility for man and his environment— through adaptive patterns of behavior.* *Unit One* *Acting in a Group* *Man learns social behavior from groups with which he interacts.*	*Emphasis on Sociology:* *A further probe into social behavior— norms, clubs, roles, customs, and other cultural traits. From the Blackfeet to the Hawaiians of Kamehameha's time, to the individual community of each child, the nature of leadership is investigated. There is focus on the boy Ikechukwu of Nigeria and his group, to study the characteristics of a group. Within the group the phenomenon of leadership—elected and hereditary—is investigated. Children examine their own roles and gain further insight into the concept of social learning, and see the relevance to their own lives of the concept-statement (at the left).*
Level 3. *Responsibility for man and his environment— through adaptive behavior of the larger group.* *Unit Three* *Groups in the Community*	*Emphasis on Sociology:* *Interaction in groups in the community. Children analyze the Moroccan girl Halima and her family, the Ghanaian boy Kwesi and his family, and the children of a Puritan family and their own community. In investigating communities in the United States and over the globe, children continue their probe into the nature of independence. They observe how environments change roles and values, and how these changes in turn affect the cultural and physical environment. They relate their increasing knowledge*

FIGURE 4-2   Continued

The characteristics of a community are the result of interactions between individuals and other groups in a specific environment.	*to the concepts of* interaction *and* social control *as epitomized in the concept-statement (at the left).*

Level 2.	*Emphasis on Sociology:*
Responsibility for man and his environment— through adaptive behavior of the basic group.	*Children investigate a variety of social groups and investigate the interaction and interdependence of people in groups, in terms of cooperative goals. They begin to understand the differences between gatherings of people and the actions of a social group. Children gain further insight into the concept of* group behavior *as expressed in the concept-statement (at the left).*
Unit Three	
Learning to Act Together The family group teaches the child the social behavior of his culture.	
	Emphasis on Sociology:
Unit One	
Learning from Others The family group teaches the child the social behavior of his culture.	*Likenesses and differences in behavior. Children investigate their own patterns of behavior and those of other children and realize that children learn their basic behavior from the nuclear group, the family. Children undertake a further synthesis of the concept of* interaction *as epitomized in the concept-statement (at the left).*

Level 1.	*Emphasis on History:*
Responsibility for man and his environment— through adaptive behavior of the individual within the group.	*Children analyze events of the past and realize that they have learned from people who have lived in the past. A first understanding of their relationship to their own ancestry and the past is established as children use the data to probe further into the concept of* social learning *as expressed in the concept-statement (at the left).*

FIGURE 4-2   Continued

Unit Seven	*Emphasis on Social Psychology and Learning*
A Look Back *Individuals learn from each other*	*Children investigate a variety of learning situations and analyze what they learn from teachers, classmates, parents, friends, and the environment. They perceive the concept of* interaction *as expressed in the concept-statement (at the left).*
Unit Three	
The People We Learn From Individuals learn from each other	

Kindergarten	
Children interact with the physical and social environment.	*Through study of the activities of a Spanish child, children will begin to analyze what children learn in their family and peer groups, as expressed in the concept-statement (at left).*

FIGURE 4-2   Continued

In discussing issues, then, the children begin to appreciate the *value* of seeing different "points of view." The analysis of values proceeds to the substantive level. In essence, this means that the teacher encourages the analysis of contrasts, encourages children to identify not only the opposite poles of an issue, but also the "gray" issues between the poles. For example, older children might discuss: What should the voting age be? For young children, the question might be: Should children be free to go to any movie? ... A variety of alternatives is considered, all views represented are heard, and the richness of human variety, yet inherent likeness, is expressed.[11]

Therefore, in Brandwein's program the pupils at each level of concept-seeking are also guided toward considering the values of the people whose way of living is being studied at the moment.

The assumption underlying the sequence in which concepts are organized from one grade to the next is that the concepts at the lower levels are easier to understand than those set for the upper grades.

[11] Brandwein, *Toward a Discipline of Responsible Consent*, pp. 24-25.

Furthermore, it is assumed that knowing the lower-level concepts is essential to—or at least helpful in—comprehending those at higher levels. The range of concepts included in the program has been determined by what the author and his colleagues believe are the most useful ideas and methods of investigation to be found in the social-science disciplines and the humanities (history, in particular).

Materials and Methods

The essential materials for implementing the concepts-and-values program are the pupils' textbooks and the related teacher's guidebooks for each grade level. To supplement these resources, the publishers issue tests, audio-visual aids, and research books—that is, "inquiry books into values and concepts—for example, Negro leadership."[12]

For nearly every lesson in the program, teachers are urged to obtain other specified materials. For example, in a sequence of first-grade lessons focusing on ways people adapt to their environment, the authors of the program suggest the use of:

1. pictures illustrating different environments, ". . . and have the children decide which season is represented in each environment. In all cases, be sure to ask, 'How do you know?' This will encourage the children to use the set of data in the picture as evidence for their responses."[13]

2. the film *Life on a Small Farm* (McGraw-Hill). "After the film, ask: 'How is a farm different from the place where you live? How is it like your home?' "[14]

3. drawings that children make of boats. The teacher can ask: "Where can your boats go? Can your boats go anywhere? How do you know? Can they go on the ocean? Can they go on the lakes? Can they go on rivers?"[15]

4. Carl Sandburg's poem "Fog," which is reproduced in the teacher's manual so that the teacher does not have to hunt it up. "You might relate the poem . . . to a discussion of the kind of weather that occurs near the ocean."[16]

5. television programs the children recall, showing desert environments.[17]

---

[12] Personal correspondence from Paul F. Brandwein, September 4, 1970.
[13] Paul F. Brandwein et al., *The Social Sciences: Concepts and Values, Blue*, p. 39.
[14] Brandwein et al., *The Social Sciences: Concepts and Values, Blue*, p. 41.
[15] Brandwein et al., *The Social Sciences: Concepts and Values, Blue*, p. 42.
[16] Brandwein et al., *The Social Sciences: Concepts and Values, Blue*, p. 43.
[17] Brandwein et al., *The Social Sciences: Concepts and Values, Blue*, p. 45.

The writing style of the children's textbooks in the Harcourt Brace Jovanovich series is illustrated by the following two excerpts. As each passage indicates, the series endeavors at all grade levels to engage the pupil in making decisions as he encounters the concepts that the program attempts to convey. To aid the child in picturing the people and places discussed in the text materials, the books are profusely illustrated with full-color photographs, diagrams, and charts.

At the second-grade level, Unit Three on group behavior (Learning to Act Together) is followed by a section entitled "Begin Your Family Book." The first page of the section shows a second-grade boy's crayon drawing of himself. The second page shows his drawing of his family. The following passage accompanies these drawings:

This year you may make a book.
You may make it from pictures you draw.
This book will be about you.
It will be about your family group.
Rusty made a family book.
Here is the first page.
Rusty drew this picture.

Draw a picture of yourself for your family book.
What could you put on the second page?

Here is the second page of Rusty's book.
Rusty drew this picture of his family group.
He made a record.
How can you make a record of your family?
Rusty used one way.
There is another way.
What is it?
Turn the page to find out.[18]

The following page of the textbook contains a photograph of Rusty with his family.

Now let us inspect the writing style at the fifth-grade level. Unit Four, labeled "A People's Choices," begins with a section on economics

---

[18]Paul F. Brandwein et al., *The Social Sciences: Concepts and Values, Red* (New York: Harcourt Brace Jovanovich, 1970), pp. 62-63. Copyright © 1970 by Harcourt Brace Jovanovich, Inc. and reprinted with their permission.

called "The Costs of Production." The photograph that accompanies the following passage shows a boy selecting a package of ice cream from a frozen-food display case in a market.

Your mother has sent you to the supermarket. She has asked you to buy a half-gallon of chocolate ice cream for your sister's birthday party. When you reach the frozen foods section, you stop for a moment because there is a *supply* of several brands of ice cream for sale at different prices.

You have $2.00 with you. Will you buy the most expensive ice cream? After all, it is for a special day. Or will you buy a less expensive ice cream? If you do, you will have enough money left to buy a package of fancy birthday napkins. The napkins sell for 39¢.

The supermarket's own ice cream, Brandex, is selling for 90¢ a half-gallon. It is good ice cream, and it is certainly cheaper than McGregor's ice cream, which is selling for $1.65. However, you choose to buy McGregor's ice cream because your mother says it is creamier than Brandex. It has greater *value* for her. She knows that it is made by a local firm. The McGregor dairy makes only ice cream and they are proud of the quality of their product.

We can say that you have made an economic choice. You have decided how to use your resources, your money, to get something you need. You've decided that you'd rather buy the creamier, more expensive ice cream and keep your mother happy than buy the cheaper ice cream and the fancy napkins. We can say that you and other purchasers of McGregor's ice cream have a *demand* for it. That is, you have the money *and* the willingness to buy McGregor's ice cream.[19]

In the pages of the textbook following this passage, the pupils read an analysis of why the prices of the two brands of ice cream differ. The analysis treats such concepts as costs of production, profit, property, labor, pricing, and costs of distribution.

With these examples of the style of textbooks in mind, let us now consider the teaching methodology recommended for the Brandwein plan. The teacher's manuals that accompany the children's textbooks at each grade level offer suggestions about teaching methods at two levels of specificity.

At the general level, the manuals explain overall instructional strategies that teachers may use. In some instances the explanations focus on a particular instructional technique, like role playing. To aid teachers

---

[19]Paul F. Brandwein et al., *The Social Sciences: Concepts and Values, Purple* (New York: Harcourt Brace Jovanovich, 1970), p. 169. Copyright © 1970 by Harcourt Brace Jovanovich, Inc. and reprinted with their permission.

in using the technique, suggestions are offered for carrying out the method successfully. In other instances, the explanation centers on the underlying pattern of most lessons that are recommended in the manuals. For example, Brandwein describes four basic elements that determine the structure of most lessons at the second-grade level:

(a) The teacher is to *create a situation* (a problem-situation based on a setting).

Of course, the teacher may plan a situation with the children, or the children themselves may suggest one. Sometimes, the teacher capitalizes on an event, such as a visiting group of children, a TV show, or a sudden change in weather.

Pictures are records of human behavior; they are data. As such, they can be used as problem-situations in concept-seeking and value-seeking. . . .

(b) As they become involved in the problem-situation created in the text, the children are encouraged by questions (developed by skilled teachers) to *explore human behavior* (their own and that of others) *and the human environment* (the people and events around them).

In the Teacher's Edition, this part of the lesson is placed under the head "Developing the Lesson." Within this section, the children

(c) *seek orderly explanations of the behavior under inquiry*, and in doing so
(d) *test their explanations.*[20]

The teacher's manuals also illustrate the varied purposes or functions of the specific questions that are recommended in lesson plans.

(a)   Knowledge: *Questions concerned with memory skills.*
Teacher: Do people sometimes waste water? How?
Child: They let water run when they wash.

(b)   Comprehension: *Questions concerned with developing understanding.*
T: Was the pond always like this? What has happened to it?
C: It must have been clean before people threw the cans into it.

(c)   Application: *Questions concerned with application of past learning.*
T: Why do factories use scrap iron over again?
C: They use it not to waste it.

(d)   Analysis: *Questions concerned with identification of different elements in a situation.*
T: Will the forest grow again?

---

[20]Paul F. Brandwein et al., *Principles and Practices in the Teaching of the Social Sciences: Concepts and Values, Red—Level 2* (New York: Harcourt Brace Jovanovich, 1970), p. T-41. Copyright ©1970 by Harcourt Brace Jovanovich and reprinted with their permission.

C: Responses include replanting, letting the forest develop from seeds, using other sources of wood, and so on.

(e)   Synthesis: *Questions concerned with separate elements in a new relationship (concept).*
T: Why must we take care of the trees and water we have?

(f)   Evaluation: *Questions concerned with judgment about the effectiveness of a procedure.*
T: Suppose you had a piece of land. What could you do with it?[21]

The foregoing varieties of general explanations regarding classroom methods is then followed in each teacher's manual with specific lesson plans to accompany each page or two of the pupils' textbooks. As the following example from the second-grade teacher's guidebook illustrates, each lesson plan is built according to the general four-step structure described earlier (create a situation, explore human behavior, seek orderly explanations of the behavior, test or verify the explanations), and questions suggested for the teacher's use are designed to carry out the functions described in the general explanation of various question types. The following lesson plan is designed for use with three pages of the pupils' textbook, each showing a picture of several elementary-school children (page 45 of children and adults in a Spanish Harlem clean-up project, page 46 of five boys in a soccer game, and page 47 of six Cub Scouts with their leader). Below each of the pictures is the question: Do they belong to a group?

Unit Three Lesson 1

Teaching Objectives

Concept-Seeking: *Children begin to gain the awareness that individuals in groups have a common interest.*
Value-Seeking: *Children begin to perceive that individuals are like other members of a group in some ways.*
Methods of Intelligence: • Observing *two groups.* • Collecting *and* Analyzing *data on group activities.* • Inferring *the criteria for a group.*

Creating the Learning Situation

Introducing the Lesson: Begin, perhaps, by asking the children to think of different things they do with others, and to identify the people with whom they

---

[21] Brandwein et al., *The Social Sciences: Concepts and Values, Red,* p. T-42.

share these activities. The children should be able to identify three or four groups of which they are members. Help them by asking:

T: With whom do you watch TV? · With whom do you eat? · With whom do you go to school? · With whom do you play?

Now, have the children turn to the problem-situation shown in the picture on the unit title page (text p. 45). The picture shows children and grownups in a Spanish Harlem clean-up project. Ask, perhaps:

T: What are they doing? · Are they a group? Why do you think so? · Are they working together? What makes you say so? · Would a person walking down the street be part of the group? Why not?

The children's responses will give you an opportunity to evaluate their present understanding of the concept of *group behavior.*

Developing the Lesson: For this introductory lesson, have the children first study the two problem-situations. Ask, perhaps:

T: Why are the children in the picture on the left playing together? · Do you think they live near each other? What makes you think so? · Do you think they all know how to play the game? Why? · Do you have a play group like these children? · Can you play alone? Is it as much fun as playing with your friends?

To show that all activities are not necessarily done in groups, ask the following questions:

T: Are there some things you would rather do alone? Name some. · Do you like to be alone sometimes? · Do you like to be in a group sometimes? Why?

Now, turn the children's attention to the situation shown on the next page. Ask, perhaps:

T: Why did the boys get together? · Do you think that they are friends? · Are they a group? · Are they learning anything? · Could they learn the same things alone? · Would it be as much fun?

To stress that most people belong to more than one group, ask:

T: Do you think the boys playing ball go to school? · Do the Boy Scouts? How do you know? · Whom do they eat dinner with? How do you know? · Do you belong to more than one group? Name the groups you belong to.

Verifying Progress Concept-Seeking: *Children should be able to hypothesize the groups the following individuals belong to:*

> *A man who wears a fire hat.*
> *A boy who wears a football uniform.*
> *A girl going out to play with a ball.*

Value-Seeking: *Ask the children to discuss the following:*

T: *Do all the Boy Scouts have to follow rules? · What do you think the rules are? · What kinds of rules might the boys playing soccer follow? · What happens if one child does not obey the group's rules?*

Alternative Experiences for a Variety of Interests

1. Ask the children whether or not the class is a group. Have them name different activities that occur in the class. Ask:

T: Do you all do them? • Do you all have to follow rules in the class-room? • Who doesn't?

2. Let each group role-play a typical class activity. If the children wish, they may select one member of their group to play the part of the teacher.[22]

To illustrate the greater complexity of lesson plans in the upper grades, let us consider excerpts from a sixth-grade plan intended for use with a unit on social behavior. The pupils have read the history of the development of several ancient cities and are now considering the fall of Rome and conditions in Western Europe during the Middle Ages. The lesson plans at the sixth-grade level, compared to those for second grade, are quite long, so we shall not quote an entire plan. Rather, we shall offer passages that illustrate several points: (1) the nature of questions and their purposes, (2) the inclusion in the plan of likely pupil answers, so the teacher might know the variety of responses to expect, and (3) the manner in which the plan bridges the gap in time between the Middle Ages and today in analyzing the phenomena of social stratification and social mobility.

Unit Two Section 4

Teaching Objectives

Concept-Seeking: *The children will reinforce their understanding of the city as an example of adaptation, interaction, and social control by recognizing the ways in which society had to restructure itself in the absence of great cities during the Middle Ages.*

Value-Seeking: *The children will identify the person to person reciprocal relationships necessary to resolve conflicts in a period in which political organization broke down.*

Methods of Intelligence: • Observing *needs for social organization after the barbarian invasions of Europe and medieval roles and norms which developed to meet those needs.* • Classifying *behaviors as roles and norms.* • Inferring *values from the development of roles and norms.* • Hypothesizing *the need for methods of resolving social conflict.* • Predicting *the need for urban centers for highly specialized economic systems.*

---

[22] Brandwein et al., *The Social Sciences: Concepts and Values, Red,* p. 61.

82921

Creating the Learning Situation

Setting: Learning situations developed around the decline and rebirth of cities during the Middle Ages and the growth of a new social structure based on feudalism, craft guilds, and the medieval Church.

Related Information: See TE p. 129.

Introducing the Lesson:

T: As you finished reading about the Roman Empire in Section 3, you learned that Rome was weakened by changes in social conditions. What do you think happened to Rome when the system of social controls and rules were weakened? Read the beginning of Section 4 to find out.

As the text suggests, the children can use the time line to figure out how long the Roman Empire existed before the German tribes captured Rome in the fifth century A.D. (509 B.C.–410 A.D., about 1000 years). Place this event on the time line, illustrating the Germanic invasions and summarizing the event.

Have the children read the subsection "A New Way of Life" to find out what happened throughout the empire when the organized government, law, and political power of the Romans were withdrawn.

T: When the towns and villages were left open to attack after the Roman troops left, what did farmers and villagers seem to value most? What evidence can you find to support your inference? Possible responses:

C: ● The farmers and villagers valued protection.

   ● Evidence was that they worked for soldiers and other Romans who offered them protection.

T: What other alternatives were open to the farmers and villagers when offered protection in exchange for their work or land? Possible responses:

C: ● None, because if they didn't give their land, the "strong men" would have taken it anyway.

   ● They had to work for the "strong men" because they had no power.

   ● They could have moved away, but then they would still be unprotected.

   ● There was no government agreement to guarantee rights to the weak. . . .

T: How could a noble be sure he'd have an army and could feed it on any day he might need to fight or to defend himself from attack? Essential response:

C: ● The vassals *promised.*

T: Why would a vassal keep his promise? Possible responses:

C: ● He exchanged promises with his lord.

   ● The noble promised to protect him.

   ● He was treated fairly. . . .

A values-seeking question for each child or for small groups of three:

T: Do you see any advantages to being a serf? Any disadvantages?

After the children have listed both advantages and disadvantages, *as they see them,* you can confront them with the consequences and protection of being a serf, even with the advantages of security.

T: If a serf gets a guaranteed job, guaranteed food, and guaranteed protection, what difference does it make if he is a serf? Possible responses:

C: ● It doesn't make a difference. He's got it made.
● That's a great life—no worries.
● If he never gets a chance to learn anything else, he's trapped.
● He can't make choices.
● He's not free to take a chance.

Responses will differ greatly depending on various socio-economic backgrounds and attitudes.[23]

After further questions of the foregoing types, the plan recommends that pupils engage in "an independent investigation into heroes and values" by reading stories of King Arthur and his knights and by answering a series of questions about what the knights valued. This activity might take from one to three days, after which the pupils return to their textbook and read about the social hierarchy under feudalism in the Middle Ages. Discussion questions of the following variety lead into another "investigation" the pupils carry out.

Now have the children turn to "An Investigation into social mobility" on text page 91.

During the Middle Ages, most people had few, if any, choices about their work roles. Thus, they could not change their statuses. Sociologists say that a person who cannot change his work role and status does not have social mobility. Social mobility means that people can move from one social class to another.

Is there more social mobility in the United States today than there was in the Middle Ages? You can find out something about social mobility in your area. With your parents' permission, ask three grown-ups what jobs they have. Ask also if they have had other jobs. If the people have changed jobs, ask the following questions:

1 Why did you change jobs?
2 Were there jobs you could have taken, other than the one you chose?
3 Can you choose to get another kind of job now?

After you have written down the answers, compare your findings with those of your classmates. Now try to answer these questions:

1 Try to make a hypothesis. Can people in the United States today choose from more work roles than could serfs? Why?

---

[23]Paul F. Brandwein et al., *Principles and Practices in the Teaching of the Social Sciences: Concepts and Values, Brown—Level 6* (New York: Harcourt Brace Jovanovich, 1970), pp. 95, 97. Copyright © 1970 by Harcourt Brace Jovanovich, Inc. and reprinted with their permission.

2   Do Americans have as many rules about work roles as people in the Middle Ages had?

3   Is there social mobility in your area? What evidence do you have?

A Search on Your Own

Why might people value social mobility? On what other values might this value be based?

Find a social system today (not the United States) in which social mobility is valued. You may want to spend some time doing research in the library. In the social system you have chosen, what do people value?

Feudalism was characterized by hereditary transmission of status based on an agricultural economy with vast differences between rich and poor.

Ideally, a democracy provides equal opportunities for each individual to participate in the decisions affecting his political life. However, an individual's social and economic life is controlled to a great extent by his social and economic circumstances. Among the circumstances are: his family responsibilities, the attitudes of the community toward him, his education and his knowledge of what choices there are, and his own values.

When an assignment goes home, it is helpful to the parents to have a written statement from the teacher explaining the purpose of the assignment and instructions on how the child is to go about completing it.

Include the first three investigation questions in your letter. The children should show the teacher's letter to the adults they interview. Answers should be written down word for word. When the children bring their results to class, you can help them classify the answers.

1.   Reasons for changing jobs:
     - Job was replaced by a machine
     - Family moved out of town
     - Health reasons
     - Boredom
     - Wanted more money
     - Learned new skills

2.   Were other jobs available:
     - Yes, but they didn't pay as well.
     - Yes, but I wanted this one.
     - No, because I only knew how to do this job at the time.
     - No, because there isn't much business or industry in this area.

3.   Are other jobs available now:
     - All of the responses listed above may be given.
     - Yes, I have new training now to do another kind of job.
     - Yes, some new businesses have opened here and they need people.
     - No, I'm too old.

Responses to the second set of questions:

1. In an urban society with division of labor and a complicated system of specialization, there are a great many work roles from which to choose, if you are skilled.

2. Specialization involves specific kinds of training which is recognized by various kinds of certification. Each work role involves certain duties and most employees have some rules.

3. Evidence of social mobility may include geographic mobility as people move to more expensive houses. Social mobility is not easy to observe even in our open-class system.[24]

In summary, the teacher's guidebooks for the Brandwein program not only give overall teaching strategies but also offer the teacher detailed lesson plans containing questions for directing class discussion and specific steps to follow in carrying out pupil investigations that use the concepts met in the text materials.

Characteristics of Learners

This curriculum pattern makes a variety of obvious assumptions about pupils.

First is the assumption that children's lives and the world about them become most meaningful when pupils develop concepts for organizing or comprehending the otherwise random experiences of their daily living. Second, it is assumed that children learn best when they are not passive receptacles for information but are considered to be active critics and investigators of problems stimulated by their experiences. Consequently, the Brandwein program places great emphasis on the children's discussing the learning stimuli (pictures, reading matter, projects) and in carrying out group and individual investigations.

A third assumption is that children conceptualize the nature of other people's lives when the children can psychologically identify with the others; and this identification is most readily achieved when the others are approximately the same age as the learners. In keeping with this belief, the authors of the *Social Sciences: Concepts and Values* textbooks build their pictorial and verbal illustrations around children similar in age to those using the text materials.

---

[24] Brandwein et al., *The Social Sciences: Concepts and Values*, Brown, pp. 100-101.

The Brandwein program further assumes that children are more capable of bridging distance in time and space as they grow older. Therefore, in the primary grades the texts concentrate more on the child's immediate environment than do the materials for the upper grades.

In regard to individual differences among children, this curriculum pattern gives more attention to variations in interest than in ability. Nearly every lesson plan suggests "alternative experiences for a variety of interests." However, relatively few plans recommend ways of accommodating for different levels of skill in reading, abstract reasoning, self-direction, or composition. Whether the planners of the program overlooked such differences or whether they expected teachers to be well prepared to meet these ability differences without aid from the program materials is not clear.

Characteristics of Teachers

An evident assumption underlying the plan is that teachers cannot carry out the program as the authors intend it unless the teachers understand the curriculum's underlying rationale. In other words, moving from step to step through a lesson plan is not enough. The effective teacher needs to embellish the basic plan with activities that suit the program to conditions in his class and community. This task of making suitable adaptations cannot be accomplished skillfully without a comprehension of the kinds of questions to ask in class discussions, the kinds of responses to make to children's expressions, and the ways to evaluate pupil progress. To help insure this comprehension, the teacher's manuals explain at some length the rationale on which the program is founded.

A second assumption is that many teachers—perhaps most—lack either the time or the talent to formulate wise ways of using the pupils' textbooks. Therefore, the authors have provided detailed lesson plans, which teachers can follow with relatively little preparation on their own.

A further apparent assumption, mentioned earlier, is that the differences in ability exhibited by the pupils in the class can be accommodated for by the classroom teacher without special recommendations from the authors of the program.

Evaluation Procedures

Brandwein's plan offers two sets of evaluation devices. The first consists of activities that are built into the daily lesson plans and pupils' textbooks as part of the regular teaching process. The second is comprised of a series of separate objective-type tests, which can be purchased for use as summary assessments at the end of units. Because the first of these varieties is the more significant from the viewpoint of the teacher's continuous appraisal of both the children's progress and the effectiveness of the instructional techniques, we shall draw the following illustrations from among the devices included in this first set.

Since the teaching methodology recommended by Brandwein depends heavily on class discussion stimulated by carefully designed questions, perhaps the most obvious evaluation device in the program is the set of questions the teacher poses. As he leads discussion, he can recognize from the pupils' answers the patterns of thought they are developing. However, since class discussion is usually carried on by the more verbal minority in the group, the teacher typically is able to use discussion periods for estimating the thinking processes of only a portion of the class. Other appraisal devices, which elicit responses from all class members, are also needed.

These other devices in the *Concepts and Values* plan include suggested pupil "investigations" and "searches on your own," which are distributed at intervals throughout the pupils' textbooks. The texts also pose problems for pupils to solve under other designations, such as "at this point in your study," "before you go on," and "using what you know." The teacher can ask for either oral or written responses to these evaluation items.

To illustrate these several varieties of assessment devices, we offer the following sample items from the unit on the Civil War in the fifth-grade textbook.

At This Point in Your Study — Do these statements seem correct?
1. "For a system of checks and balances to work, each branch of government must be able to limit the powers of the other branches."

    During Reconstruction, the system of checks and balances worked poorly. Which branch of government took charge? Why was this possible? Does the system of checks and balances work well today?

Before You Go On — Choose the ending for each of these sentences.
1. Black codes were laws that
    (a) gave voting rights to former slaves
    (b) limited the roles black Southerners could perform
    (c) both
2. Radicals in Congress wanted the South
    (a) to settle its own problems
    (b) to change much of its old way of life
3. During Reconstruction, the executive branch of the government
    (a) was more powerful than the legislative branch
    (b) could not limit the power of Congress very well

Using What You Know — Hiram R. Revels, a black man, was a United States Senator from Mississippi during Reconstruction. He was elected to the Senate seat once held by Jefferson Davis. As a Senator, Revels worked to give back the right to vote to all white Southerners who had lost this right. He believed all citizens should be able to take part in choosing their leaders.

Joseph Rainey was the first black man elected to the House of Representatives by citizens of South Carolina. He had helped to write a new constitution for South Carolina so that the state could take part in the national government again. Black people had a great majority at this state constitutional convention. But the new constitution, Rainey said, gave equal rights to black and white because ". . . we did not discriminate, although we had a majority."

1. What values about government do you think Revels and Rainey shared?
2. Which of the following people, if any, seemed to share these values?
   Give evidence for your answers.
   President Andrew Johnson
   Radicals in Congress
   Members of the Ku Klux Klan[25]

For an example of an "investigation" and of searches or problems "on your own," we turn to the third-grade pupils' textbook and a unit entitled "Communities and Their Wants."

An Investigation into the Goods and Services You Use. First, list the outer clothes you are wearing today. We might say, list the *goods* you are wearing today.

Then empty your pockets or your purse. List the goods you find there. Make a list in a table, as shown below. (A few examples are given.) If you do not know where the goods were bought, ask your parents.

Goods I Have	*Where They Came From*	
	Producer of Goods (Who Made Them?)	Producer of Services (Who Sold Them?)
Shoes	Doe Shoe Co.	Acme Shoe Store
Sweater	Tru-Knit Mills	Hink's Furnishings
Toy truck	Contempo Toy Co.	Spector's Toy Shop
Pocket knife	Hardin Steel Co.	Sam's Drugstore
Pencil	Mars Pencil Co.	Jones Dept. Store

[25] Brandwein et al., *The Social Sciences: Concepts and Values, Purple*, pp. 277-278.

Problems on Your Own

1. List five goods you use in your classroom. Find out who helped produce these goods.
2. List five kinds of services you use in school, or on your way to and from school. Who produces these services?
3. Do you produce any goods? What?
4. Do you produce any services? What?
5. Who uses them?
6. What goods might you produce when you are older?
7. What services might you produce for your community when you are older?[26]

In relation to the foregoing types of evaluation devices that are interspersed throughout the pupils' texts, the teacher's manuals furnish suggested answers to the evaluation questions and also add other questions and activities the teacher can use to supplement those in the textbooks.

As noted earlier, the Brandwein program includes separate sets of objective-item tests that schools can purchase for assessing pupils' accomplishment after they have completed a series of units. However, the chief evaluation techniques are incorporated into the pupils' textbooks.

Conditions Affecting the Adoption of the Concepts and Values Curriculum Plan

The Brandwein design seems suited to the purposes of those school systems that wish (1) to inaugurate a program emphasizing social-science concepts and the values that underlie people's behavior but (2) not to abandon more traditional concerns with family, neighborhood, and community in the primary grades or with historical eras in the upper-elementary grades. The *Concepts and Values* textbooks for the lower grades emphasize social phenomena in the pupils' immediate environment, like family groups and playgrounds, comparing them to similar phenomena in other contemporary societies. Texts for the upper grades focus on more complex phenomena from the distant past, comparing them to similar present-day phenomena that pupils experience directly.

---

[26]Brandwein et al., *The Social Sciences: Concepts and Values, Green* (New York: Harcourt Brace Jovanovich, 1970), p. 165. Copyright © 1970 by Harcourt Brace Jovanovich, Inc. and reprinted with their permission.

The *Concepts and Values* plan fulfills the needs of schools that seek teaching materials that picture people of various ethnic backgrounds in diverse social roles. For example, the photographs and drawings that abound in the textbooks show brown, black, red, and yellow people as well as whites at all levels of the socioeconomic structure.

Furthermore, this curriculum pattern is compatible with the needs of teachers who seek suggestions for activities that engage children actively in investigating social phenomena through the use of the concepts and methods of social scientists.

The plan also meets the requirements of school administrators who want a coordinated program from one grade to the next, clearly described lesson plans for teachers to follow when they lack the time or skill to devise suitable lessons of their own, evaluation techniques integrated into the pupils' reading materials, and attractively illustrated textbooks.

The Brandwein program does not appear well suited to classrooms in which there is a range of ability levels among the children and the teachers need recommendations for adapting the curriculum to these varied levels. In other words, the *Concepts and Values* teacher's manuals give little guidance in adjusting the program to different levels of pupil talent, though some suggestions are offered for meeting differences in pupil interests.

Nor does the program seem appropriate for classrooms in which teachers wish to stress the debate and resolution of social controversies, the emotional adjustment of the individual child within his social environment, or the in-depth study of a single social science, such as geography or economics.

5

Taba's Teaching Strategies

After years of distinguished contributions to intergroup education and curriculum development at the University of Chicago, Hilda Taba in the early 1950s joined the faculty of San Francisco State College. This move provided her an opportunity to work on the improvement of teaching in Contra Costa County, east of San Francisco, and in other nearby school districts. In cooperation with county personnel and with colleagues at the college, she fashioned a social-studies program for grades 1 through 8. Beginning in 1965 the work was supported by a grant from the United States Office of Education. After Taba's death in June 1967 her associates named their organization the Taba Curriculum Development Project in her honor and continued the work.

At first glance the plan appears similar to many others in that its gross structure follows the expanding-environments or expanding-communities model. However, closer inspection reveals major internal differences, which result from the detailed rationales that underlie the selection of goals and teaching strategies. Since the classroom procedures—interaction between teacher and children—represent the most significant and unique contribution of Taba's work, we shall place particular stress on that aspect of her design. However, as an orientation to the program in general, we shall preface a description of teaching strategies with (1) Taba's own statement of why a new curriculum seemed to be needed,

(2) her conception of the program's four kinds of objectives, and (3) Jack R. Fraenkel's explanation of the criteria used for specifying objectives and for establishing a logical scope and sequence. (As a professor at San Francisco State College, Fraenkel has headed the Taba project since 1967.)

The Need for a New Curriculum

Today's curriculum must cope with many problems. One is the explosion of knowledge. A vast array of ideas has been added and is being added to the curriculum each year. Since the curriculum is already overcrowded, the pressure to cover an increasing range of content creates a severe problem. To encompass expanding knowledge without aggravating the problem of coverage, it is necessary to make a new selection of content. Otherwise, additions of content without deletions will dilute what is being offered.

Obsolescence of descriptive knowledge creates still another difficulty. Much of what is covered in schools, such as political boundaries or production statistics, changes constantly. This means, for example, that much of the descriptive knowledge learned by a fifth grader will be out of date before he reaches the twelfth grade.

There is also a need in curriculum for concepts from a wider range of the social sciences. If students are to acquire the needed knowledge and skills for effective living in the complex society of today, which includes an understanding of the many cultures in the world, it is necessary to introduce concepts not only from history and geography but also from anthropology, economics, sociology, political science, philosophy, and psychology.

The cumulative effect of these problems requires a new look at what kind of knowledge is most durable and valuable. We must reconsider the role of specific descriptive knowledge in curriculum implementation. If descriptive knowledge changes rapidly, we are wasting time with any attempt to cover specifics for permanent retention. A new function must be found for descriptive knowledge.

To complicate this matter further, recent studies of learning and experimentation with curriculum have greatly extended the scope of responsibilities of the schools. For example, the current emphasis on creativity, on autonomy of thinking, and on the method of inquiry represents a renewed concern with thinking and cognitive skills. The development of cognitive powers now is recognized as an important aspect of excellence. This extension of objectives beyond the mastery of knowledge requires us to reexamine learning experiences. We no longer can assume that mastering well-organized knowledge automatically develops either autonomous or creative minds.

Another problem is that the range of ability and sophistication in any classroom has expanded both up and down. In many ways the students of today are more knowledgeable and capable than we assume. At the same time, because of a higher retention of students in schools, there are students in the ninth grade whose intellectual equipment is functioning on the level of an average second grader. This problem of heterogeneity may be severe enough to require measures other than ability grouping or changing the pacing while covering the usual ground. When the heterogeneity in ability is combined with the problems of emotional disturbance, frequently created by increasing urbanization, offering a fixed traditional curriculum becomes futile.

In other words, the curriculum must simultaneously build a more sophisticated understanding of the world, use a greater range of knowledge, be applicable to pupils having a greater range of abilities, and deal with expanding content. All of this has made it necessary to develop a new curriculum pattern.[1]

Elements of the Pattern

Taba's design, originally explicated in her volume *Curriculum Development—Theory and Practice* (New York: Harcourt, Brace, Jovanovich, 1962), consists of five major components—objectives, content, learning experiences, teaching strategies, and evaluative measures. It also considers the influence of such factors external to this model as "(1) the nature of the community in which any particular school is located—its pressures, values, and resources; (2) the policies of the school district; (3) the nature of a particular school—its goals, resources, and administrative arrangements; (4) the personal style and characteristics of the teachers involved; (5) the nature of the student population."[2]

We shall inspect these elements by starting with the initial component, objectives.

Objectives

In keeping with the first element of this curriculum, which states that the curriculum is addressed to multiple objectives and takes seriously the implementation of each, four categories of objectives are outlined: (1) basic knowledge; (2) thinking; (3) attitudes, feelings, and sensitivities; (4) skills.

---

[1] Hilda Taba, *Teacher's Handbook for Elementary Social Studies* (Reading, Mass.: Addison-Wesley, 1967) pp. 1-3.

[2] Jack R. Fraenkel, "A Curriculum Model for the Social Studies," *Social Education*, 30, No. 1 (January 1969), 41-47. Reprinted with permission of the National Council for the Social Studies and Jack R. Fraenkel.

Basic Knowledge

The first category of objectives, basic knowledge, has been subdivided into three additional categories or levels of knowledge: (a) basic concepts, (b) main ideas, (c) specific facts. Each level of knowledge serves a different function in the development of the curriculum.

(a) Basic concepts are high level abstractions expressed in verbal cues (e.g., interdependence, cultural change, cooperation, causality, differences). The basic concepts encompass large amounts of specifics and are the threads that occur and reoccur in connection with different content. They are of sufficient importance and complexity to serve as threads throughout the entire program.

(b) Main ideas represent important generalizations (e.g., the geography and use of natural resources of a country influence how people live and what people do). The main ideas are drawn from a variety of social sciences—anthropology, economics, geography, history, political science, and sociology—and are set in a context which is appropriate and meaningful to the grade-level themes. The main ideas are the most durable form of knowledge because they do not change as rapidly as does specific information. They serve not only as centers around which to organize the units but also as criteria for determining which concrete details are relevant and which are not.

(c) Specific facts (for example, population statistics) serve to develop the main ideas. They are rarely important on their own account, and since many different samplings of facts can be used to develop the same main idea, it is possible to use alternative sets of facts with different student groups. While concepts are to be studied repetitively and ideas need to be covered, specific facts should be sampled selectively rather than covered.

Thinking

Thinking, the second category of objectives, has long been considered important in curriculum planning. However, this objective has been implemented poorly because there has been insufficient analysis of the skills that thinking involves. This lack of analysis made it easy to assume either that the capacity to think depended on native ability or that it was an automatic by-product of studying certain "hard" subjects, such as mathematics, without regard to how they were learned or taught.

Current curriculum theory, supported by recent research, assumes that thinking consists of specific describable processes which can be learned. To achieve this objective the model curriculum has attempted a specific analysis of the various tasks of thinking and of the skills that are necessary to perform these tasks. Three different tasks are identified:

(a) Concept formation, or the ways in which students can interrelate and organize discrete bits of information to develop abstract concepts (e.g., the concepts of cultural change, of interdependence, and of standard of living)

(b) Inductive development of generalizations, or the ways in which students interpret data and make inferences that go beyond what is given directly in the data

(c) Application of principles, or the ways in which students use acquired knowledge—facts and generalizations—to explain new phenomena, to make predictions, and to formulate hypotheses

Attitudes, Feelings, and Sensitivities

The third category of objectives in the model curriculum is attitudes, feelings, and sensitivities. This objective suggests that students participate in the curriculum in such ways as to develop:

(a) The capacity to identify with people in different cultures (this by necessity includes avoiding or overcoming stereotypes which hinder understanding and respect for other ways of living)

(b) The self-security that permits one to be comfortable in differing from others

(c) The open-mindedness that permits the examination of opinions and of individual ways with reasonable consideration and objectivity

(d) The acceptance of changes that allows one to adjust as a matter of course to new ways and events

(e) The tolerance for uncertainty and ambiguity with minimal anxiety

(f) The responsiveness to democratic and human values that enables responsible conduct and effective societal participation

The model units provide specific materials and sequential learning experiences for the attainment of these objectives. There is special emphasis on the extension of sensitivity to cultural differences and to the dignity and worth of all people.

Academic and Social Skills

The fourth category of objectives emphasized in this curriculum includes such academic and social skills as the ability to read and to interpret maps, to construct time lines, and to use multiple references. A whole series of research skills is also emphasized. The research skills include reading selectively, asking relevant questions, organizing information around study questions, and developing reasonable hypotheses.

Social skills emphasize group work and include the ability to participate productively in discussions, the ability to develop ideas through interaction with others, and the ability to plan cooperatively.

Implementing the Objectives

The differentiation of the four areas of objectives is necessary for effective planning of curriculum because each objective requires a slightly different learning-teaching strategy. A different strategy is needed for learning to think than is necessary for learning facts. The ways in which attitudes are changed and acquired differ from the ways that students learn to think. For example, it is possible to learn the date of the discovery of America by remembering that date once it has been heard; but learning to make inferences from data takes frequent practice over a period of time. Nor are attitudes and feelings changed by studying facts. Attitudes and feelings are changed by experiences, real or vicarious, which have an emotional impact.

It is important to note that the selection and organization of content implements only one of the four areas of objectives—that of knowledge. The selection of content does not develop the techniques and skills for thinking, change patterns of attitudes and feelings, or produce academic and social skills. These objectives only can be achieved by the way in which the learning experiences are planned and conducted in the classroom. Therefore, learning experiences must be selected and designed to serve more than one objective. In other words, achievement of three of the four categories of objectives depends on the nature of learning experiences rather than on content.

Recognition of these multiple objectives leads to two significant consequences regarding the organization of curriculum. First, if the four categories of objectives—knowledge; thinking; attitudes, feelings, and sensitivities; and skills—are to be implemented thoughtfully, curriculum planning must occur in two streams: the planning of content and the planning of learning experiences.

The simultaneous pursuit of multiple objectives as well as the planning of curriculum in two streams introduces several complications. First, incremental learning needs to be provided in all four areas of objectives. It is possible, for example, that at present we are underteaching the cognitive skills because no one knows what the upper limits of intellectual potentiality would be if teaching and learning were more directly focused on the sequential development of these skills.

The second consequence of multiple objectives for curriculum organization is the need to plan scope and sequence for each of the four objectives (basic knowledge as well as the other objectives). It is necessary, for example, to see that content has appropriate breadth and that the concepts and main ideas offer increasing challenge from unit to unit and from year to year. It is equally necessary to assure increments in the capacity to interpret data, in the ability to read maps, and in the ability to construct time lines.[3]

Stated in the foregoing general form, the four sets of objectives provided the overall guidelines for personnel in the Taba project. However, as Fraenkel has pointed out:

... these overall goals are not precise enough to indicate clearly what we want to accomplish. They must be broken down into a number of more specific behavioral sub-objectives. But what criteria should we use as a basis for formulating these behavioral objectives? The following questions might be helpful:

[3]Taba, *Teacher's Handbook,* pp. 7-12.

1. Do our sub-objectives provide over a period of time for continual student development in knowledge, thinking, attitudes, and skills?
2. Do our sub-objectives indicate clearly the precise behaviors that we desire in our students?
3. Do our sub-objectives suggest certain kinds of learning experiences that may help us promote these behaviors in our students?
4. Are these sub-objectives both logically and psychologically obtainable by students?

Behavioral objectives provide a focus. They specify what it is that we expect students to be able to do upon completion of a certain amount of study. In each unit in the Taba curriculum, therefore, overall goals such as learning to think, acquiring information, and acquiring skills are broken down and expressed in behavioral terms. For example, in a unit for grade three, students are expected to describe the life of a Bedouin in the desert and compare it to their own. This represents a behavioral sub-objective of the overall goal of acquiring basic information. As another example, students in a unit for grade seven role play a number of situations involving individuals different from themselves, and then evaluate their feelings. This represents a behavioral sub-objective of the overall goal of becoming committed to the welfare of mankind.

But it is not enough to list objectives no matter how behaviorally we state them. Students also need to know why we expect them to do such things in the first place. When we determine why something is worth teaching, we clarify its significance for both ourselves and our students. Hence, the underlying rationale for each of our behavioral objectives needs to be made clear. Perhaps the following examples of behavioral objectives together with underlying rationale will illustrate the point more fully.

Objective (Knowledge): Describe the life of a Bedouin in the desert.
Rationale: So that students will realize the fact that life in different parts of the world is in many ways both similar to and dissimilar from their own.
Objective (Attitudinal): Participate as a member of a research group.
Rationale: So that students will gain some understanding of the views of others, and realize that others may react and see things differently than they do, but that this, in itself, is neither good nor bad.
Objective (Thinking skill): Generalize and make warranted inferences after examining pieces of previously unconnected data.
Rationale: So that students will realize that when one is able to perceive relationships and connections, one's knowledge becomes more useful.

Notice that the rationale for a given objective indicates *why* the objective is considered important. By making it clear to both students and teachers why we think something is worthy of consideration, we establish a logically and psychologically sound position for ourselves. Others may not agree with our particular estimate of what is significant. That is not, in and of itself, important. What is important is that we professional educators can explain why we want to accomplish certain objectives. If students and teachers, before they begin a unit of study, know what is to be studied and why it is considered important, learning becomes more a mutually interactive enterprise than a one-way directive.

The objectives listed above are examples of certain desired behaviors. When students exhibit these behaviors, then we have some evidence that they are progressing toward the goals expressed in our rationale. Of course, different types of objectives require different types of desired behaviors. To insure comprehensiveness, objectives need to be classified in terms of the different types of accomplishments we expect. What do we expect students to accomplish in the categories of thinking processes, knowledge, attitudes, and skills? Grouping objectives in terms of these categories helps us to insure that we do not neglect student development in any of them.

To summarize briefly: Our curricular efforts suggest that when we prepare our objectives, we should select from a variety of sources, break down our overall goals into behavioral statements, classify these behavioral objectives in terms of the different types of accomplishments we expect, and then justify the objectives we do select on the basis of logically and psychologically defensible criteria.[4]

Selection and Organization
of Content: Grades 1 through 8—
The Scope-and-Sequence Rationale

The logic by which the curriculum builders established a scope and sequence has been explained by Fraenkel in the following manner:

Once objectives have been decided upon and stated in terms of desired behaviors, we are faced with the selection of content. What themes and topics do we want to emphasize? Why? What kinds of content within these themes and topics do we need to consider? What criteria shall we use? How shall we organize the content selected?

Our first task is to determine the major themes of the curriculum. What do we want to emphasize at each grade level? What cultures do we want to analyze? What historical periods do we want to develop? What groups shall we study? What geographic areas will we consider?

Themes establish the parameters for a year's study in a particular grade. A wide variety of themes is possible in the social studies. The important thing is that clear, intellectually defensible reasons exist for the themes we choose. For example, the themes for the first six grades in the Taba curriculum are as follows:

---

[4] Fraenkel, "A Curriculum Model," pp. 42-43.

Grade	Theme
One	The family and the school
Two	The local community
Three	Communities in other cultures
Four	The state
Five	The United States as a nation
Six	Nations in Latin America

As you can see, the emphasis is on expanding communities. The reason for such an emphasis is based on the hypothesis that students will gain a greater understanding of their own culture if they compare and contrast it with other cultures. With this in mind, communities and cultures that differ in a number of ways from the United States were selected for comparison.

Once the themes at each grade level have been selected, our next task is to select topics for units. For example, in the seventh grade in the Taba curriculum, five of the world's major faiths—Hinduism, Buddhism, Islam, Christianity, and Judaism—were chosen for study because they are sufficiently different to permit adequate contrast, yet all are examples of the same phenomenon—institutionalized religion. It was hypothesized that when students understand the role that religions have played in the lives of men, they might try to determine what beliefs they themselves consider important.

Once a topic is chosen for development, the types of knowledge within it need to be selected.

Yearly
THEMES
Composed of a Variety of
↓
Unit
TOPICS
Consisting of Different
↓
TYPES OF KNOWLEDGE
That Include Concepts and Ideas
Supported and Exemplified by a Number of Specific Facts

One Way of Organizing
Content in the Social Studies

In the Taba Curriculum, the three blocks of knowledge—*key concepts, organizing ideas,* and *specific facts*—are considered and organized in a manner that departs from more traditional arrangements. . . .

Regardless of the level of content under consideration, we . . . need clearly stated criteria to serve as a basis for selection. But what criteria? The following questions may be suggestive:

1. Does the content have scientific validity and universal significance?

    a. Does it reflect the most valid and up-to-date knowledge available?

    b. Does it reflect fundamental knowledge that has wide application?

    c. Does it offer important insights to help students gain self- and world-understanding?

    d. Does it promote a spirit of inquiry?

2. Is the content socially and culturally significant?

    a. Is it consistent with the realities of today's world?

    b. Does it examine values and value-conflicts?

    c. Does it promote an understanding of the phenomenon of change and the problems which change produces? Does it develop minds that can cope with change?

3. Does the content relate to the needs, interests, and development level of students?

    a. Can it be learned by the students—does it consider the abilities of the students concerned?

4. Does the content promote breadth and depth of understanding?

    a. Does it develop the capacity to apply what is learned in one situation to a new and different situation?

Answers to such questions suggest criteria that we can use as a basis for content selection in the social studies. No matter what our content, however, it must be organized and placed in sequence. And so, once again, certain questions prove helpful:

1. Does the order in which the material is to be studied help us achieve the knowledge objectives of the curriculum?

2. Does the content of each grade level relate to that developed earlier?

3. Have we organized our content so that it becomes increasingly more abstract, complex, and difficult as we develop it throughout the grades?

4. Does the content organization help us develop our key concepts and organizing ideas?

Such questions are important, for the manner in which content is selected and organized is a key factor in attaining our objectives.

To summarize, we would suggest that content selection involves deciding upon what themes and topics to emphasize, what levels of knowledge to select, what criteria to use for such selection, and how to organize and order the content that is selected.[5]

---

[5] Fraenkel, "A Curriculum Model," pp. 43-45.

Methods and Materials:
Sequential Learning
Experiences and Teaching Strategies

We noted earlier that the Taba program lays particular stress on the type and order of classroom procedures. As Taba has written, three central aspects of her plan—content, learning experiences, and teaching strategies—"represent a system of thinking about and planning of curriculum. If teachers are to use such a curriculum intelligently, they need to understand the theoretical basis for this system as well as to master the special teaching skills for implementing it."[6]

Space does not permit us to offer a definitive treatment of the entire system of learning experiences and their accompanying teaching strategies. We can, however, inspect criteria used in the selection of experiences and strategies and can illustrate several of the teaching methods as they appear in classroom practice.

Fraenkel explains that:

Proceeding simultaneously with content designation . . . is the selection and organization of learning experiences. But, have clear criteria been established that we can use as a basis for selecting learning experiences? Will the learning activities be psychologically and pedagogically appropriate? How will we organize these learning experiences?

Regardless of the type of learning experience under consideration, we are always faced with the question of selection. What criteria shall we use? Again we must ask ourselves certain questions.

1. Do our learning experiences help us achieve all our objectives?
2. Do we have a definite purpose in mind for each learning experience?
3. Do our learning experiences require students to deal with content that is new and increasingly more difficult?
4. Do we ask students to take what they have learned and apply it in new and different situations?
5. Are the learning experiences relevant to the concerns of today's students?
6. Have we provided a sufficient variety of tasks so as to appeal to many different types of students?
7. Do we encourage students to inquire into the nature of themselves and their world, and to try out their own ideas?

Once again, answers to certain kinds of questions suggest criteria which in this case can help us select and design learning experiences. But social studies

---

[6]Taba, *Teacher's Handbook*, P. viii.

objectives require that different types of behaviors be attained. It is important, therefore, that our learning experiences provide for the acquisition of knowledge, the development of thinking processes, the formation and fostering of attitudes, and the acquisition of social and academic skills. Learning experiences must be designed for each of these areas if we are to attain all of our objectives. . . .

Whatever the learning experiences we choose, they, together with the content of the curriculum, must be sequentially organized. Here again the Taba Curriculum departs from what has been done in the past through establishing an organizational sequence that emphasizes:

continuity of learning. Each learning experience serves as a prerequisite for learning experiences to follow, and builds on those which have come earlier; providing a challenge without going beyond the students' capabilities;

building from the concrete and specific to the more abstract;

moving from the experientially close to the experientially distant;

requiring increasingly more abstract reasoning on the part of the students;

serving a variety of functions.

Not all learning experiences have the same function. Some provide for intake of information (for example, reading or interviewing). Others help students to organize information which they have acquired—to order and reorder their data (for example, charting, and map-making). Still others help students express and demonstrate in a new way what they have learned (for example, role-playing). All three types of learning experiences must be present in order for learning to take place in the social studies.

In short, our work suggests that in the selection and organization of learning experiences, one needs to establish criteria to use as a basis for selection, insure that the learning experiences selected develop knowledge, attitude and skill objectives, and then check to make sure that these experiences are pedagogically and psychologically appropriate.

At the same time that objectives, content, and learning experiences are being selected and organized, teaching strategies must also be planned and developed. Teaching strategies perform the equivalent task for the teacher that learning activities perform for the student. They indicate the actual procedures that the teacher will use in order to implement the objectives and content of the curriculum. Once more, a number of basic questions can be suggested:

Do our teaching strategies take into account the type of content being taught? (For example, the kinds of teaching strategies needed to help students learn factual information are different from those needed to help them acquire concepts.)

Will our teaching strategies develop all of our objectives? (For example, the strategies a teacher uses will vary considerably according to the ability levels, socio-economic backgrounds, and age levels of his students.)

Are our teaching strategies in harmony with established principles of learning?

Have our teaching strategies been designed so as to permit individual adaptation by the teacher? That is, a teacher must be well enough informed about the strategies required to accomplish a given objective in order to be able to adapt them to his particular teaching style.

Do our teaching strategies require special arrangements or facilities? (For example, large group lecturing necessitates adequate space arrangements; certain kinds of discussion strategies may be unfeasible unless appropriate reading materials are available.)

A Generic Strategy—
Comparing and Contrasting

Comparing and contrasting is referred to as a generic strategy because it appears to be applicable to any kind of subject matter and because it can be used with any type of student, regardless of ability level. Students can study similar aspects of previously unrelated content, and then be asked identical questions about the content. For example, if it were desired that students should be able to describe how Southern slaves felt during the period immediately preceding the American Civil War, we might ask them to read two accounts of slave experiences—one account being that of a slave who had a benevolent master; the other that of a slave with a harsh master. We might then ask questions similar to the following about each instance:

What is happening in this experience?
Why do you suppose it is happening?
How do you think the individual feels?
In what ways are the feelings of these individuals similar? different?
How would you explain these similarities and differences?

Notice that the same questions are asked of both accounts and that they are arranged in a definite order. This order is intentional. Students must understand what is occurring in each instance before they will be able to explain why it is occurring. They must determine how others feel in a particular situation before they will be able to identify with them.

It is important that we develop such teaching strategies. We must first specify our objectives, of course. But we cannot leave the accomplishment of our objectives to chance if we want to promote student learning. It is for this reason that the Taba Curriculum includes within it especially designed strategies that identify specific procedures that teachers may use.[7]

Methods and Materials:
Their Variety and Specificity

Unlike the complete programs issued by most commercial publishers, the Taba plan does not center around a single textbook series. Nor does it depend on the use of a specific set of workbooks, filmstrips, recordings, or

---

[7]Fraenkel, "A Curriculum Model," pp. 45-46.

charts. Instead, it takes the form of a sequence of teacher guidebooks, one for each grade, which suggest a variety of materials to use in pursuing the program's goals. In this sense the Taba curriculum is similar to state, county, and city courses of study. However, it differs from the usual course of study in two important ways. It is published commercially (by Addison-Wesley Co.), and the rationales underlying its teaching methods are far more sophisticated than those found in either the typical text series or the typical course of study. As noted earlier, this complexity and refinement of teaching strategies is the most distinctive feature of Taba's system.

The teacher's manuals present methodology on two levels of specificity. First, they describe six general strategies of teacher-pupil interaction, each designed to achieve a particular cognitive skill, attitude, feeling, or value. The purpose is to have teachers understand the nature of each strategy so that they can formulate their own lessons and not be bound by a strict lesson plan whose underlying strategy they do not comprehend. As illustrated in Charts 5-1 through 5-6, the intellectual skills children develop depend on the route of thinking along which the teacher's questions lead them. One pattern of questions leads to a different system of thinking than does another.

In addition to describing the general teaching strategies of Charts 5-1 through 5-6, the Taba guidebooks specify learning activities for each of the units that compose the year's social-studies program. The first few pages of Unit 1 of the fifth-grade teacher's guidebook (*United States and Canada—Societies in Transition*) illustrate the level of detail and the variety of materials suggested in the plan.

As the following six charts and sample pages of learning activities illustrate, the Taba plan offers both general teaching strategies and specific suggestions for using the strategies with the subject matter that composes the year's social studies. At appropriate points in each unit, the names of texts, trade books, filmstrips, and similar teaching materials for achieving the goals are listed. However, these materials are ones obtained on the general commercial market and have not been designed precisely for the Taba program. In fact, no particular book or filmstrip is a necessary part of the plan. Substitutions of similar materials can be made. But what cannot be neglected are the recommended teaching strategies, for the essence of instruction is found in the carefully designed sequences of questions and problems posed for the pupils by the teacher.

**Characteristics
of Learners and Teachers**

In regard to the project staff's assumptions about pupils, Fraenkel has explained that [page 157]:

TABLE 5-1   Developing Concepts*

Listing, Grouping, and Labeling

This task requires students to group a number of items on some kind of basis. The teaching strategy consists of asking students the following questions, usually in this order.

Teacher Asks:	Student	Teacher Follow Through
What do you see (notice, find) here?	Gives items	Makes sure items are accessible to each student For example: Chalkboard Transparency Individual list Pictures Item card
Do any of these items seem to belong together?	Finds some similarity as a basis for grouping items.	Communicates grouping. For example: Underlines in colored chalk Marks with symbols Arranges pictures or cards
Why would you group them together?†	Identifies and verbalizes the common characteristics of items in a group.	Seeks clarification of responses when necessary.
What would you call these groups you have formed?	Verbalizes a label (perhaps more than one word) that appropriately encompasses all items	Records
Could some of these belong in more than one group?	States different relationships	Records
Can we put these same items in different groups?††	States additional different relationships	Communicates grouping

*Alice Duvall, Mary C. Durkin, and Katharine C. Leffler, The Taba Social Studies Curriculum—Grade Five: United States and Canada—Societies in Transition (Reading, Mass.: Addison-Wesley, 1969), p. xxii.
†Sometimes you ask the same child "why" when he offers the grouping, and other times you may wish to get many groups before considering "why" things are grouped together.
††Although this step is important because it encourages flexibility, it will not be appropriate on all occasions.

TABLE 5-2 Inferring and Generalizing*

This cognitive task requires the students to interpret, infer, and generalize about data. The teaching strategy consists of asking the students the following questions, usually in this order.

Teacher Asks:	Student:	Teacher Follow Through:
What did you notice? See? Find? What differences did you notice (with reference to a particular question)?	Gives items	Makes sure items are accessible, for example: Chalkboard, Transparency, Individual list, Pictures, Item card. Chooses the items to pursue
Why do you think this happened? or How do you account for these differences?	Gives explanation which may be based on factual information and/or inferences	Accepts explanation. Seeks clarification if necessary
What does this tell you about . . . ?	Gives generalization	Encourages variety of generalizations and seeks clarification when necessary

This pattern of inviting reasons to account for observed phenomena and generalizing beyond the data is repeated and expanded to include more and more aspects of the data and to reach more abstract generalizations.

*Duvall, Durkin, and Leffler, The Taba Social Studies Curriculum, p. xxiv.

TABLE 5-3 Applying Generalizations*

This cognitive task consists of applying previously learned generalizations and facts to explain unfamiliar phenomena or to infer consequences from known conditions. It encourages students to support their speculations with evidence and sound reasoning. The teaching strategy consists of asking the following questions, usually in this order.

Teacher Asks:	Student:	Teacher Follow Through:
(Focusing question). Suppose that a particular event occurred, given certain conditions, what would happen?	Makes inferences	Encourages additional inferences. Selects inference(s) to develop.
What makes you think that would happen?	States explanation; identifies relationships	Accepts explanation and seeks clarification if necessary.
What would be needed for that to happen?	Identifies facts necessary to a particular inference	Decides whether these facts are sufficient and could be assumed to be present in the given situation.
(Encouraging divergency). Can someone give a different idea about what would happen?	States new inferences that differ in some respects from preceding ones.	Encourages alternative inferences, requests explanations and necessary conditions. Seeks clarification where necessary.
If, as one of you predicted, such and such happened, what do you think would happen after that?	Makes inferences related to the given inference.	Encourages additional inferences and selects those to pursue further.

This pattern of inviting inferences, requiring explanations, identifying necessary conditions, and encouraging divergent views is continued until the teacher decides to terminate the activity.

*Duvall, Durkin, and Leffler, The Taba Social Studies Curriculum, p. xxv.

*TABLE 5-4 Exploring Feelings**

Students are presented with a situation involving emotional reactions on the part of one or more persons.[†]
The teaching strategy consists of asking the following questions, usually in this order.[†]

Teacher Asks:	Student	Teacher Follow Through:
What happened?	Re-states facts	Sees that all facts are given and agreed upon. If students make inferences, asks that they be postponed
How do you think . . . felt?[††]	Makes inference as to feelings	Accepts inferences
Why do you think he would feel that way?[††]	Explains	Seeks clarification, if necessary
Who has a different idea about how he felt?	Makes alternative inferences and explanations	Seeks variety, if necessary. Asks for reasons, if necessary
How did . . . (other persons in the situation) feel?	States inferences about the feelings of additional persons	Seeks clarification, if necessary. Encourages students to consider how other people in the situation felt
Have you ever had something like this happen to you?[††] §	Describes similar event in his own life	Insures description of event
How did you feel?[††]	Describes his feelings. May re-experience emotions	Seeks clarification, if necessary. Provides support if necessary
Why do you think you felt that way?[††]	Offers explanation. Attempts to relate his feelings to events he has recalled	Asks additional questions, if necessary to get beyond stereotyped or superficial explanation.

*Duvall, Durkin, and Leffler, The Taba Social Studies Curriculum, p. xxviii.
[†]Sometimes only certain of the questions are asked. The teacher should omit questions if students have answered them spontaneously.
[††]These questions are repeated in sequence several times in order to obtain a variety of inferences and later personal experiences.
§If students have difficulty responding, you may wish to ask: "If this should happen to you, how do you think you would feel?" or, "Has something like this happened to someone you know?" Another useful device is for the teacher to describe such an event in his own life.

TABLE 5-5 Interpersonal Problem Solving

Students are presented with a problem situation involving interpersonal conflict.

Teacher Asks:	Student	Teacher Follow Through
What happened? or what did . . . you do?	Describes events	Sees that all events are given. Tries to get agreement or, if not possible, a statement of differences in perception of what occurred
What do you think . . . (a protagonist) should do? Why?†	Gives response	Accepts response, seeks clarification where necessary
How do you think . . . (others) would react if he did that? Why?†	Makes inference and explains	Accepts. Seeks clarification, if necessary
Has something like that ever happened to you?††	Relates similar event in his own life	Provides support, if necessary
What did you do?†	Relates recalled behavior	Seeks clarification, if necessary
As you think back now, do you think that was a good or bad thing to do?†	Judges past actions	Encourages student to judge his own past actions. The teacher may need to prevent others from entering the discussion at this point
Why do you think so?†	States reasons	Accepts reasons. If necessary, asks additional questions to make clear the criteria of values which the student is using in judging his actions.
Is there anything you could have done differently?††	Offers alternative behavior	Accepts. Asks additional questions to point up inconsistencies where they occur, e.g. "How does that agree with reasons you gave earlier?"

*Duvall, Durkin, and Leffler, The Taba Social Studies Curriculum, p. xxix.

†These questions are repeated in sequence several times in order to obtain a variety of responses.

††If students have difficulty responding, you may wish to ask: "If this should happen to you, how do you think you would feel?" or "Has something like this happened to someone you know?" Another useful device is for the teacher to describe such an event in his own life.

TABLE 5-6 Analysis of Values*

Students are asked to recall certain behaviors and are asked to make inferences as to what values are involved, and how they differ from the values of others involved in analogous situations.†

Teacher Asks	Student	Teacher Follow Through
What did they do . . . (e.g., to take care of their tools)?††	Describes behavior	Sees that description is complete and accurate
What do you think were their reasons for doing/saying what they did?††	States inferences	Accepts, seeks clarification, if necessary
What do these reasons tell you about what is important to them?††	States inferences regarding values	Re-states or asks additional questions to insure focus on values
If you . . . (teacher specifies similar situations directly related to student, e.g., "If you accidentally tore a page in someone else's book,") what would you do? Why?§	States behavior and gives explanation	Accepts, may seek clarification
What does this show about what you think is important?§	States inferences about his own values	Accepts, seeks clarification, if necessary
What differences do you see in what all these people think is important?	Makes comparisons	Insures that all values identified are compared

*Duvall, Durkin, and Leffler, The Taba Social Studies Curriculum, p. xxx.
†Sometimes all questions are not asked. However, the question exploring the students' own values should not be omitted.
††This sequence is repeated for each group or person whose values are to be analyzed. Each group is specified by the teacher and has been previously studied.
§This sequence is repeated in order to get reactions from several students.

UNIT I   Main Idea: New Discoveries Result from the Application of Previously Learned Knowledge to the Solution of Current Problems. Organizing Idea: New knowledge and inventions encouraged world exploration during the fifteenth century.

Notes to the Teacher	Learning Activities
Communication is important in the dissemination of knowledge. In the following sequence (Opener - Act. 3), students consider the explorations of the Vikings and the type of records left.	**Opener**
	List on the chalkboard a number of inventions with which the students are likely to have had first-hand experience, for example:
	Pencil sharpener
	Stapler
	Scissors
	Pencil
	Vacuum cleaner
	Have the students work in pairs. Tell them to select one invention and list
	What materials a person would need in order to invent it
	What he would have to know in order to invent it

UNIT I   Continued

After the pairs have worked for three or four minutes, let pairs working on the same invention form groups of four to:

Combine their lists
Choose someone to report for the group

In order to facilitate the sharing of information and, at the same time, recognize the contributions of all groups, list the contributions, as they are reported by one group, on the chalkboard. Then ask:

How many other groups working on the (invention) had some of these same items?
What different items do you have on your list?

Continue until the students have had an opportunity to respond to the invention on which they worked.

Have each student write his answer to the question:

What do you think people knew or did that helped the inventor of the (pencil, vacuum cleaner, etc.)?

Development

1.   Show a map of North America and locate the state the school is in.
Ask the class to recall from the fourth grade:

Who explored our state?

Save the responses of the students to this last question. The papers will be used again in the Conclusion.

Experience has shown that at this point the fifth-grader responds in terms of chains of workers—or not at all. Responses tend to be:

People would have to cut down trees for wood.
He would have to buy lead.

UNIT I   Continued

From where did these people come?
What other parts of North America did these people explore?
What people did they find already settled in the land we call America?

The purpose of this question is to see how many students are aware of the role of communication in shaping man's activities. Encourage students to respond but do not press. The topic will be discussed later in the unit.

Ask the students to write a sentence to answer the question:

How do you suppose that explorer got the idea that there was land here to be explored?

2.   *Have the students read about Viking expeditions to North America. Tell them to read to find out:*

Intake of information

From where the Viking came
When they came
What and whom they found
How we know about the trips of the Vikings

Suggested References:

Texts[†]

Story of our Country, The (Ver Steeg), pp. 35-39, 46-49

_____   pp. _____

_____   pp. _____

[†] *Reference is made to the California state-adopted text.   Space is left to enter the titles and appropriate page numbers of other texts.*

UNIT I   Continued

Trade Books

Leif Eriksson: First Voyager to America (Shippen)
Lief, the Lucky (D'Aulaire)
Viking Adventure (Bulla)
Vikings, The (Donovan)

Filmstrips:

Lief Ericson
Norsemen, The

3. Discuss the voyages of the Vikings.

Suggested question sequence:

1) What did you find out about the Vikings?

The students will have heard tales of the Vikings in their study of the Norweigan fisherman-farmer in Grade III.

Help them recall these tales.

As the students respond to the question, encourage them to suggest a word or very brief phrase that can be written on the board to remind them of that piece of information.

Ask additional questions, if necessary, to help the students recall the evidence, such as the Viking cross, the remainder of homes, accurate descriptions. Do not label these as evidence when you are asking the question.

UNIT I Continued

Have the students work in pairs for three or four minutes. Tell them to list the items (from the chalkboard) that answer this question:

2) Which of the things we have listed do you think show that the Vikings really did come to North America?

As the students share their decisions, ask

3) Why do you think this is proof they came?
Does anyone have a different idea about this?

4) How do we know about the other events we have listed?

5) Which ways of getting information do you think are most reliable? What makes you think so?

Inferring and Generalizing This is a task that requires students to interpret, infer, and generalize about data. Through carefully organized question sequences, students are asked to compare and contrast data that they have previously collected, to formulate inferences on the basis of these data, and to state a generalization that they feel is warranted. (See introductory material for a full statement on this task.)

New inventions and new knowledge can result in an explosion of knowledge when they are communicated to others. In the following sequence (Act. 4-17), the students consider the accumulation of information that followed Columbus' voyage and subsequent explorations.

4. Display reading materials on Columbus, Cabot, Esteban, Magellan, and Cartier. Let the students browse before selecting one explorer for depth study.

Start a couple of students who communicate well with the other students reading about Americus Vespucci. The material will be used in Act. 11.

After the students have selected an explorer, ask:

What do you think would be important to know about this person?

Suggested Reference:

Amerigo Vespucci, Scientist and Sailor (Syme)

UNIT I   Continued

List the questions suggested by the students.

Have the class read widely for several periods to answer the questions they raised and the following broad question:

What happened in the exploration of _____ ?

*Duvall, Durking, and Leffler, The Taba Social Studies Curriculum, pp. 4-8.

. . . the main principles of learning which the Taba curriculum is based upon and is attempting to implement are the following:

1. Individuals learn by responding to (i.e., "interacting" with) their environment.
2. Learning is essentially an active process whereby a change takes place in the ways in which individuals perceive and give meaning to their environment.
3. Man is an adaptive creature who can organize his subsequent responses on the basis of his earlier experiences.
4. Since every individual has a unique set of experiences, a variety of responses to any given stimulus is possible. Therefore, provision for individual differences in learning is crucial.
5. Current experiences are influenced by, and thus can build on, preceding experiences.
6. The cultural environment in which an individual finds himself shapes what he perceives and values.
7. Man has the capacity to perceive relationships, and to guide his actions accordingly.
8. Learning is facilitated when an individual is motivated and interested in what is to be learned.
9. Practice is important.
10. When a "dissonant" object or fact is inserted into any sequence of objects or facts, attention, curiosity, and interest often increase.
11. The breakdown of a task into its component parts is necessary if maximal learning of the task is to be accomplished.
12. Transfer of learning is not automatic, but it is more likely to occur when an individual learns the underlying principles of a subject or problem.[8]

The most crucial assumption the Taba program makes about teachers is that they have the time and capacity to master the six chief instructional strategies upon which the success of this curriculum pattern depends. The teacher's manuals for each grade level appear sufficiently specific in their directions to enable the diligent, apt teacher to comprehend and practice these basic strategies on his own. However, optimal use of the strategies is more complicated than Charts 5-1 through 5-6 suggest at first glance. The Taba staff intends the teacher to do more than ask the suggested questions in proper order. To do the job correctly, a teacher should be prepared to develop cognitive maps of the pattern of a class discussion so as to pose questions in a sequence that leads children

---

[8] Fraenkel, "A Curriculum Model," p. 45.

from one level to another in their thinking. In her general *Teachers' Handbook for Elementary Social Studies*, Taba explained the idea of mapping in this fashion:

> Cognitive maps take several forms. They appear as notes of points to emphasize, as sequential steps within a teaching strategy, as diagrams of probable outcomes, or as end-products from a strategy. Figure 5-1 is a cognitive map of a discussion focused on the question, "What would happen to the way of life in the desert if sufficient water became available?"
>
> The vertical lines on Figure 5-1 show divergent lines of hypotheses that third graders could project. Awareness of these divergences helps the teacher avoid fixing on "the right" line of answers and, therefore, being insensitive to a fuller range of possibilities which the student might suggest.
>
> The horizontal lines suggest the levels of predictions which consolidate leaps from the original condition, namely, the presence of water in the desert. These lines may emerge in several different ways. Some verbal "leapers" may jump from water to making farms and to building cities. More often, a suggestion by one student triggers a response from another student, and there is a logical building of a ladder from the more immediate to the most distant possibilities.
>
> A cognitive map, such as the one illustrated in Figure 5-1, suggests some of the directions and the levels of ideas responses in a discussion could take as pupils pursue a question. The map helps the teacher to anticipate the discussion because it demonstrates any number of acceptable answers to a question. As the teacher listens to the contributions of the pupils, he can anticipate where a particular remark may lead the class discussion; he is able to distinguish valid and promising leads from irrelevant, unfruitful, or illogical ones.
>
> However, when a teacher makes a cognitive map from a single class discussion, it will be less complete than the map shown in Figure 5-1, which is a composite of several discussions. A single discussion is apt to be more like the cognitive map shown in Figure 5-2. (To assist teachers who want to make cognitive maps for their class discussion, the sequence of remarks by both teacher and students is indicated in Figure 5-2.[9])

This description of cognitive mapping is intended to be only illustrative, not definitive, for the process involves other nuances and uses for the maps. In addition, Taba has recommended the mapping of content to help the teacher differentiate relevant from irrelevant subject matter and to point up facts useful to pupils as they gain the information needed to achieve the goals. As a further guide to developing children's cognitive skills, she has suggested the creation of retrieval charts that enable pupils to place in parallel form information about several different units of

---

[9]Taba, *Teachers' Handbook*, pp. 64-67.

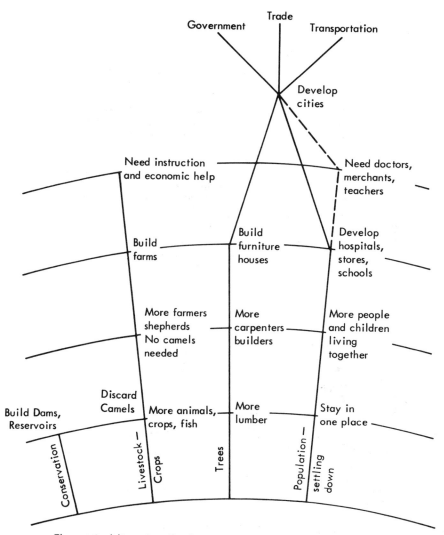

The vertical lines describe the divergent lines of predictions;
The horizontal lines describe the levels of "leaps" in these predictions.

FIGURE 5-1   Cognitive Map of Content in Third-Grade Discussion
              Question: What Would Happen to the Way of Life in
              the Desert if Sufficient Water Became Available?

Sequence of Remarks	Speaker	
1)	Teacher	Think about the boys and girls of the desert and the big changes that might happen if they had water.
2)	Gary	Lots of people will start moving there.
3)		They would have a big city with schools.
4)		They would have machines and streets and cars.
5)		They won't need the animals, because the people
6)		will go to school and learn how to drive cars.
7)	Mary	When they have cars and everything they would be more like our country.
8)		They could learn from the things that we do.
9)	Alan	If they have streets like we do, we could teach them some of our sports.
10)	Andria	They could have better schools, bigger play-grounds, and better books to read. They could have the new type of arithmetic.

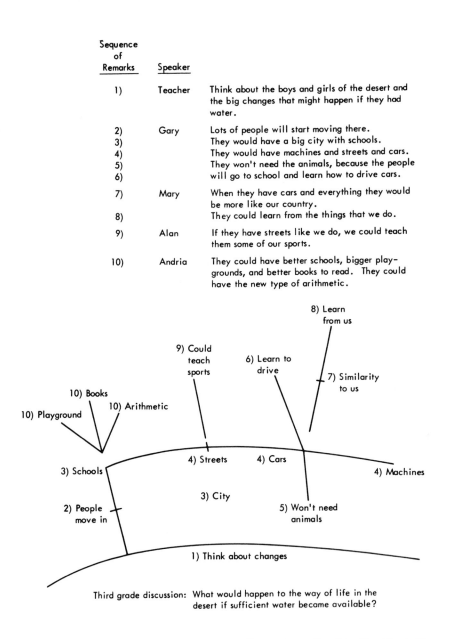

Third grade discussion: What would happen to the way of life in the desert if sufficient water became available?

FIGURE 5-2   Translation of a Discussion Excerpt into a Cognitive Map (Grade 3)

society—nations, for example—and thus more easily compare and contrast them. In sum, the skills expected of the teacher are considerable. Mastering these skills may require more application and wisdom than many teachers, working on their own, may be able to muster. Therefore, it appears that the Taba pattern might succeed best in those school systems that conduct in-service education sessions to provide guidance, practice, and incentive for teachers to master the instructional strategies. In her own work in Contra Costa County, Taba began the project with a small core of teachers and supervisors as a pilot project. Subsequently, the program was disseminated to other schools by assigning the members of the pilot program as aides or supervisors to teachers in the other schools. In later stages, teachers from these second-stage schools could be assigned as aides in a third echelon of schools, and thus the program could be expanded to an ever-widening population.

Evaluation

The attitude that the Taba project staff adopted toward appraisal has been explained by Fraenkel:

A major question for any teacher or curriculum developer is how well have the objectives of the curriculum been accomplished? Thus, evaluation becomes necessary.

Many people conceive of evaluation as something which takes place only at the end of a prescribed amount of content and process. In actuality, it occurs throughout the process of curriculum development.

Evaluation occurs in the description of a particular behavior which represents some evidence of accomplishment of an objective of the curriculum.

Evaluation occurs in the development of a variety of ways to obtain evidence of any changes in students.

Evaluation occurs in the determination of appropriate means of summarizing and interpreting such evidence.

And evaluation occurs in the use of any information gained from student achievement or setback to improve the organization of the curriculum.

The following questions may prove helpful in determining necessary kinds of evaluative data.

1. What are the objectives of the curriculum? What kinds of evidence will be needed in order to determine whether or not progress toward these objectives is being made?
2. What external factors (for example, the socio-economic environment of the school, cultural backgrounds of the students) may affect achievement of the objectives?

3. What student characteristics (for example, peer relations, intellectual ability, motivation) may affect achievement of the objectives?
4. What teacher characteristics (for example, personality, teaching methods) may affect achievement of the objectives?

When we know what kinds of evaluative data we will need, the necessary evaluation instruments must be selected or constructed. These instruments may be of several types (for example, fixed or free response tests, attitude scales, interviews, questionnaires, performance tests). It is essential that the items in these instruments be chosen or prepared on the basis of clearly stated and intellectually defensible criteria. Before we prepare any evaluative program, we might ask the following questions:

Can the items in our evaluative instruments measure student progress toward all of the objectives that we are trying to develop?

Can our evaluative instruments assess strengths and weaknesses in individual student achievement?

Are our evaluative devices valid—that is, do they measure whether or not students have learned what they are supposed to learn?

The most appropriate use of the various evaluation instruments should then be considered, for they can serve different functions at different times. When beginning a unit of instruction, diagnosis of student strengths and weaknesses should be undertaken. As a student continues his studies, his achieving the objectives of the curriculum needs to be measured; and, of course, upon completion of a unit of study, the degree to which the objectives have been accomplished needs to be determined. Our project efforts in this regard suggest that it is only through such a continual analysis of student progress that the effectiveness of any curriculum in facilitating student learning can be determined, and then, when necessary, changes in the curriculum can be proposed and enacted.[10]

To bring this appraisal scheme to practical reality, the formulators of the teacher's guidebooks for individual grades have interspersed evaluation exercises among the learning activities. For example, at the beginning of Unit 2 in the fifth-grade guidebook, the pupils are asked to work in pairs to list all of the things that come to mind when they hear the question "What is an American?" Following the activities of the unit and intermittent assessments throughout, they are asked to examine their list from the first day and to answer the question "Do you have any different ideas now about what an American is?" They are then permitted to alter or extend their original lists to reflect their new understandings.[11]

[10]Fraenkel, "A Curriculum Model," pp. 46-47.
[11]Duvall, Durkin, and Leffler, *The Taba Social Studies Curriculum*, pp. 29, 48.

However, in the Taba program much of the appraisal is in the form of the teacher's impressions about student comprehension as reflected in pupil comments during the frequent class discussions.

Conditions Affecting the Adoption of the Taba Pattern

The Taba curriculum is best suited for adoption in California schools, since its detailed teacher guidebooks focus on topics and teaching materials that parallel the course of study for that state. However, the basic teaching strategies and many of the unit topics featured in the Taba plan are appropriate for schools in any geographical setting.

To be most successful, the Taba pattern should be instituted in school systems in which the following conditions exist:

1. The administrators and teachers believe that the prime outcomes of a social-studies program should be the particular cognitive skills, attitudes, values, and concepts the plan is designed to promote.
2. Systematic in-service education or supervision is carried on for all teachers by someone skilled in the instructional techniques essential to the plan's success.
3. The year-to-year turnover of teachers is not great, or else intensive in-service training in the use of the Taba approach is provided for all teachers new to the staff.
4. The suggested materials—texts, supplementary books, filmstrips—are readily available to teachers.

The Taba program does not seem well suited to schools which:

1. Wish to have their program center around a single textbook series.
2. Want a system that is, as far as possible, "teacher proof." By a "teacher proof" instructional system we mean one that will succeed if pupils are systematically assigned to use texts, workbooks, and films, regardless of any lack of training or talent on the part of the individual teachers.
3. Do not furnish teachers guidance in learning the instructional strategies that are the core of the plan.

6

The History-Geography Tradition

A review of articles about elementary social studies in education publications in recent decades suggests that the history-geography pattern of the early 1900s has been driven out of American schools by newer curriculum designs. But this impression is far from accurate. While discussions of innovative curricula have dominated the pages of professional journals, a large number of the nation's schools have stayed with the history-geography tradition, particularly in grades 4 through 6.

The general form of the history-geography pattern has remained much the same as it was years ago. However, publishers of history-geography materials have taken advantage of recent developments in textbook design and instructional techniques, so that present-day texts and teacher's guidebooks represent improvements over those available in the past. In the present chapter we consider what these modern versions of an old tradition have to offer.

To illustrate this curricular approach, we have chosen two popular textbooks intended for use in upper-elementary grades: *America's Old*

World Frontiers[1] and *The World Around Us.*[2] Each is accompanied by a detailed teacher's manual. We selected these volumes because they are representative of history and geography texts, not because they are unique. Any number of texts from other publishers would serve our purpose equally well.

Both of the textbooks we shall consider seem to be written at the comprehension level of most fifth or sixth graders and of junior-high students. However, the publishers of these books have not labeled them for specific grades, as some school districts teach the history of Western civilization in grade 5, others in grade 6, and still others in the junior high school.

Despite the lack of a specific grade designation for our two illustrative textbooks, we shall assume for discussion purposes that both are being considered for use at the sixth-grade level in a school system whose social studies are taught during two separate periods of the day. One period is dedicated to history and the other to geography. There is no attempt on the staff's part to integrate or correlate the two subjects. The curriculum planners for the school system assume that the integration of knowledge occurs as a result of the personal experience of the learner rather than because of its form of presentation by a teacher. In other words, the planners believe that each person serves as his own integrator, interpreting all new information and experiences in terms of his own unique intellectual past.

Just as history and geography are separated in the school program, so shall we separate the discussion of the two textbooks that provide the core of social studies in the history-geography tradition. The earlier part of the chapter focuses on *America's Old World Frontiers*, the latter part on *The World Around Us.*

The Study of History

The study of history in elementary-school classrooms does not have to depend heavily on a basic textbook for its point of view, its scope and sequence, its materials and methods, and its evaluation procedures. But in practice, teachers usually do follow the textbook rather closely, supplementing it with materials and activities of their own devising.

[1] Thomas D. Clark and Daniel J. Beeby, *America's Old World Frontiers* (Chicago: Lyons and Carnahan, 1962).

[2] Zoe A. Thralls, *The World Around Us* (New York: Harcourt Brace Jovanovich, 1961).

Consequently, an examination of the basic textbook and its accompanying teacher's manual is our best single guide to the nature of typical history teaching. In reality, the text and manual become the curriculum.

The Value Orientation

America's Old World Frontiers, like the other volumes that compose the Lyons and Carnahan Frontier Series, proposes to teach American pupils ". . . to take pride in their unique heritage, and be aware of their responsibilities as citizens in the conquest of *new* frontiers."[3] Such pride and responsibility, the authors state, can be based on an understanding and appreciation of ". . . the foundations and achievements of American civilization. History tells of the conquest of many frontiers, among them frontiers of religion, culture, political organizations, and natural environment."[4] "Briefly, the purpose of *America's Old Frontiers* is to show its readers how our American civilization grew from a long and exciting past."[5]

The volume is typical of the history-textbook tradition. It does not ask readers to analyze historical data and draw their own interpretations. Rather, it offers ". . . the reader a graphic picture of the unfolding of civilization"[6] as interpreted by the historians who wrote the text. "We have organized our book so that it is both a running narrative and an elementary analysis of the time which it treats."[7]

Scope and Sequence

As the table of contents of the children's textbook shows, the historical scope encompassed by the text's 464 pages ranges from the Early Stone Age to the time of Columbus. The titles of chapters indicate that the book treats the evolution of civilization in the Middle East and Europe and accords almost no attention to the development of cultures of Central and Eastern Asia. In other words, it is a narrative tracing the expansion of Western civilization rather than world civilization in general.

---

[3] Thomas D. Clark and Daniel J. Beeby, *Teacher's Handbook: America's Old World Frontiers* (Chicago: Lyons and Carnahan, 1962), p. 2.
[4] Clark and Beeby, *Teacher's Handbook*, p. 2.
[5] Clark and Beeby, *America's Old World Frontiers*, p. 2.
[6] Clark and Beeby, *Teacher's Handbook*, p. 2.
[7] Clark and Beeby, *Teacher's Handbook*, p. 2.

The sequence of topics is also typical of traditional history instruction. The narrative is carried chronologically from one epoch to another, according to a design based upon the implicit rationale that a chronological narrative is the best pattern for illustrating cause-and-effect relationships in the development of the natural world and human cultures.

In the teacher's manual the authors give passing recognition to the fact that some instructors may wish to contrive their own sequence of topics. ("The textbook is composed of 23 chapters to allow the teacher the greatest possible freedom in devising an individual organization."[8]) However, the manual itself is clearly organized in chronological steps, with the content of one lesson often dependent on a comprehension of the content of previous ones. Thus, the authors' preference for the traditional pattern of historical writing is quite clear, and it seems unlikely that many teachers would choose to deviate from it.

America's Old World Frontiers—
Table of Contents

---

[8]Clark and Beeby, *Teacher's Handbook,* p. 2.

Materials and Methods

Although the most essential teaching material is the children's textbook, the authors recommend that children also read "folklore, poetry, tales of adventure, and biography . . ."[9] in supplementary books found in libraries. The teacher's manual also suggests the use of films, filmstrips, recordings, pictures and study prints, and such community resources as museums and historical sites. The special study of maps and globes is also recommended. Lists of supplementary books for children, films, and recordings are provided at the end of the manual.

The authors' recommendations for teaching methodology are of two varieties, one general and the other, in the form of a lesson plan to accompany each chapter of the text, quite specific. We shall first illustrate the general suggestions about teaching history, then reproduce two of the lesson plans along with segments of the children's textbook.

A General Methodology

General approaches to teaching history are described for the teacher in the following manner:

> Reading for information is basic to a successful study of history. In addition, wide reading of adventure stories, biography, travel, and other literature is essential to gain a "feeling" and appreciation for history.

---

[9] Clark and Beeby, *Teacher's Handbook*, inside front cover.

The textbook is an invaluable tool for both kinds of reading. *America's Old World Frontiers* provides detailed information about the way people lived. It is recommended that pupils use it as a basic source of information and that pupils use the index to locate specific information they may be required to find. At the close of the study, or near the end, when a pupil has a background of information, he can gain a deeper understanding by rereading the book as he would a story book. . . .

A study of history which follows the plan developed in this manual calls for countless situations that require the problem-solving technique. The teacher should use these numerous occasions to develop this skill. The textbook, *America's Old World Frontiers*, is excellently adapted to the basic information needs of this age group. To enrich the program, however, all sources of information should be used to answer the problems that arise from the study. The artistic, masterful teacher guides pupils through the steps of a lesson so that they think through the problem or question themselves. *How* and *why* questions usually are the ones suitable for this type of lesson. Here is one way such a lesson is developed:

a. The question arises out of the activities or study (or is posed by the teacher).

b. The teacher decides what sources are best to answer this problem and makes the sources available to the pupils.

c. The exact question is stated by pupils, and is recorded by the teacher (usually on the chalkboard).

d. The pupils talk about the question, and in so doing suggest possible solutions.

e. The teacher records these suggested solutions on the chalkboard, under the question.

f. The pupils then try to find the exact answer(s) in one or more of these ways:

reading
using films or other audio-visual aids
experimentation
observation
consulting authorities

g. The findings are then discussed and compared with the solutions originally suggested by the pupils. Findings that are not previously thought of are noted.

h. A decision is made as to the correct solution.

i. The pupils restate the problem and now supply the agreed-upon conclusion.

j. The learning is used by the pupils—applied in some way (dramatization, construction, written summary, drawings, etc.).

Construction activities contribute greatly to the growth of pupils when they have a real purpose and the products are used by the pupils in a culmination program or to help clarify concepts. Pupils need to establish standards for conduct during these periods. They need to plan the objectives carefully and to carry through their project. The mechanics of the activity would be the responsibility of the pupils under the guidance of the teacher. (Teachers will find excellent help for construction activities in the references listed in the Teachers Bibliography.)

Group discussions are vital in the planning, problem-solving, sharing of information, and evaluating activities that are carried on throughout a study. It is important that the pupils themselves decide upon the standards for their discussion periods and are helped to attain them if they are to develop skill in discussion techniques. This type of oral exercise is one that offers the teacher an opportunity to achieve many of the goals of the elementary school.[10]

Specific Lesson Plans

For each chapter in the children's textbook the authors of *America's Old World Frontiers* offer a lesson plan consisting of four parts: (1) pupils' problem for study, (2) introduction, (3) finding the solution to the problem, and (4) conclusion and summary. This structure for lessons indicates that the writers do not believe that a procedure of simply assigning pupils to read a chapter and answer questions at the end of it is a satisfactory way to teach history. Rather, they feel that one or more problems should first be posed for the pupils. Then the reading they subsequently do in the test has a purpose: it helps them answer the questions contained in the problem.

To illustrate the level of specificity of the lesson plans and the nature of the activities they contain, we shall reproduce the plan for Lesson 41, a segment of study the pupils will meet near the end of their textbook. In order to show the authors' approach to presenting historical material to upper-elementary pupils, we shall reproduce the lesson plan, followed by a passage from the pupils' textbook. The passage is drawn from the opening portion of Chapter 20, at which Lesson 41 is directed.

Lesson 41

Pages 375-380. Pupils' problem for study: *What important freedoms did the English people win or keep?*

Introduction

A. "What are some freedoms that we in this country have today?" (List them on the chalkboard.)

B. "Which freedoms do you think are most important?" (Stress the *big* freedoms such as representative government, trial by jury, and freedom of religious worship.)

---

[10]Clark and Beeby, *Teacher's Handbook*, pp. 3-4.

C. "Did people in the Middle Ages have these freedoms?"

D. "Let us find out how the English people won some of these freedoms." "Read pp. 375-380 in the text."

Finding the solution to the problem

A. "What two important freedoms did the English win?" (List them on the chalkboard.)

B. "Can you explain what is happening in the picture on page 377?"

C. How do we find out today whether or not a man is guilty of a crime?" "What punishments do we inflict on a guilty person?"

D. "What ways did the early British people have for finding out whether or not a man was guilty of a crime?" "How did they punish a guilty person?"

E. "Why is trial by jury more just than trial by ordeal?"

F. "Tell how trial by jury first began, and how it was brought to our country."

G. "What important freedom did Henry II give to the English people that John tried to take away?"

H. "What is a charter?" (Have the pupils add this word to their dictionaries.)

I. "What did King John promise in the Great Charter?"

Conclusion and summary

A. "Why do you think the Great Charter is important to us today?"

NOTE: The teacher should stress the following points:

1. A *precedent* (discuss the meaning of the word) was established by the King admitting in writing that the people have a right to say something about the laws that govern them.

2. Certain freedoms were guaranteed the people that previously had been left to the kindness of the king.

B. "Can you think of any other document that guarantees the people freedom?" (Constitution)

C. "What important differences are there between the Magna Carta and our Constitution?" (Have the pupils reread page 381. Ask them to notice if it says that *all* Englishmen were to have a say in their own government.)[11]

The following material from the first four pages of Chapter 20 in *America's Old World Frontiers* is accompanied by two reproductions of

---

[11] Clark and Beeby, *Teacher's Handbook*, pp. 60-61.

paintings: one illustrating trial by ordeal (a woman running over hot plowshares in her bare feet) and the other illustrating trial by jury (12 men in ancient days deciding whether or not an accused man is guilty).

Chapter 20
The Growth of English Liberty

Trial by Ordeal

One of the principles which the English colonists brought to America was the right of trial by jury. This right developed slowly in England, for when the uncivilized Saxons conquered the country they introduced some cruel ways of trying men who were accused of crime. These forms of trial do not seem at all sensible to use. Strangely enough they were used in England for several centuries.

One kind of trial was called the "ordeal by water." The accused was bound hand and foot and thrown into the water. It was thought that the water would refuse to receive him if he were guilty. Hence a guilty man would float. If the accused was lucky enough to sink, he was pulled out and set free, for he had been proved innocent.

Another form of trial was called "ordeal by fire." The accused was forced to take three steps while carrying a red-hot iron in his bare hand. His hand was then bandaged. If the hand was found to be healing rapidly at the end of three days the accused man was declared innocent. If the hand was still badly blistered, he was declared guilty.

In another form of trial by fire the accused was made to plunge his hand into a kettle of boiling water. If the hand was badly burned the man was proved guilty. It was thought that God would protect an innocent man from all harm.

We must remember that these ordeals were not punishments for crime, but were merely ways of finding out whether or not the accused was deserving of real punishment.

Trial by Battle

After the Norman Conquest trial by battle was introduced into England. In this form of trial the accused man and his accuser were placed in a small enclosure. They were armed with spears, swords, battle-axes, or clubs. If the two contestants belonged to the nobility they would be dressed in heavy metal armor.

Churchmen and women, who could not fight, were allowed to choose a champion to fight for them. It was supposed that God would give the victory to the man who had justice on his side. We may be sure that a skillful fighter would be anxious to choose this kind of trial especially if his accuser was inexperienced in the use of weapons.

All these old forms of trial were unsatisfactory even though the people of that time were very superstitious. They knew very well that innocent men were often punished, while guilty men often escaped.

Trial by Jury

In the United States today when a man is accused of crime, he is tried before a body of twelve men and women called a jury. First the jury hears the witnesses for and against the accused man. Then it listens to the arguments of the lawyers on both sides of the case and to the advice of the judge. The jury then goes to a private room to decide whether the accused man is innocent or guilty. Let us see how this system of trial by jury developed in England.

About eight hundred years ago England had a wise and just king named Henry the Second. He was a grandson of William the Conqueror. King Henry knew that his people could not be tried justly by the old methods of ordeal and battle. He did away with those trials and selected judges and sent them to the various parts of England to settle disputes among the people and to try all men accused of crimes. Henry's judges used to choose twelve men of the vicinity to tell all they knew about the accused man. These men were called "jurors." Often it happened that the twelve jurors knew little or nothing about the facts of the case they were helping to try. In that event other persons who had seen the crime committed or who knew about it in some other way were called before the jurors and asked to give all the facts they could. Later it became customary for the jury to decide cases entirely from the facts told them by the witnesses.

You can readily see that the system of trial by jury was a great improvement over trial by ordeal or battle. The jury trial was used by the first English settlers in our country. It is still used in all our states as well as in all the other English-speaking nations in the world.[12]

Although every lesson directs the pupils' attention to passages in the textbooks, the plans frequently differ from each other in the other teaching techniques they suggest. For example, the first lesson in the year's work begins with the teacher's drawing a time line on the chalkboard and asking pupils to think of important dates in history that can be charted on the line. The fifth lesson plan suggests that the teacher create a picture exhibit of Egyptian masterpieces of art, architecture, and technology. As a summary activity for Lesson 13, the teacher's manual recommends that the pupils "Pretend your father is a Cretan sea captain and that you are accompanying him on a trading voyage for the first time.

---

[12] Clark and Beeby, *America's Old World Frontiers*, pp. 375-378.

Describe the places you might visit and give reasons for visiting these places." As a summary activity for Lesson 16, pupils are to create a newspaper for their bulletin board to report what might have occurred if the Greeks had not beaten the Persians at the Battle of Marathon. By deliberately choosing a topic that is contrary to historical fact, the authors intend to force pupils to consider the ways events are linked in cause-and-effect relationships. So it is that the teacher's manual recommends a diversity of methods that are designed to make history both more interesting and more meaningful to the pupils.

Assumptions about the Learners

Two of the authors' apparent beliefs about upper-grade children have been touched upon earlier in our discussion.

First is the assumption that pupils best comprehend the "message of history" when they meet historical events in chronological sequence. The chronological approach, which traditionally has been by far the most popular, is in contrast to such alternatives as counter chronology (tracing from a present-day event back through its antecedents) and historical themes (inspecting a single theme at a time—for example, armed revolution or economic systems or educational institutions—to see its diverse forms during different historical periods and in different places). Since available research on pedagogical approaches to history does not indicate that one of these alternatives is necessarily better than another, the chronological tack of *America's Old World Frontiers* seems as defensible as any other approach.

A second assumption is that children derive the most benefit from their reading in a textbook if that reading is motivated by a desire to answer particular questions or solve a given problem. In line with this apparent conviction, the teacher's manual suggests that each lesson be initiated by the teacher's posing a historical problem for the pupils or by his stimulating the pupils to pose the problem themselves. Then they read to solve the problem. It should be understood, however, that the kind of problem solving that the authors of *America's Old World Frontiers* have in mind is somewhat different from what many other social-studies educators mean when they talk about a problem-solving approach. For Clark and Beeby, the authors of this textbook, the "problem" is really a question that the passages in the text can answer. It is not a controversial social or historical issue that the children might conceive on their own. Nor, in most cases, is it an issue that is to be viewed from different perspectives so that reasonable alternative answers can be considered and the children can determine which answer they judge is most sensible. In other words, the "problem" with which a lesson is begun is a pedagogical lure or bait to capture the pupils' curiosity. The authors do not consider it to be controversial, since the only real answer or solution to it is the one they subsequently offer in the children's textbook. There are educators who would contend that this variety of lure is not so effective for motivating pupils to learn—nor so significant for producing decision-making citizens in a democracy—as is a social-studies program that focuses on problems requiring the pupils to weigh alternative solutions and select the most convincing of them. We do not seem to have sufficient research evidence available to indicate which of these two approaches to motivating pupils—the pedagogical lure or the "real" problem to be solved—is generally the more successful. So each teacher is left to follow his own convictions in the matter.

What Clark and Beeby have assumed about the nature of individual differences among children is not entirely clear. If we are to take their text and teacher's manual at face value, the authors seem to believe that all, or nearly all, upper-grade pupils are capable of reading their textbook with understanding. However, a host of evidence about the range of reading skills within any elementary grade suggests that such an assumption cannot be supported. A substantial minority of fifth-, sixth-, and seventh-grade students would not comprehend the text, if left to their own devices. They would likely have particular difficulty understanding the placement of different events in an historical relationship. That is, how close was one event or person to another, and how did one of them affect the other? On the other hand, the authors have suggested in the teacher's manual that a diversity of methods in addition to reading the textbook be used during each lesson. This provision of diversity of media—time lines, map study, picture stories created by the pupils, filmstrips, dramatizations—may be intended as a means of providing for individual differences in reading abilities and learning styles. In any event, the authors have not given any specific recommendations about teaching that would suggest they recognize the problems of individual abilities and interests that a typical classroom of children poses.

Assumptions about Teachers

The contents of the instructor's manual indicate that this curriculum plan is based upon two beliefs about teachers' preferences and abilities.

First is the assumption that some teachers will prefer to create their own methods and their own sequence for using the chapters of the text; however, others will wish to follow the authors' lesson plans, perhaps embellishing the plans as time and ingenuity permit.

The second assumption is that teachers who use the lesson plans will profit most from great specificity in terms of questions to ask the pupils and projects to assign. Examples of great specificity are the following:

> Guide a class discussion with the following questions:
>   1. "How did the Greek city-states lose their independence?"
>   2. "Explain how Alexander came to love and respect Greek learning."
>   3. "List the reasons why Alexander is called 'the Great.' "[13]
> Make sure the pupils understand the difference between the Arab world and the Moslem world. Point out that the Moslem religion is practiced by many people who are not Arabs and that some Arabs are Christian rather than Moslem. . . .
> Divide the class into groups and have them work on the following projects . . . :
>   A. Construct a relief map of Europe, Africa, and Asia, showing the spread of Mohammedanism to various parts of the world. Use flags to show important battles or milestones. . . .
>   B. List all the Roman numerals and their Arabic equivalents. . . .
>   C. Prepare a group report, illustrated by drawings and pictures, on the achievements of the Moors in Spain.[14]

Although such specific suggestions as the foregoing are given, the authors of the manual assume that the teacher already knows how to guide children successfully in carrying through the steps of such activities as a class discussion, the compilation of individual reports on historical topics, and the construction of historical maps.

Evaluation Procedures

Both the children's textbook and the teacher's manual give considerable attention to devices for assessing children's knowledge of the contents of the text. Although some assessment activities require the pupil to exhibit his ability to reason out the answer to a question, most of the evaluation items test for his memory of facts and generalizations given in the text. The authors have gone to some lengths to devise a variety of

---

[13] Clark and Beeby, *Teachers Handbook,* p. 26.
[14] Clark and Beeby, *Teachers Handbook,* p. 40.

types of evaluation items, apparently in an effort to provide a sort of novelty that might sustain pupil interest. For example, at the ends of chapters of the children's textbook there are the following kinds of items:

Questions and topics, such as:

Why was it easy for the Phoenicians to become sailors and traders? Tell how the men of Tyre obtained their beautiful purple dye. How did the Greeks improve the Phoenician alphabet?[15]

Matching items, such as:

Fill each blank in the following sentences with one of these words: *orator, philosopher, Plutarch, astronomy, Mussolini, botany, independent, Hitler*
1. _____ was dictator of Italy.
2. Demosthenes was a great Greek _____ .
3. In _____ one studies about plants.
4. _____ wrote many stories about the men of ancient times.
5. Aristotle was a Greek _____ .
6. _____ was dictator of Germany.
7. We study about the stars in _____ .
8. Greece became an _____ country in 1854.[16]

Activities to carry out, such as:

Draw a map showing the land and the water routes from western Europe to the Holy Land.
Dramatize the great meeting at Clermont, France, in 1095.[17]

Vocabulary use, such as:

Write ten sentences in which you use each of these words or groups of words: Renaissance, Revival of Learning, science, magnet, astrolabe, astronomer, astronomy, telescope, magnify, Milky Way.[18]

---

[15] Clark and Beeby, *America's Old World Frontiers,* pp. 97-98.
[16] Clark and Beeby, *America's Old World Frontiers,* p. 168.
[17] Clark and Beeby, *America's Old World Frontiers,* p. 340.
[18] Clark and Beeby, *America's Old World Frontiers,* p. 409.

So that the teacher does not have to puzzle about what the answers to these questions might be, the answers that the authors consider correct are listed in the teacher's manual along with additional questions that the teacher can ask at the end of each section of the textbook. Some of the questions are of the true-false, matching, or multiple-choice variety. Others are in the form of historical puzzles, such as this one:

> To conquer Greece was my intent;
> My Persian force was great,
> Across the Hellespont we went,
> And on to Greece's "Gate."
> Who am I? . . . . (*Xerxes*) . . . .[19]

In summary, this textbook curriculum plan furnishes a variety of specific test items and evaluation activities for each stage of the year's study.

Conditions Encouraging the Adoption of This Variety of History Curriculum

The curriculum pattern represented by *America's Old World Frontiers* would probably be most welcome in schools that value the study of narrative history as a means of guiding upper-elementary children toward an understanding of, and a pride in, "their American heritage." Like nearly every history textbook, this one presents its data and generalizations more as truths to be believed than as select items of information accompanied by the authors' interpretations. Consequently, this typical history curriculum approach would not suit the interests of schools that choose to feature social-science inquiry techniques or a critical examination of American society and its problems, past and present. It would not be appropriate for a classroom in which the teacher wants pupils to practice fashioning their own interpretations of events and to examine the value commitment of the writers of history—such commitments as might be associated with an author's national origin, his religion, or his political party.

---

[19] Clark and Beeby, *Teacher's Handbook*, p. 29.

From the viewpoint of the ease with which teachers can be prepared to use a curriculum pattern, the traditional history model has a variety of advantages. First, nearly every student has studied narrative history at some point in his school career, so when students graduate from college and become teachers, they need not alter their existing ideas of what social-studies teaching is all about. Second, the pattern is so familiar that school administrators can expect new teachers to carry out the program without the special in-service preparation required in order to succeed with such patterns as Taba's (Chapter 5), Oliver's (Chapter 9), and Brown's (Chapter 10). Third, narrative history is not likely to stir up controversy among members of the community, since virtually all adults studied history in a like manner when they were in school. In other words, the pattern does not evoke feelings of antagonism as do some inquiry approaches to social studies.

On the other hand, some members of religious and ethnic minorities in the community may object to what they consider a distortion of their group's role in history as it is portrayed in existing text materials. Their objection is usually not to the program's approach. They agree that narrative history is a good thing to teach. But they feel their group has not been accorded as much favorable attention in the story as it deserves. To settle these complaints, the school system may adopt different textbooks or may supplement the existing materials with ones offering a different view of the concerned minorities.

The Study of Geography

The authors of *The World Around Us* and the accompanying teacher's manual are like the authors of other present-day geography text materials in explaining that the curriculum they espouse encompasses a far greater number of concerns than did the geography books of the past.

> In past generations the study of geography dealt almost exclusively with place locations, or with the detailed study of land and water forms, or with rote learning of long lists of crops and products. . . . But modern geography includes much more than place location, physiography, or crops and products. The older concepts of geography are still present but are only a small part of a richer and more meaningful body of ideas. Modern geography deals with the arrangements, distributions, associations, and relationships among people and their natural cultural environments. Its emphasis is on an understanding of people, their land, and how their activities affect one another. . . .

The "why" of living is best explained in terms of the adjustments each society has made to its natural environment—the things it has had to do to come to terms with nature in its particular part of the earth and the things it has been able to do to make nature serve its basic needs better. . . .

The many different societies of people around the world are not shown as separate and isolated groups. They are shown as parts of the total and complex society of mankind. . . . [The student] . . . learns that there are people in the southern United States, Asia, South America, Africa, and Australia who face similar problems in their day-to-day lives. He learns that these people face their problems in ways that are more similar than they are different.[20]

The authors of this program in geography summarize their purposes in the form of six primary objectives:

1. To acquaint students with the earth on which they live, the kinds of people who live on the earth, and the ways in which these people live.

2. To acquaint students with their own country so that they will have a better knowledge and understanding of its position in the world today.

3. To show the interrelationship between man and his natural environment and how man has learned to change, control, and direct his environment.

4. To promote peace by emphasizing the interdependence of all peoples in the world and the problems of these peoples.

5. To teach the value of natural resources and the need for making better use of them through conservation.

6. To develop a real interest in worthwhile leisure activities, such as travel, reading, lectures, museum visits, and observations that will result in a better understanding of the land of the world, the peoples of the world, and their occupations.[21]

Scope and Sequence

The general scope of the field of geography, as the authors see it, is reflected in the foregoing statements of the concerns encompassed by modern geography. However, to understand more precisely which areas of the world the pupils will study, we can analyze the textbook's table of

---

[20] Zoe A. Thralls, Edward L. Biller, and William H. Hartley, *The Teacher's Manual and Resource Book for use with The World Around Us* (New York: Harcourt Brace Jovanovich, 1962), pp. intro., 3. Copyright © 1956, 1957, 1962, by Harcourt Brace Jovanovich, Inc. and reprinted with their permission.

[21] Thralls, Biller, and Hartley, *Teacher's Manual*, p. 4.

contents. Inspecting the table of contents also reveals the pattern for the sequence in which various sections of the world are studied. Specific countries, or portions of them, are grouped according to their similarities in climate. Nine climatic regions form the basis for nine units that are studied throughout the school year. The units proceed in sequence from the hottest, wettest lands to the coldest. The rationale for viewing the world as a series of climatic zones is explained by the authors as follows:

> More than half a century ago professional geographers began to see that they could gain new insights into mankind and his earth if they gave closer attention to the different natural environments in which men live. . . . They probed, analyzed, and classified many things that go to make up any natural environment: elevation of the land, water bodies, soil, flora and fauna, rainfall, temperature, humidity, and so on. . . . [They] found that the most useful universal factor of environment, for purposes of analysis and classification, was climate. Man can alter many things in his natural environment, but climate he must learn to live with as he finds it. . . .
>
> In *The World Around Us* . . . we have borrowed from the "climatic" geographers those facts, insights, and learnings that we believe to be appropriate for young teen-agers. [22]

As the following table of contents indicates, each unit is composed of three chapters, some of them identified by numbers and others cited as *features*. Whereas a chapter describes a geographic setting and its people in some detail, a feature is a vignette of from one to three settings. The first 57 pages of the text furnish both an overview of climatic regions and some preparation for understanding maps.

The World Around Us—Table of Contents[23]

<table>
<tr><td>People and Places</td><td>8</td><td></td></tr>
<tr><td>This Living Earth</td><td>34</td><td rowspan="2">*The Climatic Regions*</td></tr>
<tr><td>Let's Look at Maps</td><td>44</td></tr>
</table>

[22] Thralls, Biller, and Hartley, *Teacher's Manual*, pp. 3-4.
[23] Zoe A. Thralls, *The World Around Us* (New York: Harcourt Brace Jovanovich, 1962), pp. 5-6. Copyright © 1956, 1961, by Harcourt Brace Jovanovich, Inc., and reprinted with their permission.

The approach to materials and methods suggested in the teacher's guidebook to *The World Around Us* is similar to that in the teacher's manual accompanying *America's Old World Frontiers*. Both manuals recommend the pupils' textbook as the central learning material, to be supplemented with reading in other volumes and with the study of maps, globes, pictures, charts, graphs, films, and recordings. Each of the guidebooks presents a general strategy for teaching as well as individual lesson plans to accompany the separate chapters of the pupils' text.

In the geography manual the general teaching strategy—discussed at some length—consists of four stages: (1) motivating the pupils, (2) gathering information, (3) organizing and discussing the information, and (4) evaluating the pupils' learning. Each lesson plan follows this general scheme, though the steps of the lesson are not necessarily identified by the labels *motivating, gathering information, organizing-discussing,* and *evaluating.* Compared to the lesson plans for *America's Old World Frontiers,* those recommended for *The World Around Us* are considerably more detailed. They suggest alternative ways to arouse pupil interest, and they describe at some length the steps that can be followed in using certain general methods—such as how to show a filmstrip, how to direct a panel discussion, or how to organize children into committees for "workshop" activities.

Following is a typical lesson plan from the teacher's guidebook for *The World Around Us.*

*Chapter 6: Lands of the
Wandering Bedouins*

Your Own Look Ahead into Chapter 6

Recently, much attention has been focused on the tropical dry lands of Africa and Asia. These dry lands, the home of both Bedouins and oasis dwellers, have become increasingly important in the news. Refugee problems and boundary disputes between Israel and her Arab neighbors, internal unrest in Algeria, as well as extreme nationalism in Egypt have threatened to turn the area into a huge battlefield. Only through the diligent efforts of the United Nations has war been averted.

Rapid changes, attracting world-wide attention, have been taking place in this important area. As you guide your class through Chapter 6, you will be able to point out some of the basic geographic factors which have brought about these changes and which are reflected in many of the news reports from the Near East. Chapter 6 is divided into a number of short sections which will help your students with their reading.

1. "Let's Look at Maps," pp. 128-129.

2. "Wanderers on the Desert," pp. 130-131, depicts the nomadic life of the Bedouins who wander about in the desert searching for pasture and water for their sheep, goats, and camels.

3. "Life of the Bedouin Tribe," pp. 131-134, shows how aspects of the wanderer's life are conditioned by climate and how the Bedouins depend upon their camels for food, clothing, shelter, and transportation.

4. "Farms and Cities in the Oases," pp. 134-136, describes life on the oases, where agriculture is made possible by irrigation. It also describes some of the larger oases that have grown into important cities such as Damascus and Baghdad.

5. "The Nile Valley, Largest Oasis of All," pp. 136-138, illustrates how millions of Egyptians are supported by the Nile River, which furnishes water for irrigation and brings fertile soil to the valley and delta. The importance of Cairo, the largest city in Africa, is also discussed.

For Your Own Reading

You may find the books listed below helpful in supplying background information about desert people.

George B. Cressey, *Asia's Lands and Peoples*,
      Ch. 24, "Arabia," Ch. 25, "Iraq."
R. J. Russell and F. B. Kniffen, *Culture Worlds*,
      Ch. 27, 28, 29, 30, 31, "The Dry Worlds."
L. Dudley Stamp, *Africa: A Study in Tropical Agriculture*,
      Ch. 10, "Egypt and the Nile," Ch. 12, "The Sahara."
Richard Sanger, *The Arabian Peninsula*.

Major Questions

Two Major Questions are developed in connection with this chapter. The first question reinforces the idea of interrelationship between man and his natural environment. The second question points out the need for conserving valuable natural resources.

Primary Objective

Major Question #1

To show the interrelationship between man and his natural environment and how man has learned to change, control, and direct his surroundings.	⟷	In what ways do the Bedouins live in harmony with their natural environment?

Ways in Which the Bedouins Have Adjusted to Their Environment

Occupation	Herd goats, sheep, and camels. Move from place to place in search of water and pasture. Several months of each year are spent at an oasis, where trading and social events take place.
Housing	The Bedouins live in tents made of camel's-hair cloth. These tents are easy to put up, take down, and transport. The tents are usually low so that they will offer little resistance to desert winds.
Food	The Bedouins live mainly on milk and cheese, which are easy to obtain from their herds. Sometimes the Bedouins buy grain at an oasis. They also buy a few luxuries such as tea, coffee, sugar, and rice. Meat, too, is considered a luxury because it means a precious animal must be killed.
Clothing	Most of the Bedouins' clothing is white. They wear loose-fitting, long-flowing robes to protect their bodies from the heat and to allow air to circulate through the garment. The burnoose gives warmth during cool desert nights. The headdress furnishes protection from sun, wind, and blowing sand.
Furnishings	The furnishings are simple. Cushions, rugs, and blankets are easy to transport and furnish the necessary comfort for living in a tent.
Utensils	Utensils are simple and include a few trays and bowls, a brass coffee pot, some cups and a mortar for making flour. All of these are transported easily in leather bags.
Transportation	The camel is the chief beast of burden because it is well suited to desert life. The Bedouin prizes his horses most highly because they furnish fast means of transportation when it is needed.
Customs	Hospitality is the keynote, since the nomad's life frequently depends on the hospitality of another. Even an enemy in distress is given food and shelter. When he leaves the camp, he cannot be pursued for three days.

Primary Objective   Major Question # 2

| To teach the value of natural resources and the need for making better use of them through conservation. | ⟷ | Why is the Nile River so important to Egypt? |

(See chart.)

Reasons for the Nile's Importance to Egypt	
1. The Nile River is the longest river in Africa; it is over 4000 miles long. 2. The Nile brings water from central Africa to the desert. 3. Millions of people live in the oasis formed by the Nile. 4. The Nile delta includes the most fertile land in all Egypt. 5. Nile floods are beneficial because they furnish water for irrigation and deposit rich silt on the valley floor. 6. Storage dams which make water available throughout the year have been built. 7. The rich delta stretches for 155 miles along the Mediterranean coast.	8. The Nile flows through the delta in streams which provide water for irrigation. 9. Thousands of irrigation canals distribute water throughout the delta. 10. Leading crops of the delta: long staple cotton sugar cane rice millet beans citrus fruit barley dates figs vegetables

Suggestions for Teaching

In the pages that follow, you will find various suggestions and ideas for teaching Chapter 6. Many of the suggestions are aimed at encouraging your students to question and investigate and to find answers or verify their own conclusions. In addition, many of the teaching suggestions given with chapters in earlier booklets may be adapted to Chapter 6.

Arousing Interest in the Chapter

Through the unit introduction on pp. 125-126, your students were introduced to the climatic characteristics of tropical dry lands. If they examined pictures of deserts in various parts of the world, they may be wondering why some of these deserts appeared barren while others seemed to be productive. You may want to kindle their interest further by using one or more of the following suggestions:

1. You might have your class continue its observation of pictures in the textbook to find out how people make their livings in tropical dry lands. The pictures on pp. 16-17 in the pictorial introduction and those included with the chapter, on pp. 127-137, are excellent for this purpose. In these early picture studies, you can help your students to develop observation skills by asking them pointed questions. In later picture observations, you can encourage students to ask their own questions and to draw their own conclusions.

In the chart that follows, any question suggested for one picture may be asked about other pictures if it applies.

Page	Question	Suggested Answer	Probable Conclusion
16 (Small picture)	Why do you think palm trees can grow in this desert? What kind of roofs do the houses have?	Since trees need water to grow, there apparently is water here. The houses have flat roofs.	There are some places in the desert where water can be found. Flat roofs indicate that there is probably little rainfall.
(Large picture)	What animals are drinking water? Where do the people live? Why do you think this makes a good home for them? Where is the water from?	Camels are drinking the water. The people live in tents. The tents are easily packed when moving is necessary. The water is coming from a pipe which is probably connected to a well or stream.	Some of the people on the desert herd camels. The people live in tents.
17 (Small picture)	What kind of furniture is in the tent? What are the people doing? What kind of household utensils do you see?	Furniture is not apparent. The people are seated on the ground. They are holding a conversation. A tea or coffee pot and several cups are in the foreground.	The household furnishings in the tents are very simple.
(Large picture)	Why are awnings hung across the street? What kind of clothes are the people wearing?	The awnings shade the street from the sun. The clothes are loose-fitting and mostly white.	Some people live in towns and cities.
127	What does this picture tell you about the deserts?	Looks like sand dunes with no vegetation. There are some gullies which show that a little rain may have fallen.	The desert is a desolate place.
130	What animals are drinking in this picture? Where do you think the people got the water for the bucket?	Goats are drinking water. The water was probably obtained from the oasis in the background.	Some of the desert people herd goats. Some water can be found in the desert.
132	What color is the man's clothing? How can his headdress protect him?	The clothing is white. It protects him from sun, wind, and sand.	Bedouin clothing is designed to protect people from the sun, wind, and sand.

Page	Question	Suggested Answer	Probable Conclusion
133	What animal is shown? How is the animal being used?	The animal is a camel. The camel has a saddle on his back and is used for riding.	The camel is used for transportation.
134	This picture shows an oasis. What activity is taking place on this oasis?	The people are growing fruits and vegetables.	Oasis dwellers sometimes farm.
135	What is the source of water in this picture? For what are the men using the water?	The source is a deep well. Water is drawn to the surface in a leather bucket by means of a pulley and rope. The men are watering their camels.	Some water can be obtained from deep wells.
136	What is the man picking? Do you think this tree grows in the desert or on an oasis?	The man is picking dates from a palm tree. These trees grow on the oases.	Dates are grown on the oases.
137	How is the available water being used in this picture?	Some animals are drinking in the background, and the canal is used for irrigation in the Nile Valley.	Farming can be carried on where there is enough water for irrigation.

Once this information has been collected, you will need to remind your class that their tentative conclusions may or may not be correct. It is up to them to study further to verify or disprove their tentative conclusions.

2. You may wish to read a good description of desert life or part of an adventure story which takes place in a desert. Your Book Committee might furnish this material, or you may want to consult the Student Reading List for Chapter 6 on p. 11 of this booklet. After your class has heard this story, you might start a discussion of how people live in the steppe and desert regions. During this discussion, your students should form probable conclusions which they might then check by reading the text.

3. Interest in this chapter can be aroused if someone in the class is able to relate a first-hand experience in a desert region. Souvenirs or artifacts displayed in class usually create enthusiasm. After you have allowed enough time for class observation or listening, you might start a discussion to bring out further information about the desert people and how they make their livings.

4. Many films and filmstrips present a good introduction and overview of desert regions. You may want to choose a film or filmstrip from the Selected Audio-Visual Aids for Chapter 6 on p. 12 of this booklet.

Getting Started (pp. 127-128). Your class gets an overview of the dry lands of North Africa and Asia by means of an imaginary airplane flight from New York City to Cairo. The small inset map on p. 128 shows the route and the global relationship between Cairo and the United States. Your students can find out how long the trip will take by working out the problem stated in the picture caption on p. 128.

Let's Look at Maps (pp. 128-129). This map study will acquaint your class with the lands that are included in the desert and steppe regions of North Africa and Asia. Some of the map skills learned earlier are reviewed and some new ones are introduced.

Map Skills

	Review	New
Direction	N,S,E,W Latitude	
Distance	Scale—recognition of differences	
Location	Latitude and North Tropic	
Symbols	Political boundaries, peninsula,	Wadies
Legend	Shading to indicate precipitation (relative differences) Shading to indicate population density (relative differences)	Hatchings to indicate deserts and steppes
Comparison & Inference	Population densities of various areas compared Rainfall of 2 regions compared Inference about climate from location	Inference about differences in population density Inference about water supply of rivers

Suggested Answers for Map Study

1. These tropical dry lands lie between $3°N$ and $38°N$ latitude. The location near the North Tropic indicates that these dry lands get direct rays from the sun during part of the year, and that the temperature is probably hot.

2. This activity requires student observation.

3. The Arabian Sea and the Persian Gulf lie to the south and east of the Arabian Peninsula. The Great Sandy Desert lies in the southern part of the Arabian Peninsula.

4. The Red Sea, the Mediterranean Sea, and the Atlantic Ocean surround parts of North Africa which have dry lands. The countries of North Africa which contain dry lands include Spanish Sahara, French Morocco, French West Africa, French Equatorial Africa, Algeria, Tunisia, Libya, Egypt, Sudan, Eritrea, French and British Somaliland, Ethiopia, and Somalia. The Atlas Mountains border the Sahara Desert on the northwest.

5. The rainfall is heavier in the steppe regions than it is in the deserts.

6. By following the directions given in the text, students learn the meaning of *wadies* and their symbol.

7. Baghdad is the large city located in Iraq. The Indus River flows through the Thar Desert.

8. The population density of Arabia is much less than that of the Nile Valley. The fact that the Nile River furnishes a dependable supply of water accounts for the fact that more people can make a living in the Nile Valley than in Arabia.

Skim Reading for Main Ideas (pp. 130-134). Your class has already had numerous opportunities to practice close reading for details in the preceding chapters. Reading for details, however, is only one of several valuable reading skills. Sometimes it is necessary to skim a great deal of material in a short space of time to gather general information. Perhaps you would like to try some skim reading with your class, using the text material on pp. 130-134.

You can instruct your class to read only the titles and sub-titles on those pages together with the first two sentences of each section. The objective in skimming these pages is to see how fast your students can find out something about the life of the Bedouins.

With *reluctant students, you might allow five minutes for skimming pp. 130-134 to gather essential information. **Average students will probably not require more than four minutes, while ***advanced students should be able to skim these pages in three minutes.

At the end of the allotted time, you might ask each group of students to write down some of the things they learned from this hasty reading. Their lists might include items such as these:

1. Bedouins wander in the desert for nine or ten months of the year seeking water and pasture for their animals.

2. The Bedouins must move to a different pasture when the animals have eaten all the grass.

3. Herdsmen take care of the camels.

4. When all the grasses and water holes are dried up during the hottest part of the year, the Bedouins gather at an oasis.

5. The Bedouin's animals provide him with food, clothing, and shelter.

6. The Bedouin's chief food is milk; but if money is available, he can obtain luxuries such as bread, dates, rice, tea and salt.

7. The clothing is loose and flowing. Most people wear a burnoose.

8. Tents are made of bought or homemade cloth.

9. Bedouins are very hospitable.

10. Camels are the center of the Bedouin's life.

11. Bedouins value their horses even more than they do their camels.

Frequently in skimming, your students may read a sentence or two which increases their curiosity to read farther for an explanation. You may want your students to reread pp. 130-134 for details, using the questions in the "Checking Up" exercises on p. 131 and p. 134 as guides.

Finally, you might want to explain to your class that both types of reading are useful, each for a different purpose. When a general overview is needed, skimming is helpful; but when details are desired, all material must be read carefully.

Reading for Comparison (pp. 134-136). Your students have already learned that there are oases in the desert and that the Bedouins spend part of each year at these oases. As your students read pp. 134-136, they will discover that still another group of people live at the oases all year round. These people, the oasis dwellers, make their livings as irrigation farmers or as tradesmen. The ways of life of the Bedouins and the oasis dwellers are very different, yet each group has adapted to the dry lands climate and each depends on the other for certain things.

You might want to have your students compare these two groups of people to discover their similarities and differences, and to find out how and why they are dependent on each other. The chart below furnishes you with some ideas for such a comparison. One-star items indicate probable answers from *reluctant students. **Average students should be able to add the two-star items. ***Advanced students may be able to give all the answers.

	Bedouins	Oasis Dwellers
Housing	*tent (movable) **camel's hair tent ***low tent	*mud houses (permanent) **flat roofs, adobe ***shaded narrow streets, houses on poor land
Food	*milk and cheese **bread and meat ***luxuries of rice, tea, coffee, and sugar	*farm products **cereal grains, dates, vegetables ***apricots, peaches, almonds, olives, nuts, wheat, barley
Clothing	*white, long, flowing **burnoose and use ***headdress and use	*white, long, flowing ***when oasis dwellers work in the fields, they sometimes shed their burnoose
Occupation	*herders **sheep, goats, camels ***horses	*farmers **"three storied" agriculture using irrigation ***there are many different ways of securing water: natural springs, wells, wadies, and pipelines
Riches	*camels and horses **camels furnish food, shelter, clothing, & transportation ***use camel's milk, meat, hide, hair, and back	*date palms **date palms furnish many necessities of life ***building material, fire wood, food, drink, mats, bowls, baskets, string, shoes, stuffing, and trade goods
Trade Items	*camels and handicrafts **wool, leather goods, and camel's hair ***goat's hair, rugs	*farm products and luxuries **clothing, food, weapons ***entertainment, dates, cereal, grains, coffee, tea, sugar

When such a comparison chart has been completed, your students will have recalled how each of these groups has adjusted to the hot, dry climate. You might want to point out the fact that the Bedouins spend about two months of each year visiting an oasis in order to trade their goods for the things they need. The oasis dwellers produce or can acquire many of the things the Bedouins need. The Bedouins and the oasis dwellers have a basis for trade since each group has something the other wants or needs.

Reading about the Nile Valley (pp. 136-138). In guiding your class in their study of "The Nile Valley, Largest Oasis of All," you might want to use again some of the reading suggestions given previously. The map on p. 137 and the "Checking Up" questions on p. 138 focus your students' attention on the importance of the Nile Valley.

Reviewing the Chapter. You will probably want your class to review the geographic vocabulary learned in this chapter by using the "Words to Understand" section on p. 138. The "Questions to Think About" are helpful in stimulating thinking about the important aspects of the chapter as a whole. The "We and They" exercises will guide your students in comparing tropical dry lands with their own local community.[24]

As the foregoing example illustrates, the teacher's manual for *The World Around Us* offers detailed suggestions about learning activities, the specific steps for carrying them out, and the kinds of answers the pupils might be expected to devise. In short, the teacher need not do much preplanning of his own if he wishes to follow the guidebook closely.

Assumptions about the Learners

Two of the principal convictions the authors hold about pupils are described early in the teacher's manual. The first relates to motivation, the second to individual differences.

The teaching plan is founded on the belief that "all of us, including teen-agers," have an "insatiable curiosity" about other people.[25] The wise teacher takes advantage of this curiosity by opening each lesson with questions or activities or objects that capture the pupils' interest in people and places. "Once the students have been well 'motivated,' the rest of the learning process—gathering information, organization and discussion, and evaluation—is plain sledding."[26]

---

[24] Thralls, Biller, and Hartley, *Teacher's Manual,* Booklet 1, pp. 2-8.
[25] Thralls, Biller, and Hartley, *Teacher's Manual,* Booklet 1, p. 7.
[26] Thralls, Biller, and Hartley, *Teacher's Manual,* Booklet 1, p. 7.

In regard to individual differences, the authors state:

> When a group of students face you in a classroom, they comprise a mixture of abilities, talents, personalities, needs, and backgrounds. . . . In the manual, these differences have been taken into consideration. . . . A simple starring system has been used to denote three types of material. One star (*) indicates material particularly suitable for use with the reluctant student. Two stars (**) indicate material effective with average students. Three stars (***) indicate material for the advanced student.[27]

A third assumption is that most pupils will not be able to read the geography text materials without some special instruction. Therefore, both the pupils' textbook and the teacher's manual are designed to furnish practice in comprehending the words and paragraphs as well as the maps, charts, tables, and pictures that are part of the textbook. For example, the lesson plan quoted earlier includes suggestions for helping children to find information in pictures and maps, to skim for main ideas, and to read for comparisons.

Assumptions about Teachers

Comments in the teacher's manual indicate that the authors of this geography plan recognize that teachers, like their students, bring diverse talents, backgrounds, and styles of instruction to the classroom. In producing the teacher's guidebook, the authors state that they are not ". . . blueprinting your course for you. . . . We have tried, rather, to compile ideas and suggestions that practicing teachers have found workable and rewarding. From these you may select, adapt, or reject as you see fit."[28]

Evaluation Procedures

Like the history program described earlier in this chapter, *The World Around Us* provides evaluation items in both the pupil's textbook and the teacher's manual. In the children's text several "checking up" questions are posed at intervals in every chapter. At the end of each

---

[27] Thralls, Biller, and Hartley, *Teacher's Manual,* Booklet 1, p. 8.
[28] Thralls, Biller, and Hartley, *Teacher's Manual,* Booklet 1, p. 2.

chapter and each unit are "Questions to Think About" and suggested activities under the title "We and They" or "Your Geography Workshop." For the teacher's convenience, the answers to the questions are listed in the manual. Following are examples of these varieties of items from the chapters related to the lesson plan reproduced earlier (Chapter 6: Lands of the Wandering Bedouins).

> *Checking up:* Why must the nomads drift about the desert for many months? What is the first work to be done when a new pasture is reached? What two foods are luxuries for the Bedouin? Why?
>
> *Questions to think about:* What is the difference in the ways in which the Bedouin and the oasis farmer judge their wealth? Why is it said that the camel is a necessity, rather than a luxury, to the Bedouin?
>
> *We and they:* How does an oasis home differ from your home? Take a sheet of paper and draw a line down the middle. On the left-hand side make a day's menu for a Bedouin family. On the right-hand side write the menu you have for a day. Why is there so much difference between the two menus?
>
> *Your geography workshop:* Make a list of activities that illustrate life in the various tropical dry lands. For example: (a) a Bedouin putting up a tent; (b) the unusual table manners of a Bedouin; (c) a Bushman hunting; (d) an Australian worker on a walkabout; and so on. In class, act out these activities in pantomime. Have the members of the class guess what activity each pantomime represents.[29]

For every chapter the teacher's manual also provides several test items intended to measure pupils' command of the textbook information. To illustrate the form and level of difficulty of such items, we reproduce below a portion of three evaluation exercises for the Bedouin chapter.

> *True-false:* (To measure your students' understanding of factual knowledge):
> - Oasis dwellers earn their living by herding.
> - Textiles are manufactured in Damascus.
> - Bedouins are very hostile, especially to their enemies.
>
> *Identification:* (To see whether students understand how the Bedouins are dependent upon their camels):
> Directions: A Bedouin might own all of the articles listed below. Place an X after any item that might have been supplied by a camel.

black tent	steamed barley	strong coffee	pillow
cheese	leather bucket	wheat bread	woven rug
roast meat	figs and dates	burnoose	rice

---

[29] Thralls, *The World Around Us*, pp. 131, 134, 138, 158.

Completion: (To see whether your students understand the importance of water conservation in the Nile Valley):

Directions: Fill in the blanks in the paragraph below. The following list furnishes you with answers. . . . There are more answers in the list than you will need. . . .

100	canal	delta	Mediterranean	thousands
1,000	clear	fertile	millions	
4,000	crops	flood	red	
camels	dams	hundreds	source	

The Nile River is over _____ miles long. It carries water and fine soil from the uplands of Africa to the _____ Sea. The yearly floods have deposited _____ soil in the river valley and have built up a _____ at its mouth. The land can be irrigated and many _____ can be grown. _____ have been built to store some of the _____ water for use during the rest of the year. _____ of people depend upon the wise use of the waters of the Nile River.[30]

In addition to offering the foregoing kinds of questions, the authors of *The World Around Us* recommend that at the end of a unit the classroom teacher

. . . may want to construct test items that check your students' skills in map work, vocabulary, reading, and picture observation. Your evaluation should measure understanding of the factual information as well as development of the skills and attitudes necessary to accomplish the Primary Objectives. . . .[31]

Teachers who use this curriculum pattern, although they may agree with the authors about the desirability of measuring skills and attitudes in addition to factual information, may feel that the authors have themselves avoided the more challenging task of evaluating skills and attitudes. As the sample assessment items in the foregoing paragraphs illustrate, the specific evaluation procedures that the children's textbook and the manual provide are nearly all limited to measuring factual knowledge.

---

[30] Thralls, Biller, and Hartley, *Teacher's Manual*, Booklet 5, pp. 10-11.
[31] Thralls, Biller, and Hartley, *Teacher's Manual*, Booklet 5, p. 28.

Conditions Encouraging the Adoption of
a Geography Curriculum of this Type

This variety of geography curriculum would probably find its greatest acceptance among educators who regard an orientation to climatic regions of the world as a significant part of the child's elementary social-science education.

Descriptive geography, like narrative history, has been a very familiar subject in the lives of older generations so that both teachers and parents are prone to accept a geography program as suitable fare in the elementary school. It is far safer from attack by parents than are curricula focusing on controversial social issues of the community or on personal-social adjustment of children and their families.

Not only do many teachers appreciate the noncontroversial character of descriptive geography, but they also find it easier to teach and the outcomes easier to evaluate than is true of other, more innovative programs. The array of detailed suggestions for instructional methods given by the teacher's manual can relieve the classroom instructor of much of the burden of devising teaching techniques. Furthermore, the essential facts that are to be learned are all contained in the children's texts and the teacher's manual, making it unnecessary to collect a variety of other teaching materials. And though the manual lists a range of desired outcomes that the program can produce in children (the learning of facts, generalizations, attitudes, appreciations, skills of investigation), it seems apparent that the chief and sometimes exclusive goal that is pursued is the learning of factual information about the world's climatic regions. Teachers find this type of learning the easiest to assess, for it can be measured with essay or short-answer questions and with objective-type test items (true-false, matching, multiple-choice, fill-in). Such outcomes as the reduction of prejudice, increased skill at social-science inquiry, and increased self-confidence—which are primary goals of other kinds of social-studies programs—are far more difficult to appraise.

In summary, many schools include a heavy offering of descriptive geography in their overall social-studies program because they consider a knowledge of peoples and places to be important in today's world of rapid communications, because the study of geography is a familiar and noncontroversial tradition in American education, and because many teachers find geography convenient to teach and to evaluate.

7

Our Working World

Economists were prominent among those academicians who, in the late 1950s and early 1960s, sought to introduce the teaching of social-science disciplines into elementary schools. Of several curriculum designs that resulted from these efforts, the best known has been one created by Lawrence Senesh at Purdue University and published between 1963 and 1967 by Science Research Associates under the title *Our Working World*.

Although economics serves as the central organizing core of the plan, Senesh does not consider his design just a partial program. Rather, he has labeled it "the organic curriculum"[1] through which children can relate their experiences to "the fundamental ideas of the social sciences."[2] Thus, economics is emphasized, but children also meet sociological, anthropological, historical, and political-science concepts throughout the program.

Senesh began to formulate his design in 1958 after he was appointed by the Department of Economics at Purdue to ". . . a special academic

---

[1] Lawrence Senesh, *Our Working World, Families at Work, Resource Unit* (Chicago: Science Research Associates, 1963), p. 1. © 1963, 1964, Science Research Associates, Inc. Reprinted by permission.

[2] Senesh, *Families at Work, Resource Unit*, p. 1.

position to promote research in economic education and increase the economic competence of teachers and pupils in the public schools."[3] Over the following years he designed and tried out economics resource units in the primary grades of such public school systems as those in Elkhart, Indiana, and in DeKalb and Glencoe, Illinois. Ultimately, teachers' guidebooks, pupils' texts, pupils' activity books, and a series of stories narrated on phonograph records were published for general distribution to elementary schools. More recently, books and recordings have been prepared for upper elementary grades. These materials are currently used as segments of social-studies programs in various parts of the nation.

The Author's Set of Values

The author's belief that the organizing concepts of the social sciences are a necessary part of the elementary-school child's education has been expressed in the following manner:

In the dynamic world in which we live today changes are taking place so rapidly, and methods of communication are so efficient, that adults as well as children are deluged with new information. . . . Unless we discover some pattern or design behind the seeming chaos of events, we may find ourselves fleeing into unreality to escape the real world of difficult and insistent problems.

Discovering fundamental patterns or principles beneath the welter of raw experience is not an easy task. A special kind of thinking is necessary to make the bridge between a person's experiences and his ideas. Up to now, training for this kind of thinking has been entrusted largely to the secondary schools. By the time youth have reached maturity, bad thinking habits have often become ingrained and respect for analytical thinking is frequently lacking. It is during the early formative years of the child, when he has an unlimited curiosity and an earnest desire for answers to his questions, that the preparations for analytical thinking should begin.

The many "why" questions that come from children stem from fundamental intellectual curiosity and honesty that drive them to search for reasons or patterns in terms of underlying principles or codes of behavior. If this search is frustrated by the child's adult guides, and if the classroom adds to his confusion by dumping quantities of unrelated information on him, the child can only sink deeper into the swamp of unrelated experiences. If, on the other hand, he is helped at an early age to discover order in the world around him, and if the

[3] Senesh, *Families at Work, Resource Unit,* acknowledgments.

discovery of the relation between events and ideas is made a part of a continuing learning process, life can become an exciting adventure from childhood to old age. . . .

The purpose of this series, *Our Working World*, is to introduce children to the fundamental principles underlying the functioning of our social world and to relate children's experiences to these principles. . . . This curriculum is based on the hypothesis that children's experiences are potentially so meaningful that the fundamental ideas of the social sciences can be related to them on every grade level.[4]

Scope and Sequence

Senesh has defended his use of economics as the focal discipline for his program by saying that:

. . . because economics plays so large a role in the child's world, and because it will continue to be so important all his adult life, . . . it has been made the core of *Our Working World*. The other social sciences, such as anthropology, geography, political science, sociology, and history, are, however, an integral part of the program.[5]

To understand the conceptual structure by which Senesh has organized economics ideas and has related them to other social sciences, we can turn to a diagrammatic view of his basic framework (Figure 7-1). With this diagram in hand, the author and his co-workers developed a sequence of units and constituent lessons for the primary grades. In broad outline, the sequence follows the expanding-environments approach. In first grade the child views economics and related disciplines within his most intimate social environment, the family *(Families at Work)*.

The first-grade program . . . is intended to familiarize the children with certain fundamental principles and ideas. While its purposes are purely introductory and little attempt is made to show first-graders how these principles are interrelated or how they evolve from one another, it is

[4] Senesh, *Families at Work, Resource Unit,* p. 1.
[5] Senesh, *Families at Work, Resource Unit,* p. 2.

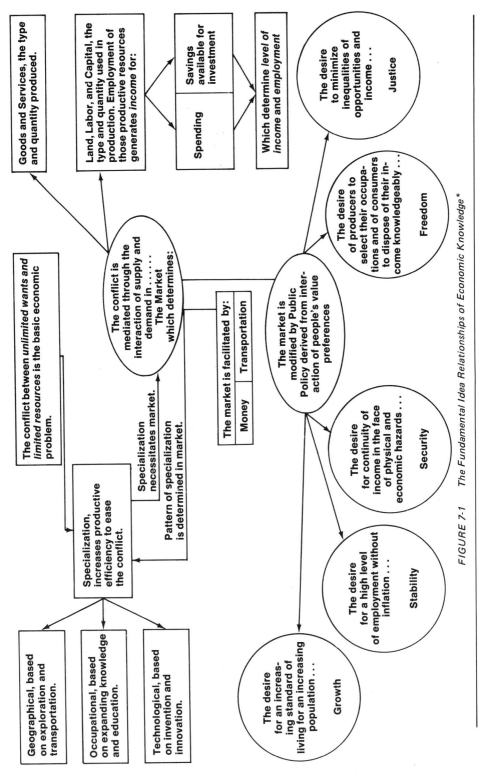

The conflict between *unlimited wants and limited resources* is the basic economic problem.

Goods and Services, the type and quantity produced.

Land, Labor, and Capital, the type and quantity used in production. Employment of those productive resources generates *income* for:

Spending

Savings available for investment

Which determine *level of income and employment*

The conflict is mediated through the interaction of supply and demand in ...... The Market which determines:

Specialization, increases productive efficiency to ease the conflict.

Specialization necessitates market.

Pattern of specialization is determined in market.

Geographical, based on exploration and transportation.

Occupational, based on expanding knowledge and education.

Technological, based on invention and innovation.

The market is facilitated by:

Money	Transportation

The market is modified by Public Policy derived from interaction of people's value preferences

The desire to minimize inequalities of opportunities and income ... Justice

The desire of producers to select their occupations and of consumers to dispose of their income knowledgeably ... Freedom

The desire for continuity of income in the face of physical and economic hazards ... Security

The desire for a high level of employment without inflation .... Stability

The desire for an increasing standard of living for an increasing population ... Growth

FIGURE 7-1   The Fundamental Idea Relationships of Economic Knowledge*

*Senesh, Families at Work, Resource Unit, p. 3.

extremely important that the teacher have these relationships in mind as each principle is presented. Hence it is important that the teacher study and understand the fundamental idea relationships of economic knowledge as indicated in the chart[6] . . . [Figure 7-1].

At the second-grade level the child focuses on a broader social environment as he studies the community (*Neighbors at Work*). The scope of concepts is suggested in schematic form in Figure 7-2.

The second grader's studies are organized in six sections. The sequence of these sections and their general contents are as follows:

I. What Is a Neighborhood? . . . the elements of a neighborhood—the most important of which are man and his relationship to other men.

II. Types of Neighborhoods . . . how neighborhoods differ in land use and in the economic and cultural behavior of the people. The analytical tool of price theory is introduced to show how the price of land guides the use of land.

III. Institutions Guided by Prices and Profit (in other words, by the Market) . . . how the fluctuation of prices for individual goods guides the construction industry, factories, and stores in deciding what goods and services should be produced, and how they should be produced. The lessons also help the children discover how the general level of spending and saving affects the jobs and incomes of people who work in trade and industry.

IV. Institutions Guided by the General Welfare . . . two such institutions are introduced . . . : volunteers and government. . . .

V. Dynamics of the Neighborhood . . . why neighborhoods change, why changes create problems, and how problems may be prevented by foresight and planning.

VI. School: Threshold to the World . . . children see that schools teach them about ideas, how ideas are disseminated, and how ideas generate new ideas. . . . how the exploration of nature and the use of such findings increase men's choices. This introduces some of the basic principles of economic growth. The children see science as a special way of looking at things. They further discover that science includes social science—a disciplined way of looking at people.[7]

For the third grade, the program moves out from the neighborhood to encompass the metropolis (Cities at Work). The nature of studies at this level is suggested by the titles of the program's 18

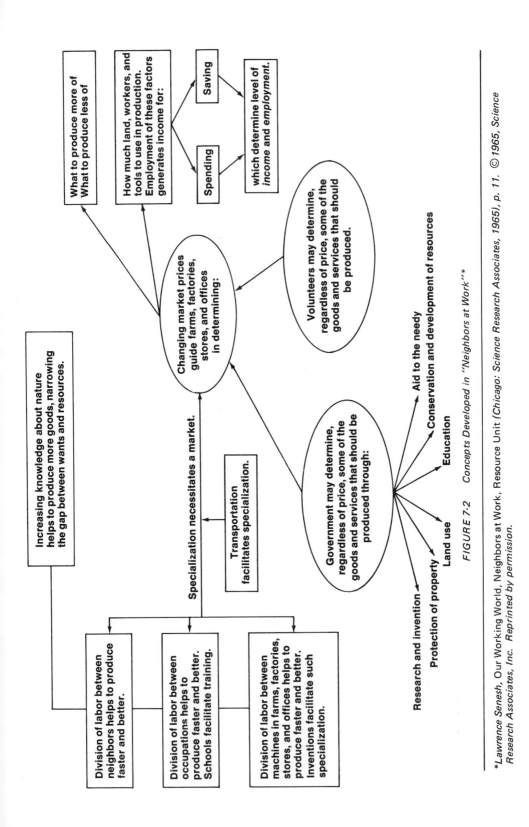

FIGURE 7-2   Concepts Developed in "Neighbors at Work"*

*Lawrence Senesh, Our Working World, Neighbors at Work, Resource Unit (Chicago: Science Research Associates, 1965), p. 11. © 1965, Science Research Associates, Inc. Reprinted by permission.

lessons: What Is a City?; Why a City Is Where It Is; Marketplace of Goods and Services; Marketplace of Ideas; Why a City Grows; What Keeps People Together?; What Keeps People Apart?; The City and Government; Why Must Cities Plan?; Keeping Cities Up to Date; The City and Transportation; The City, Water, and Air; The Precious Gifts of a City (Athens); The City That Swallowed Villages (London); A City Married to the Sea (Venice); A City Rises from Ashes (Rotterdam); A City That Has More People Than Jobs (Calcutta); A City That Uses Its Wits (Singapore); The Future of Cities.[8]

As many of the foregoing lesson titles indicate, a variety of social-science disciplines other than economics play important roles in the third-grade program—sociology, political science, geography, anthropology, and history.

In summary, the scope of this curriculum is determined by principal economic concepts and related ideas from other social sciences as they promote children's understanding of families, neighborhoods, and cities at work.

Materials and Methods

There are two general categories of instructional materials recommended in the Senesh curriculum. The first category contains coordinated materials furnished as part of the program itself: pupil textbooks, pupil activity books, phonograph records with an accompanying script book, and a teacher's manual referred to as a "resource unit." The second category involves other materials, such as maps and pictures, that are recommended in the resource unit but must be obtained by the teacher on his own initiative.

The overall teaching plan that the author suggests for grades 1 and 2 consists of introducing each of the year's *lessons* (which are actually teaching *units*, since each involves a variety of activities carried on over a period of several days or weeks) with a phonograph record designed for that lesson. The session of listening to the record is followed by a diversity of learning activities, many of which involve use of the hardcover textbook and the pupils' activity book for that grade level.

[8]Lawrence Senesh, *Our Working World, Cities at Work, Resource Unit* (Chicago: Science Research Associates, 1967), table of contents. © 1967, Science Research Associates, Inc. Reprinted by permission.

The type of general guidance furnished the teacher in the manual is illustrated by the following excerpt from the second-grade resource unit:

> Each lesson is best introduced by the recorded lesson. However, the children do not get the full value of the recording unless it is presented in a specially created atmosphere. The teacher should prepare the children for listening as if they were entering upon an adventure.
>
> The listening technique should be carefully explained. If the furniture is movable, best results are obtained by clustering the seats around the record player. The teacher should make sure that the children's textbooks are open to the proper lesson *before* the record is played. This is important because each of the recorded lessons refers directly to the big picture that introduces each lesson in the textbook.
>
> The teacher should indicate to the children the main theme of the lesson. If the record has been organized around a central character, he may introduce the character and suggest that the children watch for certain things.

Using the Resource Unit

The resource unit is like a cookbook. It contains a large collection of classroom activities—many more than any teacher could possibly use in one year. The large assortment enables the teacher to select activities that are suitable to the experience of the class or to the school neighborhood. The assortment also enables each teacher to make a variety of choices from year to year, so that the menu will not become monotonous. The teacher's selection will also depend on his ability to coordinate social sciences with the skills of reading, writing, and arithmetic. The activities and stories have been selected with these skills in mind. The teaching of skills and the teaching of social sciences should enrich each other.

The activities and stories cover the various areas of the social sciences. Economics is the core around which the other areas of social science—political science, anthropology, history, sociology, geography—are clustered. Some of the activities have also built a bridge toward the natural sciences. A whole lesson unit has been devoted to the study of scientists and the impact of their work upon society.

The teacher will observe that the same economic concepts are repeated in many lessons. For example, prices, profit, and risk are taught in the first eight lessons. This repetition gives the children an opportunity to discover the same concepts in a variety of situations. The same practice has been followed with other topics and lessons. The repetition also gives the teacher an opportunity to select from all the lessons those combinations of activities that may be closest to the experience of his class. If the school is located in a rural neighborhood, the teacher may prefer to emphasize the teaching of price, risk, and competition as they relate to the farm; if the school is in an urban neighborhood, the teacher may emphasize price, risk, and competition as they relate to industry and commerce.

The teacher who is new to this program will have to plan carefully so that he does not give too much attention to a few lessons, thus neglecting the others. The most effective use of this resource unit will depend on the care with which the teacher plans the lessons and the extent to which he is acquainted with the material.

The following study plan is suggested for teachers who are using the resource unit for the first time. It gives one of many possible combinations of activities that might be used within the school year. With time and experience, the teacher can take advantage of the great variety of activities, add to them, and suggest activities of his own. Fundamental questions have been drawn from the purposes of each lesson. The study plan recommends class activities. It is expected that the children will also fully utilize the textbook and recorded lessons.

Suggested Study Plan

Lesson 1: What Is a Neighborhood? (2 weeks)

1. What is a neighborhood? (Part I, Activities 1 and 2)
2. What keeps the people of a neighborhood together? (Part II, Activities 3 and 5)
3. How are neighborhoods different from each other? (Part I, Activity 14)
4. How do people choose their neighborhood? (Part II, Activities 11 and 14)
5. What do you have to know to draw a map of your neighborhood? (Part III, Activity 1)[9]

In a manner similar to that outlined for Lesson 1, the teacher's manual suggests a study plan for the remaining 14 lessons that compose the second-grade program. The rest of the manual is dedicated to a description of learning activities—of alternative teaching methods—from which the teacher may select ones to use with this year's class. As an illustration of the range of activities included, we offer the following six examples chosen from the pool of 39 alternatives available for the first unit (entitled Lesson 1).

To give the children a sense of the great variety of American neighborhoods in real life, the teacher can have them turn to "Let's Take a Trip" on page 6 of the text. In discussing the pictures, the class should touch on such questions as

---

[9] Senesh, *Neighbors at Work, Resource Unit*, pp. 15-17.

these: How do the amount of land available and its price affect the character of the neighborhood? (If land is scarce and its price high, buildings are usually built taller or closer together than in neighborhoods where land is more plentiful or cheaper.) How do the customs of the people who live there affect the life of the neighborhood? (The kinds of stores, houses, and churches, and the types of recreation available are affected by the customs and beliefs of the people.) How do the materials available and the climate affect the neighborhood? (Buildings are often constructed of materials that are near at hand—adobe in the Southwest, wood in Alaska—and must provide protection against the elements.) How does the geographical location of a neighborhood affect the people who live there? (Fishermen must live near water. Farmers must have fertile land.)

To enable the children to see neighborhood differences at first hand, the class can take a short trip and observe their own neighborhood and another nearby. This observation can also be made while they are traveling to some other destination on a regular field trip. A trip to a rural point of interest would be particularly valuable for urban children. After the trip the class can discuss the differences they noted. Some children may also be able to recall neighborhoods they have visited on trips with their families and share their observations with the class.

The discussion should bring out that neighborhoods can differ in a number of ways: (1) The land itself may be different (hilly or flat, wet or dry). (2) The land may be used in various ways (for single-family houses, for apartment buildings, for stores or factories, for parks or highways, and so forth). (3) The people may be different (have different incomes, come from different ethnic groups, have different customs, religions, and so forth).

The following activities can be completed in the Activity Book.

(a) 1A: "Different Ways Land Can Be Used." The children should be able to match each picture with its title, indicating some of the varieties of land use. After completing the activity, the class can discuss examples of various land uses in their own community.

(b) 1B: "What Does Your Neighborhood Have?" The children should recognize the basic features of a neighborhood as indicated in the lesson—land, buildings, and people. Discussion should point out that the kinds of houses, people, and so forth, may vary just as kinds of neighborhoods vary.

(c) 1C: "How Many Neighborhoods Are in Each Picture?" In determining the number of neighborhoods shown, the children should recall from their activities and the statements in "What Did We Learn?" on page 11 of the text how neighborhoods may be divided from one another.

To bring out the elements that go to make up a neighborhood, the class can construct a movie about the neighborhood as follows: The children draw pictures of people who live in the neighborhood, of children playing together, different kinds of houses, parks, the school, stores, a fire truck or police car, and other things that they feel are important and that they can draw. Pictures for the movie should then be chosen to give the best composite picture of the neighborhood; at least some of each child's pictures should be used, so that all the children will have a feeling of participation. The selected pictures should then be pasted in a predetermined order on a long strip of wrapping paper or similar material. This picture sequence should be attached to and rolled about a dowel or roller (the end of a broom handle serves well), and the free end attached to a second roller. A large cardboard box can be used as a screen. The rollers are inserted into holes cut in the top and bottom of the box near its front corners. The paper is rolled from one roller to the other, displaying the pictures in sequence. Such a movie can be called "A Neighborhood Is Made Up of Land, Buildings, and People," and the class can compose a narrative to be read as the pictures are being shown.

To make the children aware that the way people behave toward each other helps determine whether the neighborhood is a pleasant one, the class can make a survey as outlined below. (Before beginning this activity, the teacher should inform the parents that their children will be asking some questions, and explain the purpose of the survey.) Each child can ask his parents the following set of questions and report back to the class:

(a) How many people in our block do you know well enough to talk to?

(b) Do you borrow things like tools from our neighbors? Do you lend things to them?

(c) Do you ever visit any of the people who live in our block?

(d) Do any of the people who live in our block visit us?

(e) Do you exchange favors (baby sitting, caring for plants or pets during an absence, helping with home repairs, making purchases, and so forth) with any of the people who live in the block?

(f) Do you do things or go out with any of the people who live in the block?

The children can prepare reports on their findings and discuss the fact that the neighborhood is a place where they and their parents have friends and cooperate with others. The children can also draw pictures of their families engaged in various activities covered in the survey. Afterward the children could act out their drawings, or the class could dramatize each of the activities discussed.

Since the class will be studying the neighborhood during most of the school year, it is important that the children prepare a table or floor map of the school neighborhood. If the teacher uses green flannel as the map base, it can be stored and reused in later years. The map can be prepared through the following sequence of activities. (Note: The preparation of the map need not be completed during the first two weeks work, but can be a continued activity over a longer period.)

(a) In many schools such a map will be identical with the children's own neighborhood. In other cases, where children are brought to school from greater distances, the area around the school should be considered an experimental neighborhood. In this way all the children can study the same neighborhood. To assure that all of them, regardless of where they live, have some knowledge of the school neighborhood, they can go for a short walk along a number of blocks in the immediate vicinity. Special attention should be paid to the landmarks observed.

Upon their return the children can discuss or write short compositions on the buildings they saw, how these were arranged (adjoining, close together, with vacant space or whole lots between, and so on), what the buildings are used for, and how one gets from one building to another (route taken).

(b) After the children have described the school neighborhood in words, the teacher can ask them how a whole neighborhood can be shown on a small piece of paper. The discussion should lead the children to the discovery that the map is an important way of doing this.

The teacher can show examples of various types of maps, blueprints of a house, a neighborhood map, a city map, an airline map, an illustrated tourist map, and a road map, and explain the various ways maps can be put to good use.

To practice mapmaking, the children can prepare a map of the classroom. The teacher can ask them to pretend that they are viewing the classroom from a perch near the ceiling. The children can imagine and then draw what the classroom would look like from that position; what shape the classroom has; where the desks are and how much space they occupy; and the size and location of the empty spaces. The teacher should make sure that the children have their maps in the proper position, so that directions on the map correspond to real directions in the classroom. After they have discovered this relation, the children can use their classroom maps to perform simple exercises in map reading, using the terms *right* and *left*, *front* and *back*. Children can then advance to the use of the map turned freely in any direction relative to the classroom, testing their ability to read the map even when it is not aligned with the classroom itself.

(c) Once the children become acquainted with scale, direction, and viewpoint, they can turn their attention to the school neighborhood. The teacher can ask them to imagine they are looking on the school neighborhood from an airplane or helicopter. To stimulate their imaginations and help them develop their ideas, the teacher can first show them aerial photographs of cities and other areas. (Such pictures can be collected from newspapers and illustrated magazines where they frequently appear.) With the teacher's help, they can now go on to the preparation of the school neighborhood map itself. The teacher should place a large sheet of paper on a table so that the children can gather round, and explain that the paper represents land. A model of the school should be placed in the center. With the teacher's help (he may use a small street map of the area as a guide), the class can draw in the streets of the neighborhood around the school. If it is convenient, the teacher can take the class outside. The map should be placed on the ground and oriented properly. To ensure that the children are always relating the directions on the map to the real world around them, they can be asked to point in the general direction of buildings and other landmarks as shown on the map.

In the classroom, models, pictures, or symbols representing the main buildings in the neighborhood (besides the school)—the children's homes, stores they frequent, the police station, the firehouse, and so on—can be constructed and placed in position on the map. (Different colors can be used to indicate different kinds of buildings. Thus the school might be red, homes green, stores yellow, offices blue, and so forth.) The teacher should establish a scale of distance so that the buildings can be placed on the map according to their relative positions in the neighborhood. Care should be taken so that the children understand that the neighborhood map does not represent the whole of the neighborhood or the city, and that streets do not actually stop at the edges of the map.[10]

To review, the Senesh program provides such teaching materials as textbooks, activity books, and recordings as well as a pool of alternative teaching activities for each *lesson* or unit in the year's plan. It becomes the classroom teacher's responsibility to choose which activities and which parts of the texts and activity books will best suit his pupils' talents and his style of teaching.

Characteristics of Pupils

The chief assumption behind the key role given to phonograph recordings in the first two grades is that young pupils' reading skills are so limited that the children cannot be expected to gain much from reading in a textbook. Consequently, the task of introducing each unit, which most curriculum designers assign to the textbook or to the classroom teacher, is assigned by Senesh to recordings at the lower-primary levels. Senesh apparently feels that by grade 3 the children, with some explanation by the teacher, can profit from the textbook's introductory overview.

Like so many elementary curriculum designs of recent decades, *Our Working World* is founded on the belief that children best comprehend social science when they begin with their immediate environment and move through expanding circles to consider phenomena that are increasingly remote in time and space. Furthermore, the authors of the recorded lessons assume that children's interest in social-science concepts is effectively aroused if the concepts are introduced through stories, especially stories involving children the same age as the pupils.

Perhaps most basic to the Senesh program is the belief that concepts underlying economic theory can be adequately comprehended by elementary-school pupils if these concepts are presented in

---

[10]Senesh, *Neighbors at Work, Resource Unit*, pp. 26-32.

simple social settings with which the pupils are familiar and if the children have enough opportunities to practice using the concepts.

Characteristics of Teachers

Compared to many other curriculum patterns that are organized around textbooks and workbooks, the Senesh program expects the classroom teacher to take more responsibility for deciding what learning activities will compose the daily lessons and in what order these activities should be presented. Rather than providing a sequence of recommended daily lesson plans, *Our Working World* offers the introductory recorded lesson and then trusts the teacher to select his own array of subsequent lessons from a broad range of alternatives.

Likewise, the Senesh plan leaves in the teacher's hands the decision about how children's individual differences in ability, experience, and interests should be accommodated. Alternative goals or activities for slow, average, and fast learners are not described, as they are in some other curriculum designs. Nor does *Our Working World* suggest criteria for the teacher to use in selecting activities suited to different ability and interest levels. In short, meeting individual differences is exclusively the teacher's business.

The fact that the plan offers resource materials rather than a set sequence of lessons for each day suggests that the authors of the plan assume that different teachers will prefer to use the program in different ways. Some may choose to have *Our Working World* constitute the entire social-studies program for their grade level. In this case, all of the textbook and activity-book pages will be used, along with a large number of the learning activities from the teacher's resource book. Others may choose to use *Our Working World* as only one portion of the class's social studies. In such an event, the teacher will select fewer sections of the books and fewer activities from the resource manual.

There is, however, one exception to the general tendency of the Senesh program to place great trust in the classroom teacher. This exception involves the recording that is recommended for introducing each unit. Apparently the authors of the plan are so convinced that the record will be superior to the average teacher's presentation that they urge the use of the recording with every unit.

The curriculum's sponsors have assumed that teachers who are contemplating the adoption of *Our Working World* will profit from seeing how other teachers have conducted activities recommended in the program plan. Consequently, Senesh offers filmstrips produced during the experimental stages of the plan's development to illustrate methods of carrying out several aspects of the classroom methodology.

Evaluation Procedures

The plan furnishes two chief channels for assessing children's achievement. One is the collection of exercises that compose the pupils' activity books at each of the three grade levels. The other is the collection of learning activities in the teacher's resource book. The following examples suggest the kinds of appraisal devices available from these two sources.

The activity books are comprised mainly of drawings so that children's lack of reading ability will not prevent them from participating in the judgments that the exercises in the books require. Near the end of the first-grade book words are gradually introduced. Over the primary grades the vocabulary increases until some lessons in the third-grade book involve a substantial amount of reading.

Many exercises in the activity books are of a multiple-choice variety. For example, at the first-grade level the pupil on one occasion is asked to choose from among eight pictures those things that his house protects him against. The pictured items include wind, witches, tigers, rain, dragons, snow, giants, and sun.[11] In the second-grade book, a drawing of a factory is surrounded by drawings of five different geographical locations: a small island, a desert, a dirt road in a mountainous area, a dam holding back a large supply of water, and a slope adjacent to a highway, railroad, and airport near a city. The child is asked to draw a line from the factory to the most desirable factory site, then be able to explain what is wrong with the other sites.[12]

In other cases the activity-book exercises are of the matching type. For instance, in a first-grade exercise, six tools are pictured on the upper half of the page (spade, sickle, broom, horse-drawn wagon, bow and arrow, and pencil). Children are to match them with tools pictured on the bottom half that perform the same function more efficiently (semi-trailer truck, rifle, typewriter, lawn mower, vacuum cleaner, steam shovel).[13] At the end of the second-grade book, the following matching item is

---

[11] Lawrence Senesh, *Our Working World, Families at Work, Activity Book* (Chicago: Science Research Associates, 1964), p. 7.

[12] Lawrence Senesh, *Our Working World, Neighbors at Work, Activity Book* (Chicago: Science Research Associates, 1965), p. 45.

[13] Senesh, *Families at Work, Activity Book*, p. 20.

used to determine "What did we learn?" Children are to draw a line from the correct sentence stem at the left to the proper completion for the sentence at the right.

We cannot	makes rules that tell how land is used.
Neighborhoods	have everything we want.
Government	are different.
Price helps decide	land, buildings, and people.
Every neighborhood has	how land is used.
The market is	where goods are bought and sold.[14]

Some items in the workbooks assess the pupils' ability to use a principle they have studied by asking them to carry out some plan. Figure 7-3 illustrates such an item from the third-grade book.

As the foregoing examples illustrate, the activity books serve as both learning experiences and evaluation devices for the pupils. Since a large number of exercises are provided for each grade level (65 in grade 1, nearly 60 in grade 2, over 75 in grade 3), the teacher has a host of opportunities for estimating pupils' understanding of the concepts treated throughout the program.

Though most items in the activity books appear readily understandable for children who have mastered the concepts concerned, some seem ambiguous enough to confuse pupils and teacher alike. For instance, early in the first-grade book the child is to identify which of twelve drawings show consumers and which show producers. In the case of a drawing of a barber cutting a child's hair, this decision is a difficult one to make, since both a producer and a consumer of service are in the picture.[15]

Some exercises suffer from the author's attempt to illustrate a basic principle of economics in everyday life without confusing the child with too many of the factors affecting economic behavior. In doing so, he has had to oversimplify cause-and-effect relationships. Consequently, the average child may mark the item as the author intended, but a particularly able or well-informed pupil can mark it "incorrectly" because he sees ramifications beyond the simplistic version of the principle that is under inspection. For example, in a lesson in the first-grade book aimed at showing the way supply and demand influence prices of goods, one exercise pictures six varieties of items and asks the child to decide which

---

[14] Senesh, *Neighbors at Work, Activity Book*, p. 63.
[15] Senesh, *Families at Work, Activity Book*, p. 10.

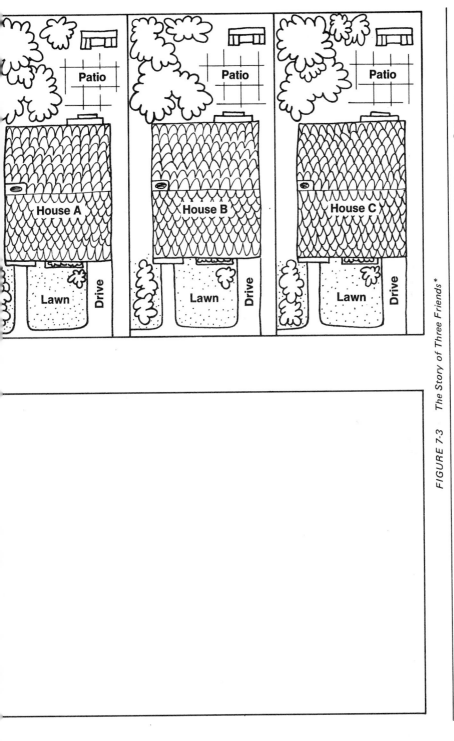

*FIGURE 7-3   The Story of Three Friends**

*Lawrence Senesh, Our Working World, Cities at Work, Activity Book (Chicago: Science Research Associates, 1967), p. 52. © 1967, Science Research Associates, Inc. Reprinted by permission.

type might be cheaper in winter and which in summer. The items are watermelons, sleds and skates, winter clothing, beach clothing, garden tools, and fresh vegetables.[16] The bright child might well be stymied by the exercise if he recognizes that a diversity of factors—not just one—affects markets—such factors as geographical location, the possibility of closing-out and off-season sales, the availability of items in mail-order houses, whether the factories producing certain of the goods have suffered a labor strike, and others. Consequently, such items as this one are better as sources of discussion than as testing devices.

As mentioned earlier, the teaching activities in the instructor's manual often provide information about pupils' progress as well as furnishing them instruction. The illustrative activities described early in this chapter include class discussions, pupils' oral and written reports, drawings children make from their observations of economic functions, the creation of maps, and the building of models. Each of these furnishes the teacher evidence of what the pupils have learned and of what they still do not accurately comprehend.

In short, the pupils' activity books and the teacher's resource unit provide a broad range of opportunities for assessing children's learning.

Conditions Influencing the Adoption of Our Working World

The Senesh curriculum appears best adapted to the requirements of two varieties of schools: (1) those that seek to devote the primary-grade social-studies program to developing an understanding of the economic world, with minor emphases on allied social sciences, and (2) those that wish to provide the primary-grade child a taste of several different social sciences—such as anthropology, psychology, and economics—each represented by a different curriculum plan. In other words, either the complete *Our Working World* plan can serve as the entire social studies of grades 1 through 3 or selected portions of it can form the economics segment of a multidisciplinary program.

The organization of Senesh's plan seems more appropriate for teachers who wish to formulate their own sequence of lessons than for those who prefer the security of an established series of lesson plans, each containing suggestions for discussion questions and pupil activities that the teacher can follow closely.

[16]Senesh, *Families at Work, Activity Book*, p. 46.

The fact that *Our Working World* follows the expanding-environments pattern so familiar in American schools in recent decades should please those teachers and administrators who are dedicated to the rationale of such a pattern and who might feel uncomfortable with a different approach.

The complaints that teachers often express about the difficulty their less adept pupils experience in trying to read social-studies texts are less likely to be leveled at the Senesh materials than at certain other textbooks in the field. As pointed out earlier, the recording designed to introduce each set of Senesh's lessons replaces the written introduction that authors of other curricula expect children to read in a textbook. Hence, the child who does not read well in grades 1 and 2 has as good a chance as his more adept classmates to understand the opening story of each unit in *Our Working World*. Furthermore, the first half of the pupils' textbook at the first-grade level consists entirely of pictures that pupils "read" under the teacher's direction. (However, unlike the pupils' activity books, the texts suddenly begin introducing vocabulary at a rather swift pace in the last half of the first grade.) All in all, from the viewpoint of reading skills, the Senesh materials can probably be used with a larger portion of the pupils in the typical classroom than is true of certain other primary-grade texts.

It should be apparent that *Our Working World* is not an appropriate program for schools that wish to give equal attention to each of several social sciences rather than emphasizing one. Nor is it designed for schools that desire to conduct an integrated social-studies program from kindergarten through grade 6.

Three

Partial Programs

The five curriculum designs that compose Part Three are labeled *partial* because none of them would be expected to function as an entire social-studies program, either in a single grade or over a sequence of grades. Rather, each is intended either as a supplement to an ostensibly complete program or as one segment of an overall curriculum that has been fashioned from a number of partial programs.

Each of the partial plans was created to fill a void that critics of current social-studies practices identified as being particularly undesirable. For example, the Jurisprudential-Teaching plan of Donald W. Oliver (Chapter 8) was devised because the author felt that students were not learning how to dispute and settle social issues upon which citizens of a democracy are expected to take action. The Confluent-Education plan of George I. Brown (Chapter 9) was designed to promote the emotional growth of children—an area that the author of the plan was convinced the schools were neglecting.

The third illustrative program in Part Three—Dale L. Brubaker's Current Social Themes and Problems (Chapter 10)—incorporates aspects of both Oliver's and Brown's concerns as it centers attention on social problems of the past decade that have been the object of public concern.

The final two programs in Part Three illustrate two quite diverse teaching methodologies that arose in the 1960s as social scientists at the university level developed partial elementary-school programs focusing on their own academic specialties. The first example is the anthropology curriculum from the University of Georgia (Chapter 11). The teaching method is chiefly deductive. Pupils learn the methods and concepts of anthropologists by reading about and discussing archeological discoveries and studies in anthropology. The second example is the social-psychology curriculum from the University of Michigan (Chapter 12). The teaching method in this case is more inductive than deductive. Children spend far more time using social-psychological methods to conduct investigations of their own than they do reading definitions of terms and results of studies by social psychologists.

As was true throughout Part Two, each of the five chapters that compose Part Three is organized according to the analytical criteria explained in Chapter 2.

8

Jurisprudential Teaching

For decades, a variety of critics of American education have charged that most students who graduate from high school are ill-equipped to make the decisions expected of citizens in a modern democracy. Recently, students themselves have joined the attack on the traditional secondary-school curriculum, claiming it lacks relevance to dealing with social issues.

As an attempt to remedy this situation, Donald W. Oliver in 1956 launched the Harvard Social Studies Project. He aimed to develop a curriculum approach that would teach junior-high and high-school students to analyze public controversy and, particularly, to argue social issues successfully. In subsequent years he was aided in this effort by such co-workers as James P. Shaver, Harold Berlak, and Fred M. Newmann, who helped disseminate the idea of the jurisprudential approach among teachers of social studies.

Although Oliver's departure was designed for grades 7 through 12, it can be adapted for use in some upper-elementary grades. Therefore, we include it among the partial programs that can be profitably considered by people interested in improving elementary social-studies instruction. (The Berlak-Tomlinson curriculum developed at Washington University and outlined at the end of Part Four is essentially an elementary-school adaptation of Oliver's rationale.)

The Jurisprudential or Legal-Ethical Model

The crux of Oliver's approach is the classroom dialogue or debate into which the teacher leads pupils to give them experience in adopting a position on controversial social issues and in defending that position against those who would assail it. Typically an instructor begins a lesson by describing to the class a specific case involving a problem such as racial discrimination, freedom of speech, property rights, ethnic integration, slander, libel, religious freedom, or the like. During the discussion that this introduction stimulates, the teacher relates the case to similar cases in other places and other eras,

> . . . appealing especially to historical analogies to broaden the context of discussion. The initial questions raised by this material tend to be "should"-type ethical questions, but the class is inevitably thrust into legal, factual, and definitional questions when the students' own views of the "good" solution are compared with other "legitimate" social solutions. It is this amalgamation of law-government, ethics, contemporary, and historical factual questions developed around perennial issues of public policy that we refer to as *jurisprudential [or legal-ethical] teaching.*[1]

Scope and Sequence

Unlike many authors of curriculum designs, Oliver and his associates have not recommended a specific range of social problems that should make up a course of study nor a particular sequence in which problems should be presented. Rather, they have described six common ways teachers select scope and sequence and have indicated which of these ways best served the needs of teachers in the project. So with the following suggestions to guide him, the classroom teacher is expected to decide which method of choosing study topics will be most appropriate for his particular classroom.

> At least six pedagogical approaches are commonly used to organize materials for the teaching of contemporary issues. These might be briefly stated

---

[1] Donald W. Oliver and James P. Shaver, *Teaching Public Issues in the High School* (Boston: Houghton Mifflin, 1966), pp. 114-115. Copyright © 1966 by Donald W. Oliver and James P. Shaver. Reprinted by permission of the publisher, Houghton Mifflin Company.

as follows: (1) the injection of contemporary issues into regular history and government courses whenever they appear relevant; (2) the treatment of the "daily news" as the main substance of the course, often through programs provided by daily or weekly newspapers or newsmagazines; (3) the treatment of "current events" periodically (usually once a week) as a regularly scheduled activity; (4) the thematic approach to history wherein a topic such as "Church and State" or "The Democratization of American Society" is injected into the regular historical content; (5) the historical crises approach, in which particularly critical historical episodes or eras are identified and analyzed in the search for useful generalizations which might help one analyze or explain contemporary problems; (6) the problem-topic approach, which gives priority to particular topics, and then seeks to develop them from some point in the past to the contemporary definition of the problem.

While there may be strengths and weaknesses in all of these approaches, the first three have a fundamental shortcoming; they make little systematic effort to integrate the historical background of an issue with its contemporary form. . . .

We would suggest that the latter three approaches have much in common and all deserve serious consideration. We have used both the historical crises approach and the problem-topic approach.

The Historical Crises Approach

One begins by looking at historical periods which are analogous to or may be contrasted with contemporary history, and which may help explain contemporary problems. Once the historical period to be investigated has been identified, the teacher must consider each of the variety of problems that converge at this point in history. In the American Revolution, for example, a number of important issues converge: the social class upheaval; the ideological revolution embodied in the words of the Declaration of Independence; the legitimacy of resorting to violence as a means of resolving political and economic questions; the formation of a new government. The New Deal likewise contains a number of interrelated problems and issues which reach crisis proportions simultaneously: the imbalance between agriculture and industry; the flood-drought problems in agriculture; the stock market crash and the consequent economic depression; the ideological assaults on free enterprise and existing political institutions; the absence of adequate political instruments to handle growing problems in labor-management relations; and internal labor disagreements caused by the rise of industrial labor unions. All of these issues have contemporary analogues.

In general, the historical crises approach to the organization of content gives initial priority to a specific historical setting and then seeks to analyze the complex interplay of problems within that setting. The study of specific historical settings clearly has two kinds of relevance to contemporary issues: (1) It allows the identification of direct or indirect causal relationships between historical antecedents and a contemporary fact or state of affairs. For example, current southern attitudes toward northern "interference" in the race problems of the South are partly conditioned by the way these problems were handled during the Civil War and Reconstruction periods. (2) It may lead toward the development of general principles of political or social behavior from analogous historical situations, i.e., what might be called "lessons of history." For example, since it is commonly believed that the appeasement of Hitler in his early days of conquest was a great mistake in the foreign policy of the Western democracies, we now operate under the assumption that future appeasement will lead to war rather than peace. The principle evolved that if force is actually used in the critical phase of a dictator's attempt to consolidate power, the dictator may be overthrown and the community of nations saved from the ravages of an outlaw state. Thus, in one sense, the French and English attacked Nasser's Egypt in 1956 "for historical reasons."

The Problem-Topic Approach

The problem-topic approach begins with the selection of a contemporary issue which is deemed important and persistent. The issue or topic then determines what data are relevant and should be presented to the student. These data may be mainly historical (which they usually are), or journalistic, sociological, etc. The approach is clearly causal or explanatory. Only those historical or social scientific facts and generalizations are sought which help clarify or explain the nature of the contemporary problem.

From our point of view there is little purpose in debating the relative merits of the thematic, historical crisis, or problem-topic approach in the development of teaching units. There is no reason to think that one approach is invariably better than another, or to think that one approach cannot be used to complement another. Certain historical periods are crisis ridden because several problems in an aggravated form converge at that point in history. One cannot understand the full impact of these problems, or their interrelationships, without studying the crisis as a whole. The problem-topic approach, however, does provide the student with a clearer interpretation of the historical development of a problem, as well as making it easier to use contemporary social science information in its analysis. For example, in studying racial desegregation as a historical topic, sociology, psychology, anthropology, and law, as well as history, can all play a major role.

Before we discuss the problem-topic approach in more detail, a note of caution should be sounded regarding the use of an explicit analytic framework to select and organize materials of instruction. However one goes about selecting and organizing specific materials for the teaching of contemporary political controversy, he should realize that once a problem has been classified and described, even in a tentative way, the student is already predisposed to deal with it as the writer or teacher has seen and presented it. . . .

We are thus faced with something of a paradox in building a curriculum. A framework is necessary to "make sense" out of problematic data and deal with them systematically. But the framework tends to predispose us to include some aspects of the problem and to exclude others. Obviously, although we hope to teach the student our particular frame of reference, it is necessary to be alert to the fact that each student will modify it to meet the idiosyncrasies of his own personal history. This, of course, is the basic corrective in any social or political theory designed for instruction in the area of public controversy: It can be communicated or taught only imperfectly, thus allowing for growth and change in the theory itself as each new mind struggles to comprehend it and apply it to the facts of the day. . . .

With these words of warning, we shall proceed to describe a set of problem areas and some specific units or topics implied by each area, admitting from the outset that our treatment is neither systematic (in the sense that it evolves from some overall theory of social conflict) nor exhaustive. The scheme is based on a problem-topic approach; the student studies the history of a single topic or problem from its first acute symptoms to its contemporary manifestations.

Table 8-1 presents an outline of problem areas, topics, and the value conflicts in each. An obvious point brought out by the table is the abundance of problem-units that could conceivably be treated in a regular . . . social-studies program. Our own experience indicates that it takes from three to six weeks, at a minimum, to provide a "one-shot" treatment for such a unit. There must, therefore, be even more selection than is suggested by the outline. The student cannot be taught the historical background of all the problems he must face as a citizen, let alone all of "history" in general.

In selecting specific problem units from among such a list, a number of useful criteria come to mind: (1) The teacher might select topics that seem most critical on the contemporary scene. (2) The teacher might select topics which are *least* understood because of the geographical area or the type of student body he teaches. (3) The teacher might select topics which he is personally most competent to handle. (4) The teacher might first select topics which are less complex and work toward greater complexity, insofar as this can be determined. Since many such criteria can be identified, these four are meant only to be suggestive.[2]

In the foregoing manner, then, Oliver and Shaver introduce their approach to establishing scope and sequence. The teacher is provided guidelines for selecting controversial problems that are to be studied, but the specific problems and the form in which they are to be presented to the pupils are to be decided by the teacher himself.

With such flexibility in the choice of scope and sequence, jurisprudential teaching can furnish an entire year's or semester's work in social studies or can appear in the curriculum as only one or a few units within the year's course of study. In other words, it can dominate the year's activities or can serve only as an occasional supplement to some other curriculum design and teaching methodology.

Materials

It should be obvious that a single textbook or workbook will not suffice as teaching material for the jurisprudential approach. A variety of

---

[2] Oliver and Shaver, *Teaching Public Issues in the High School,* pp. 138-141.

TABLE 8-1   Identification of General Problem Areas*

Problem Areas	Sample Unit Topics	Conflicting Values[+]
Racial and Ethnic Conflict	School Desegregation Civil Rights for Non-Whites and Ethnic Minorities Housing for Non-Whites and Ethnic Minorities Job Opportunities for Non-Whites and Ethnic Minorities Immigration Policy	Equal Protection Due Process Brotherhood of Man v. Peace and Order Property and Contract Rights Personal Privacy and Association
Religious and Ideological Conflict	Rights of the Communist Party in America Religion and Public Education Control of "Dangerous" or "Immoral" Literature Religion and National Security: Oaths Conscientious Objectors Taxation of Religious Property	Freedom of Speech and Conscience v. Equal Protection Safety and Security of Democratic Institutions
Security of the Individual	Crime and Delinquency	Standards of Freedom Due Process v. Peace and Order Community Welfare
Conflict Among Economic Groups	Organized Labor Business Competition and Monopoly "Overproduction" of Farm Goods Conservation of Natural Resources	Equal or Fair Bargaining Power and Competition General Welfare and Progress of the Community v. Property and Contract Rights
Health, Education, and Welfare	Adequate Medical Care: for the Aged for the Poor Adequate Educational Opportunity Old-Age Security Job and Income Security	Equal Opportunity Brotherhood of Man v. Property and Contract Rights

TABLE 8-1   Continued

Security of the Nation	Federal Loyalty-Security Programs [Foreign Policy] [†]	Freedom of Speech, Conscience, and Association Due Process Personal Privacy v. Safety and Security of Democratic Institutions

Oliver and Shaver, Teaching Public Issues in the High School, *pp. 142-146.*

[+]*The "v." in the listing of values suggests that the top values conflict with the bottom values. While this is generally true, there are, of course, many exceptions. One can argue, for example, that a minimum wage law was a violation of property and contract rights and that it also was against the general welfare.*

[†]*This topic obviously should be the center of a new curriculum, extending our analysis of domestic problems. It might consist of a wide variety of subtopics, such as disarmament, the uncommitted nations, the stabilization of central Europe, the underdeveloped countries, etc. Such a curriculum would have to deal with a totally new problem: the relationship between power and law in the international scene. This problem is handled in our curriculum by the concept of constitutionalism and its subsidiary legal concepts. There is, however, no general constitutional framework within which world problems can now be worked out. Current work at Harvard does include not only an exploration of the problem of developing a legal-ethical frame for international problems but also development of teaching materials and strategies to implement this framework.*

materials are required, including newspapers, magazines, historical novels, short stories, history textbooks, cases from courts of law, radio and television news commentaries and dramas, motion pictures, tape recordings of controversies, and sociology, anthropology, and psychology texts. Not only must the materials relate to the controversy at hand, but the teacher must select some sources that serve to engage the pupil emotionally in the issue at hand and some other sources that provide the learner with factual information and theories that help him understand the varied facets and interpretations of a social controversy. Oliver and Shaver have recounted their own experience in choosing materials:

> To discover types of instructional materials necessary to lay the foundation for a critical political judgment, we first asked ourselves what information and commitments the student is likely to bring to a discussion, what information we must give him before a dialogue can begin, and what additional information he is likely to need to seek as he gets deeper into a problem. Certain distinctions in types of materials became apparent as we discovered that simply "presenting" the issue was an extremely difficult task which could not be handled by a single type of document. (Our first impulse had been simply to use "cases.") We found it difficult, for example, to meet the competing demands of *complexity* and

saliency. An issue must be presented as personal, relevant, and salient to the student if he is to become sufficiently concerned to want to handle it or structure it in his own mind. Yet we want him to see the problem in broader, more complex terms than those which will appear relevant or important at first encounter. To meet these competing demands, several different types of materials were developed.

Materials to Effect Empathy and Emotional Impact. Political and social problems begin in personal emotional reactions to concrete situations, and it is then that people begin to reflect about and rationalize reactions. It is therefore not enough to "tell" the student how others conceptualize the problem or have reacted to problem situations. He must see the controversial situation in a "raw" concrete setting; and he must experience, at least vicariously, the emotional reactions of the antagonists in the problem situation.

We have found that materials most appropriate for this purpose tend to be in art form, including both fiction and history. The main requirement of empathic materials is that they be highly personal so that the student can identify with individuals who are actually involved in the problem situation. . . .

Materials for Historical and Conceptual Clarification. Before a student can intelligently develop a position in a controversy, he must certainly become familiar with its broad historical, sociological, economic, and political background, as well as with the technical language in which this background may be presented. In discussing race problems in America, for example, he should know the distinction between race and culture, the differences between the Negro and the white which are attributable to each, and sufficient psychological and sociological conceptual background to evaluate controversies over which characteristics may be attributable to race and which may be attributable to culture. Furthermore, the student obviously should know why and under what circumstances the Negro came to America, and something of the bitter sectional rivalry culminating in the Civil War and Reconstruction Period around which revolved the Negro's destiny on this continent. . . .

Cases to Provide Situational Referents for Abstract Social and Political Procedures. The purpose of conceptual case material is to provide specific referents for general ethical, legal, or social science concepts. The term *collective bargaining*, for example, describes a complex set of procedures and is often related to such concepts as *strike, strike settlement*, and *union contract*. While the general abstract characteristics implied by these terms can be described, it is doubtful that the concepts can really be understood before the student has actually seen one or more examples in operation.

Conceptual case materials can, of course, be either simple and brief or elaborate and complex. Conventional textbooks are sprinkled with short examples illustrating general conceptual information. Characteristically, however, the examples are not sufficiently detailed to handle the complexity of many of the concepts which must be understood in order to cope with social and political problems.

The Controversial Case. The controversial case describes a specific situation about which there are controversial ethical, legal, factual, or definitional interpretations. It may be a classic historical or legal situation, like *Plessy* v. *Ferguson* in race relations, or the Wagner Act or Kohler strike in labor relations. Or it may be a short story or fictionalized account of a situation which expresses the essential nature of societal controversy, e.g., Orwell's *Animal Farm*. These cases are designed to provide a focus for controversial dialogue between teacher and student or among students. . . .

Takeoff Materials. The general teaching model within which we have operated gives the dialogue a central position. Although initially the student is given information that makes it easy for him to empathize with antagonists who differ over a political or social issue or that will allow him to understand the background and circumstances surrounding the issue, "teaching" takes place when the teacher begins a dialogue with the student. We assume that the ultimate purpose of teaching, however, is to make the student independent of the teacher. Specifically the student should learn to carry on a dialogue or argument and counterargument with himself and his peers. He should learn to question his own statements as well as those made by others outside the classroom. The implications of this position for instructional materials are obvious: The student must learn to seek out newspapers, including both news accounts and editorials, magazines, journals, books, and TV and radio accounts presenting positions which lend themselves to critical evaluation. When he does this spontaneously, without prodding from the formal sanctions of school, we may say that he has arrived at "takeoff."[3]

As the foregoing description indicates, the case study serves as the most important material in the jurisprudential approach, chiefly because Oliver and his co-workers are convinced that case studies elicit pupils' enthusiastic involvement with social issues and that ". . . intensive study of detailed situations will lead the student toward valid generalizations."[4] In Oliver's system, a case study can assume any of a variety of forms, including these:

1. *Story.* It portrays either actual events or fictitious happenings. It has a plot that traces events, showing the way people act and talk and feel.

2. *Vignette.* The vignette does not contain a complete plot, as does a story, but simply pictures a slice of life. Its writing style may be similar to that of the story, with dialogue and descriptions of people's actions and feelings.

3. *Journalistic historical narrative.* In the form of a news story, the journalistic narrative depicts happenings without attempting to construct a plot or delineate character. It may either describe the acts of individuals and groups or tell how some institution has operated.

---

[3] Oliver and Shaver, *Teaching Public Issues in the High School,* pp. 143-146.
[4] Fred M. Newmann and Donald W. Oliver, "Case Study Approaches in Social Studies," *Social Education,* XXXI, No. 2 (February 1967), 108.

4. *Document*. "... court opinions, speeches, letters, diaries, transcripts of trials and hearings, laws, charters, contracts, commission reports."[5]

5. *Research report.* This typically describes an experiment, survey, or poll, with accompanying statistics that serve as evidence useful in testing theories or checking the accuracy of factual statements.

6. *Text.* A text presents a description and explanation of general social phenomena, which the reader is to regard as true.

7. *Interpretive essay.* The essay is designed to explain, interpret, and assess some abstract issue such as these: What are the components of *good* government? Who was to blame for the outbreak of the First World War? Is free medical care for the aged a proper responsibility for the state? Essays try to convince the reader of the validity of their appraisal or explanation of events and institutions. Essays assess the past and present and often attempt to predict what will occur in the future.

Methods

As mentioned earlier, the real core of jurisprudential teaching is the dialogue that is stimulated between teacher and pupils, and among the pupils themselves, by the cases of public controversy they inspect. As Oliver has written, "... our central objective is to teach the student to carry on an intelligent dialogue bearing on important public issues."[6]

The proponents of jurisprudential teaching have referred to the variety of classroom discussion they espouse as *socratic* teaching. Rather than asking students to describe the facts and theories they have taken from their reading or lectures (a pattern of pedagogy called *recitation* teaching), the instructor using a socratic approach "... requires the student to take a position on the [controversial] issue, state that position, and defend it. Here the emphasis is not only on knowledge provided by the teacher as background for the discussion but on the process by which the student arrives at a decision about the topic under consideration, on the careful consideration of alternative decisions, and on the

---

[5] Newmann and Oliver, "Case Study Approaches in Social Studies," pp. 108-113.
[6] Oliver and Shaver, *Teaching Public Issues in the High School.*

utilization of analytic concepts and strategies, regardless of the position which is finally reached.[7] In other words, Oliver is more interested in the students' improving their techniques of securing information and analyzing it than he is in their acquiring particular social-science facts.

Thus, jurisprudential teaching places the pupil and teacher, or the pupil and pupil, in an adversarial position. The classroom atmosphere is argumentative and therefore elicits more emotion, including negative affect, than recitation teaching typically does.

The following excerpt from a classroom discourse on full voting rights for Negroes in the South illustrates the intellectual agility the teacher must display in order to force students to inspect all facets of an issue and defend the stance they have adopted. The annotations in the right-hand column trace the design of the teacher's instructional tactics. As Oliver has noted, a well-ordered dialogue serves two functions: "It reveals the implicit framework of the student, and it allows the teacher to intervene in the functioning of this framework to add elements and clarify inadequacies in it."[8]

*Excerpt of a Discussion That Has Focused on
the Question of Full Voting Rights for Negroes[9]*

Dialogue	*Annotation*
Teacher: What do you think, Steve?	
Steve: I think that the police power of local government can go only so far, that the constitutional rights of voting—maybe the Negroes should have them.	
Teacher: Negroes should have the right to vote, even though there may be all kinds of violence and resistance. We should send troops into the South and protect every individual's right to vote?	The teacher suggests that providing voting rights may threaten a second important value: the safety of the community; and this in turn may threaten local control by the states, if federal intervention is required to keep order.
Steve: I'm not saying that. I don't think that we would have to send down troops.	Questions factual assumption of teacher. The teacher can, at this point, choose to debate the factual

---

[7]Oliver and Shaver, *Teaching Public Issues in the High School*, p. 177.
[8]Oliver and Shaver, *Teaching Public Issues in the High School*, p. 152.
[9]Oliver and Shaver, *Teaching Public Issues in the High School*, pp. 150-152.

Teacher: But what if it did go that far?

Steve: Probably; yes.

Teacher: Suppose people called Negroes on the phone who intended to vote and said, "If you vote tomorrow, something might very well happen to your kids." Do you think we should send the FBI down there to investigate these intimidations?

Steve: No.

Teacher: Why not?

Steve: If the threat is carried out; then I would send down troops or the FBI.

Teacher: After something has happened to the courageous Negro's family, then you would send someone down to stop it.

You don't go along with the notion that if there is an atmosphere of fear and intimidation we should do something to change the atmosphere so that people will be free to vote. We shouldn't do anything until there is actual violence?

Steve: In the case of Negroes, yes.

Teacher: Why?

Steve: Because I don't want to give them the complete power to vote. This is taking a little of it away.

Teacher: You want to deny some Negroes the right to vote, a right you are willing to give whites?

Steve: Yes.

Teacher: Why?

Steve: Because I feel that Negroes are inferior to whites.

assumption or treat the assumption hypothetically and clarify the value commitment of the student.

The teacher chooses the latter course.

The teacher modifies the hypothetical situation to determine the point at which the student's position will change in favor of local control and against federal intervention. He is shifting the meaning of "violence" to do this.

The student reverses his position with the shift in the situation.

The student is aware of the reversal of his position and explains the essential criterion determining the reversal: overt use of force to prevent the Negro from voting. The student has qualified his position.

Emphasizes the negative consequences of the student's position.

The teacher now raises the definitional question: Do we have to commit an act of physical violence against a person before we have violated his rights? Is threat of violence, to some degree, also "violence"?

The student is operating with two categories of citizenship. The teacher is here asking him to justify classification on the basis of race.

Children are classified as different from adults and denied full rights of citizenship. In a sense, it is because they are "inferior." This response does have a rational component which the teacher feels obligated to explore.

Teacher: In what respect?

Steve: In intelligence; in health; in crime rates.

The student states the criteria on which his classification is based.

Teacher: You are suggesting that if a person is tubercular or sick, you should deny him the right to vote.

The teacher is here challenging the relevance of a criterion on the basis of which the student is making his classification.

Steve: No.

Teacher: But if a Negro is sick we don't let him vote?

Steve: Let him vote, sure. It is just that I think they are inferior for these reasons. I'm not saying because of these reasons I'm not going to let him vote.

Teacher: Then for what reasons aren't you going to let them vote?

Steve: Because I think they are inferior because of these reasons. (Student then laughs self-consciously, aware of his inconsistency.)

At this point the student has contradicted an earlier position.

Characteristics of Learners

The jurisprudential model of instruction is founded on several assumptions about the learners' experiential backgrounds, their personal motives or interests, their intellectual abilities, and their learning styles. When a teacher considers adopting a jurisprudential approach, it is appropriate for him to estimate whether he can validly accept these assumptions as applicable to his own pupils.

In regard to the learners' previous experiences, Oliver and Shaver have posited that

Any social studies program must face the fact that the student comes to class with a "social theory" already in mind, one which allows him to function quite well. He brings to the instructional setting a fairly stable set of interrelated personal constructs which affect how he reacts, both emotionally and intellectually, to political and social events. Instruction must be seen, therefore, as a more challenging task than simply providing the intellectual tools of the academic; rather it is one of shaping, changing, and developing intellectual and emotional orientations already present. . . . What makes social science theory or knowledge especially exciting, in fact, is its potential for feeding, expanding, or contradicting the student's already existing personal theories of social reality.[10]

A second assumption that the proponents of this system make is that pupils most readily engage themselves in investigating political controversy if they can emotionally identify with people and institutions involved in the dispute. To encourage this identification, the system uses the several varieties of case study and obligates the teacher to press each pupil to take a position in the controversy and defend it in debate.

Critics of curricula that focus on social problems often contend that secondary-school students are too immature to deal with public issues. They say, "If the world's most experienced statesmen are confounded by such issues as race relations, competing economic systems, human rights, and ways of settling international disorders, how can inexperienced adolescents be expected to deal with these problems in any adequate manner?" In response, Oliver and his associates have written:

Youth in other societies facing difficult survival problems assume adult roles at an early age. With our society now facing its own survival problems, the assumption of adult concern for the society should and undoubtedly could be brought about at a much earlier age. Maturity in the understanding and practice of social graces and heterosexual behavior has been pushed back from college to junior high school. Why not give intellectual maturity the same push? . . .

Admittedly, further research is needed before firm answers can be given to questions about the age at which students should be confronted with the basic problems of our society. Despite occasional warnings that our curriculum would "pull the rug" from under "children," however, it has been our experience that exposure to a jurisprudential approach is not disconcerting to the student. If anything, the opposite tends to be true. The student gets an awakened sense of his own intellectual power. He also finds the approach stimulating and satisfying as he enters into the debate of problems meaningful to the society rather than rehashing historical facts or discussing the abstract problems of the social scientists. . . . On motivational grounds alone, a social studies curriculum that involves the students in discussion and analysis of public issues has much to commend it.[11]

---

[10] Oliver and Shaver, *Teaching Public Issues in the High School*, p. 232.
[11] Oliver and Shaver, *Teaching Public Issues in the High School*, pp. 236-237.

Such is the Oliver-Shaver defense of using controversial social issues as the focus of secondary social studies. But what about the suitability of such a curriculum for elementary-school pupils? The answer to this query would appear to depend on the adequacy of answers to four groups of questions.

1. Is it desirable to confront preadolescent children with the conflicts of the adult world? Does this not tend to make them pessimistic? Is it not better to teach them the strengths and positive factors of their society and nation than to stimulate the doubts that arise in their minds when they face political controversy?

Since there appear to be no very adequate research data bearing on this first cluster of questions, the answers depend upon the teacher's own value system. Some people would contend that children's basic security as individuals and citizens depends upon their developing a faith during their early years that their world is basically well ordered, that they will be able to deal with it successfully, and that things are going to turn out all right. Exponents of this view of the child often support elementary-school curricula that emphasize descriptive, noncontroversial material about American society and its past history. They believe that a suitable glorification of the nation builds a sound foundation for citizenship, and that the task of confronting the reality of social conflicts can best wait until the senior high school or even later.

In contrast to the foregoing point of view, other teachers and parents believe that the young child should not be sheltered from the social conflicts of the real world but should be aided in facing and solving controversies. They believe that if the child is forever shielded from reality, when he finally is confronted by it he will not be equipped to handle controversy. They say that many of the disillusioned, bitter youth of today are the products of a system that has unduly sheltered the young from the conflicts of their world so that when they have had to face controversies, the foundations of their faith have been shaken or shattered.

Again, since we lack adequate research to settle this difference of opinion, each teacher or school is left to determine on the basis of personal experience and conviction whether it is best for elementary-school children to deal with political controversy. Or perhaps the question is better stated as What kinds of controversies should children face, at what rate, and in what grade levels? The answer depends somewhat on a consideration of the next three of the four clusters of queries.

2. Can elementary-school children be stimulated to address themselves enthusiastically to social controversies?

As an attempt to answer this question, a brief project was launched at the University of Wisconsin, Milwaukee, under the direction of one of the present authors. The effort was aimed at adapting Oliver's jurisprudential approach to elementary-school classes at different grade levels. A series of controversial issues and everyday social-conflict problems was devised, case studies were prepared for presenting the problems to pupils, and elementary-school teachers were instructed in the general process of jurisprudential dialogue.

The outcome of these tryouts was no real surprise. Children engaged most readily in discussing the kinds of controversies that had the most immediate bearing on their own lives and experiences. Furthermore, the higher the grade level, the more willing the children were to consider problems farther removed in time and space from their immediate experiences. So it was that issues of racial discrimination were of greater interest to pupils of racial minorities and to those in racially integrated schools than to pupils in all-white classrooms. It was difficult to evoke much enthusiasm for such problems as labor-management disagreements or territorial conflicts in the Middle East or Southeast Asia. It was relatively easy to capture pupils' interest in controversies centering on safety in the schoolyard, dealing with a new student, or settling territorial conflicts involving a playground used by gangs of children from rival neighborhoods.

Another obvious outcome of the lesson tryouts was the demonstration of significant individual differences among pupils in their level of enthusiasm about different social controversies. Some fifth and sixth graders willingly grapple with problems of war, revolution, social discrimination, and religious prejudices, whereas many others regard such matters as a great bore.

The conclusion we have drawn from these trial efforts with a case-study and jurisprudential approach is that a few of the issues used successfully by Oliver's project members in the secondary school will readily interest a significant proportion of fifth and sixth graders. The nature of the issues that are of interest depends somewhat upon the children's own social setting—their home and community atmosphere, their race, their religion, their parents' occupations, the topics their parents discuss at home. The topics that lend themselves to the case-study and argumentation approach in the middle and lower elementary grades are not broad political issues but issues involving social relations that children personally experience. It is true, however, that principles of human interaction as analyzed in these immediate social relations are profitably applied toward explaining conflicts in the broader political world.

3. Have elementary-school pupils' past experiences armed them with social knowledge sufficiently varied that they can comprehend the complexities of social controversies and not cling to

simplistic solutions to social problems? Are pupils' reasoning skills sufficiently advanced that they can perceive inconsistencies in their logic, or in the logic of others, as the jurisprudential dialogue develops?

Our own experience in adapting Oliver's approach to elementary grades supports what one might expect. Children vary significantly both in the richness of their social experience and in their reasoning capacities. Some fifth and sixth graders manage to argue their case with greater sophistication than many adults. Others appear distressingly naive and illogical. But this is the challenge of trying jurisprudential teaching—to broaden children's social understanding and sharpen their perceptions of logical reasoning. If a particular social issue is relatively strange to the class, the teacher faces the responsibility of providing learning materials (verbal case studies, films, stories, text materials, newspaper articles, visitors who tell their personal experiences) that fill in the empty areas of their background. And the process of the dialogue is intended to reveal to the pupil the inconsistencies in his own defense of his position and in others' defenses of theirs.

In sum, to answer the above questions, a teacher must try out several social issues from a jurisprudential approach. In the early stages of the discussion that follows the presentation of a stimulating case, the gaps in the pupils' background knowledge and in their patterns of reasoning will reveal themselves. Knowledge of these gaps helps the teacher decide what other teaching materials or practice in argumentation will be needed to meet the pupils' needs. If the social issues that are attempted are beyond the children's capacities, the pupils' inattention, their inept arguments, and their "misbehavior" should reveal the difficulty.

4. Is jurisprudential teaching appropriate for all varieties of pupil personalities? Are not some children poorly suited to the adversarial or combatant relationship with the teacher and with peers?

In our experience, there are indeed some children who appear quite uncomfortable with the argumentation that jurisprudential teaching entails. They are embarrassed when the teacher or a classmate challenges their line of reasoning or notices a gap in their store of facts. Such children tend to avoid participating in the dialogue.

Some other children willingly take part when they themselves are engaged in the debate, but when another member of the class is involved in dialogue with the teacher, their attention wanders to other concerns. In effect, they are not interested spectators and do not learn from their classmates' participation.

Because of such attitudes, and because of other factors that determine individual differences in learning styles, the socratic dialogue is not equally well suited to all children. A similar observation was made by Oliver following his experimentation with jurisprudential teaching in secondary schools. He concurred with McKeachie's comment that "Students who profit from one method may do poorly in another, while other students may do poorly in the first method and well in the second."[12] When measuring the final quality of students' learning in classes using jurisprudential teaching as contrasted to classes using more traditional recitation, the Harvard Project staff found that "... the analysis of learning outcomes affected by these quite different teaching styles revealed no discernible differences. We did find that the ability of the group had a systematic effect regardless of the style used by the teacher...."[13] It seems likely that this lack of difference between the jurisprudential and recitational groups might have resulted, at least in part, because some students in each group found the particular method employed to be well suited to their learning style, while other students found the particular method inappropriate. Taking an average score for a class serves to obliterate the significant differences among pupils within the class. So it becomes important for the classroom teacher to observe how individual pupils progress under various teaching methods in order to provide, as far as possible, suitable opportunities for each child to study according to his own style of learning.

In summary, we believe that when a teacher adopts the jurisprudential approach with elementary-school pupils, he must assume that (1) the controversial issues posed for the class are ones that will interest most of the pupils, (2) the children have sufficient wit and background knowledge to comprehend the interaction of the varied forces involved in the controversy (or at least they can gain the background and ability in logic during the study of the unit), and (3) the jurisprudential dialogue is compatible with the personalities and learning styles of a majority of the class members. In order to estimate whether these assumptions are valid for his particular class, it may be necessary for the teacher to try a short unit of jurisprudential teaching and observe the results.

---

[12]W. J. McKeachie, "Motivation, Teaching Methods and College Learning," in Marshall Jones, ed., *Nebraska Symposium on Motivation* (Lincoln: University of Nebraska Press, 1961), pp. 111-112. As quoted in Oliver and Shaver, *Teaching Public Issues in the High School*, pp. 308-309.
[13]Oliver and Shaver, *Teaching Public Issues in the High School*, p. 302.

Jurisprudential
Teaching for Elementary Grades

In the foregoing pages we have suggested modifications that may be desirable for adapting jurisprudential teaching to elementary schools. To illustrate one attempt at such adaptation at the fourth-grade level, we offer the following transcript of a case study and a subsequent discussion. The 25 children in this classroom were from lower- and lower-middle socioeconomic-level families in a "run-down" section of a large city. Fifteen of the pupils were black, five were Latin-American, and five were Anglo-European.

To initiate the lesson, the teacher read *The Bus Incident* aloud while the children followed the narrative on mimeographed copies of their own. Before reading the case, she told the children that they would be expected at the end of the narrative to write down their feelings about the incident. She requested such written responses so that (1) all pupils would be obligated to pay close attention to the case, (2) she could learn something about each child's reaction to the case before he might be influenced by classmates' views expressed during open discussion, and (3) pupils would have at hand a written record of their initial opinions to which they could refer as they discussed the case.

The Bus Incident[14]

"You owe another dime," the bus driver told Melvin, a black sixteen-year-old.

"Who, me?"

"That's right. It costs a quarter to ride this bus, not fifteen cents. Come on and give the company another ten cents. Okay?"

"But I put a quarter in already. Somebody else must have put in fifteen cents. Not me."

"Look," said the driver. "There were four passengers getting on the bus. You were the last one. You put fifteen cents in the box. What's it going to be? Are you going to pay up, or what?"

"I told you I didn't put no fifteen cents in there," replied Melvin. "I ain't putting no more money in."

After a few seconds of silent staring, the driver closed the bus door and drove into the downtown traffic. Melvin sat in an empty seat near

---

[14]*The Bus Incident* was developed in a police-community workshop sponsored by the Civic Education Project under the leadership of Dale Flower, University of California at Santa Cruz, 1969.

the back. All seemed settled, though Melvin was still angry about being accused in front of the fifteen white passengers.

Then the bus stopped at a hamburger eatery. The driver got off and entered the restaurant. Five minutes later he returned and again drove into the traffic.

At the next stop the bus dropped off three passengers and five more got on. One of the new passengers, a friend of Melvin's, moved to the back of the bus and sat next to him.

The bus did not move. The driver watched out the front window until a police car drove across in front of the bus and parked. Two young officers got out and entered the bus. One of them pulled a small tablet from his pocket and began to write on it as he talked with the driver. The driver talked angrily and pointed to Melvin. Then he led the two policemen to where Melvin sat with his friend.

The driver said, "He just walked on the bus and put fifteen cents in the box. When I caught him at it, he got smart and said he wouldn't put any more in."

"Okay," said the first officer. "let us handle it." He asked Melvin, "Is that true, young man? Is what the driver said true?"

"No. I had twenty-five cents in my pocket—just enough to ride the bus home. I put it in the box. See, I don't have any money on me. That's how I know I put a quarter in the box."

"I see," said the officer. "Was this young man with you at the time?" He pointed to Melvin's friend.

"No, he just got on," Melvin replied.

The driver began to yell, "I want him off my bus. These wise kids are always giving us trouble."

"Okay," said the officer. "Please let us handle this."

But the driver continued, "This bus isn't going to move till you get that guy off. Why do we pay you police anyway? Bus drivers are attacked all over the city, and I can't even get two cops to help me when I find a criminal."

"But it's your word against the kid's," the second officer said.

"There you go, taking the side of the colored. It seems like today the colored can get away with anything. They rob and beat up us bus drivers all over town, and now you take their side."

"Look, nobody's taking sides," the first officer said. "The young man has a right to speak in his own defense."

"Just get this colored boy off my bus," the driver shouted.

"Don't call me 'boy,' " said Melvin. "An' I ain't 'colored.' I'm a man, and I'm black. I'm a black man."

"There he's talking about Black Power and all that stuff," said the driver.

"Wait a minute," said the first officer. "Let's not get off onto race problems."

"What's your badge number?" the driver demanded. "If you don't get this punk off my bus, I'll report you to your department. You've already made me late."

"I'm not getting off," said Melvin. "I paid my fare."

The second officer asked the driver, "How about making an exception this one time? The company can stand to lose one dime."

"There you go," said the driver, "letting the criminal off."

"Won't you let him ride this time?"

"No."

Melvin said, "I'm not paying more money."

"Get off," shouted a passenger. Several others joined in, "Get off. We want to get home."

"That's right," said the driver. "See, the passengers are on my side. They know this guy didn't pay a quarter."

The two officers looked at each other, sighed, and shrugged their shoulders. "Come on," one of them said to Melvin. "You have to leave the bus."

After the teacher finished reading the incident aloud, the pupils read it silently, while the teacher walked around the class, helping individuals with words or phrases that were difficult for them. Finally, each pupil wrote a reaction to the story. In the following chart the left column contains five representative reactions. The right column contains the teacher's annotations about the written comments.

Written Comments	*Annotations*
Wendell: "I don't think it's fair. If he was white the bus driver won't have done that. I don't think the bus driver was fair."	Many of the black pupils' comments show they identify with the black youth and consider the white in general oppressive.
Shar: "I don't think it fair, and he should of got his money back. Maybe he did pay the right amount."	
Diana: "I would tell the bus driver that he did put in all the money he was suppose to. Or I would give the black man 10 cents."	Some pupils picture themselves as passengers on the bus with a chance to influence the outcome of the incident.
George: "I think the bus driver was not fair. The cop was not fair either, because he didn't ask the black man as much as the driver."	Many of the pupils link the police and driver together as allies in the "white establishment."
Bob: "If he was white, it wouldn't of happened. Just because the man was black the bus driver said he did not have enough money. The driver was prejudiced. The policeman was fair because he was doing his duty."	This child sees a conflict between the way the bus driver behaved and the role expected of a bus driver. But the pupil sees no role conflict for the police.

As the first steps in initiating a classroom dialogue focusing on the bus incident, the teacher wished to (1) clarify terms not understood—or not agreed upon—by all pupils and (2) secure agreement among the pupils about what facts were presented in the case and what questions should be asked about factual issues that the narrative did not make apparent. Therefore, after several pupils read their written comments aloud, the teacher's first question was: "Bob said the bus driver was prejudiced. What does the word *prejudiced* mean?"

Class Comments	Annotations
Shar: "It means you don't like somebody because he's black." Bob: "Not just black. You can be prejudiced against people for different reasons."	The definition of terms is an important aspect of analyzing controversial issues, since disagreements often center on the meaning of words rather than on the substantive issues in the case. Clarifying meanings sometimes solves the controversy.

Subsequent comments from a variety of members of the class convinced the teacher that the children understood what *prejudice* meant. She then turned to the matter of the facts in the narrative.

Class Comments	Annotations
Teacher: "What facts—what we know for sure—can you tell me about the situation Melvin was in?" Janet: "Melvin was kicked off the bus and didn't have a ride." George: "The driver was prejudiced." Teacher: "How do we know that?" Larry: "He called Melvin a colored boy." Teacher: "Would that always mean the person who said it was prejudiced?" Larry: "Around here it does."	 The teacher wishes to illustrate that the meaning a listener attributes to a term is not always the meaning the speaker intended.

After some minutes of discussing clues from the driver's behavior, the class agreed that he was prejudiced. The pupils then described a variety of other facts in the case—the driver stopped at a restaurant, a boy boarded the bus and sat next to Melvin, the police asked Melvin's opinion, Melvin claimed to have paid the full fare. The teacher then wanted the pupils to identify the kinds of information they needed that was not provided in the narrative.

Class Comments	Annotations
Teacher: "What do we still need to know about the situation? What questions should we ask and try to answer to help us understand what happened?"	
Bob: "We still don't know for sure if Melvin put in fifteen cents or a quarter."	
Teacher: "Good. Now, we read that the police were young, but were they black, white, or brown?"	The teacher had hoped a pupil would ask about race. But since no one did, she raises the question herself.
Diana: "It doesn't say. I guess we all thought they were white."	
Teacher: "Why?"	
George: "Most cops are white."	
Teacher: "Then would it make a difference in your judgment of the case if you knew whether the police were black, brown, or white?"	The teacher tries to alert the pupils to their hidden assumptions in matters of controversy.

Pupil responses at this point indicated that the race of the policemen was an important consideration. A few pupils did not think the matter was important because the policeman's role is defined regardless of race. "Police are police, no matter what."

The teacher next wanted to bring up the values involved in the case, to illustrate ways some of the values were in conflict, and to consider alternative solutions for the conflicts.

Class Comments	Annotations
Teacher: "Let's talk about what different people in the bus thought about what happened. We'll talk about what they thought was really important. We'll call this their values."	In raising a new facet of public controversy, the teacher introduces a new term and its definition. She writes on the chalkboard "*Values—what you think is important, good, or bad.*"

George: "They were mad. They wanted to get where they were going, and the fight slowed them down."

Teacher: "Who knows what *efficiency* means?"

Charlotte: "Getting things done without bother."

Teacher: "Yes, getting it done quickly and not making mistakes or too much trouble. Who else seemed to want efficiency?"

Fred: "The driver. He said he was late."

Teacher: "Good. Now, what did the police want or value?"

James: "Blood!"

Teacher: "What did the police want in this situation?"

Warren: "They wanted to clean up the mess—the whole mess."

Teacher: "Say a little more about what you mean, Warren."

Warren: "They thought the bus driver was stupid and the kids were wrong to be noisy and angry. They just wanted to stop the fight—clean up the whole mess without taking sides."

Teacher: "By the way you're nodding, you all seem to agree. What did the bus driver want?"

James: "He wanted to show he was the man—the boss telling everybody what to do."

Teacher: "What did Melvin want or value?"

Richard: "He just wanted to do his thing—to be left alone. He was tired of being put down—just like all blacks."

The teacher writes *efficiency* on the board. She wishes to abstract a general value from the concrete situation. The teacher draws as many definitions as possible from the class rather than simply offering meanings to the class. Her purpose is to encourage active participation and to learn the nature of the pupils' present ideas. The teacher seeks additional applications of the general value.

The teacher decides James' response detracts from the discussion, so she ignores it by restating the same question. She could pursue the *blood* remark by quizzing James about why he holds that value and what it means to him.

The teacher encourages the boy to elucidate what he intends by giving examples.

The teacher writes *keep the peace* and *order* on the board. These ideas are general values drawn from a concrete situation. Pupils do not yet perceive conflicts between general values.

Teacher tries to summarize opinions, then moves another step toward uncovering bases for the conflict.

Teacher writes *authority* on the board, writes *person in charge* next to it.

Bob: "Yeh, but if he didn't put the quarter in, he was just hustling the driver."

James: "He put the money in."

Teacher: "Remember, we said that one thing we didn't know for sure was if Melvin put the money in or not. Let's just say we do know that Melvin didn't like what happened, whether or not he put in the money."

Teacher has pupils recall facts of the case.

At this juncture the teacher wrote *anti-authority* on the board, and the pupils discussed what it means. As a result, the word *driver* was written below *established authority* and Melvin's name was written below *anti-authority*.

Class Comments	*Annotations*
Teacher: "What did Melvin's friend want or value?"	Teacher directs attention to a person playing another role in the drama.
Shar: "He stuck up for his friend just as he should of."	Teacher writes *loyalty to friend*.
Teacher: "So he wanted to help his friend. All right, now let's talk about what you think should have happened. How would you have changed the way it went?"	Teacher directs pupils to next step, that of considering alternative solutions for conflict situations.
James: "They should have kicked the bus driver off the bus."	Teacher accepts all suggestions without evaluating their worth. She does this in order to encourage widespread participation and obtain many possible solutions. Later in the discussion the worth of the solutions will be appraised.
Wendell: "Yeh, fired him."	
Teacher: "How could that have happened?"	
Wendell: "Tell the driver's boss."	
James: "Nobody listens to kids."	
Bob: "You could have your parents tell the driver's boss."	
Teacher: "What else could have happened?"	
Richard: "The cops could have put in a dime for Melvin."	
James: "Yeh, or somebody in the bus should of."	

Bob: "The police should have given Melvin a ride instead of just leaving him there."

Diana: "Yeh."

If we compare this fourth-grade modification of the jurisprudential approach with the high-school dialogue quoted earlier in the chapter, we can identify several ways they are alike and are different. Both discussions were launched with a case study illustrating a controversial social issue. In both instances the case successfully engaged the interest of the pupils. Likewise, both teachers focused pupils' attention on their value commitments as well as on the facts included in the narratives. The teachers encouraged the pupils to express their own values as well.

But there was a prominent difference in the conduct of the two dialogues. The high-school teacher spent some minutes in discourse with a single student in order to reveal varied facets of the student's belief system and to press the boy into recognizing the consequences and logical inconsistencies of the position he espoused. In contrast, the fourth-grade teacher moved quickly from one pupil to another, seeking their opinions without challenging their remarks or pressing them to debate the reasonableness of their views. The principal goal of the fourth-grade teacher was to illustrate to pupils various ways of viewing controversial situations. She also wished to demonstrate the way general conditions—such as authority conflicts and role expectations—are shown in concrete incidents. As desirable as these purposes might be, they represent only a part of the jurisprudential approach as represented in Oliver's work. To use the approach fully, the fourth-grade teacher on other occasions will need to challenge the value stands adopted by individuals and to press them into recognizing weaknesses in their logic as well as the worth of different stands that other people might take.

Teacher Characteristics

Jurisprudential teaching is founded on assumptions that the teacher:

1. Is an effective extemporaneous debater. Not only does the teacher need a sound background of information in the field that the social controversy covers, but he also must display the intellectual acuity required to assess the pattern of reasoning students are employing and to pose the kinds of questions that reveal strengths and weaknesses in their logic. Because the path the class discussion will take cannot always be predicted, the instructor must constantly be prepared to deal with unexpected turns in the argument. Teachers unwilling to take this risk of facing the unexpected are not comfortable with the jurisprudential approach.

2. *Is prepared to accept the negative emotions that arguments evoke.* The verbal confrontations elicited by jurisprudential methods excite strong emotions, many of them negative—anger, fear, confusion, shame. A teacher unwilling to accept these feelings as a necessary part of the classroom climate is poorly equipped to use a jurisprudential approach. Furthermore, the teacher must be prepared to control his own negative feelings during debate so that he deals rationally and fairly with pupils who express views contrary to his own. Otherwise the negative emotions can get out of hand, giving the classroom atmosphere such a negative charge of contentiousness and fear that the pupils are unlikely to learn much that the teacher has intended. The dialogue can deteriorate into irrational name calling or seething silence.

3. *Is willing to face objections from colleagues or the community.* A social-studies program centering on public controversies is clearly not the safest from attack by parents, school officials, and other teachers. Many people believe that the elementary classroom is not the proper place for arguing the merits of different positions in labor-management disputes, public-welfare provisions, social-class conflicts, and race relations. Some parents believe preadolescent children are too young to assess the merits of different positions in controversies. Others fear that the teacher or the authors of text materials will indoctrinate children with the wrong beliefs or will cause children to question values that the parents hold. Consequently, teachers who employ jurisprudential teaching can expect occasional criticisms of their social-studies program. Some teachers, to forestall such attacks, inform parents ahead of time about the purpose of a unit on controversial issues and about the advantages of the approach. This preview may be in the form of a parent-teacher meeting or a letter to the home.

Just as some parents object to children debating social problems in the classroom, so some teachers and administrators in the school may also disapprove. In this event, a conference with the critics or a description of the program during a faculty meeting may be used to encourage acceptance of the value of jurisprudential teaching.

4. *Has the time and interest for developing or collecting the necessary teaching materials.* As noted earlier, Oliver's approach depends on case studies of controversies—past and present—and on materials containing facts, theories, and analyses of issues that bear on the controversies. The Harvard Project staff compiled such materials for treating only a limited number of public issues at the high-school level. At the elementary level this task is left entirely up to the individual school or teacher. Therefore, teachers who choose to organize their social-studies

program around established textbooks or pamphlet series will find jurisprudential teaching—at least in its present stage of development—ill suited to their desires.

Evaluation Procedures

The Harvard Project directed careful attention to the problem of appraising how well students achieve the goals of analyzing public issues after participating in jurisprudential discussion sessions. For purposes of the formal appraisal of student progress, the staff used three kinds of measures: (1) established tests of critical thinking, (2) two multiple-choice tests devised specifically for the project, and (3) two oral-analyses tests created by project personnel. Undoubtedly the teachers who employed the jurisprudential approach also made their own informal observations about how adequately students performed during classroom dialogues, but such informal observations were not reported in the Harvard Project's official account of the experiment. Thus, we shall direct our attention chiefly to the three varieties of formal measures employed.

Several previously published measures of critical thinking were tried. They included the Watson-Glaser Critical Thinking Appraisal, several tests from the American Council on Education's Cooperative Study of Evaluation in General Education, and some that had been part of the Progressive Education Association's Eight Year Study. However, these tests, which were composed of items treating individual segments of pupils' thinking rather than students' overall patterns of thought, proved to be a disappointment.

> (1) While some instruments attempt to assess various fragments of a critical thinking process, none of these assesses the student's ability to follow a sequence of operations within a dialectical framework—e.g., the sequence that two individuals might go through of stating a generalization, questioning a generalization by providing a contradictory example, qualifying a generalization to take into account the contradictory example, and supporting it with authoritative evidence, including the credentials of the authority. (2) It is possible that a student might perform important operations on a paper-and-pencil test, yet be totally inept at performing the same operations in a "real" setting, e.g. in a street-corner argument. . . . And . . . little evidence is available on the usefulness of the tests in predicting performance outside of the testing situation.[15]

[15] Oliver and Shaver, *Teaching Public Issues in the High School*, p. 185.

To illustrate their point, Oliver and Shaver have provided the transcript of a segment of dialogue in an eighth-grade class that was concerned with the desirability of school desegregation measures. Following the transcript, the authors have commented on aspects of the pupils' performance that could not readily be assessed by means of typical objective-type critical-thinking measures.

> Doris: I'd like to tell the people who say the Supreme Court does not have a right to tell us to integrate the schools: it is a fact that you're not giving Negroes their constitutional rights. That's why they're telling you to integrate. It's not that they're trying to interfere with your school system, but the Negroes don't get their constitutional rights, their natural rights. The Supreme Court can rule on this.
>
> Jean: The Supreme Court has no right to tell us what to do; it's a state right; and I believe the schools are run right.
>
> Doris: But what about the constitutional rights, their natural rights? They're not getting an equal schooling.
>
> Jean: They have the same schools; they have good schools.
>
> Bill: Right here it says segregation harms the Negroes by making them feel inferior. It doesn't matter whether the schools are equal or not. Segregation always makes the children feel inferior.
>
> Jean: I don't think the Supreme Court has any right to make any such decision or any such generalization. Our schools for the Negroes are better than the schools for the whites. You could reverse that and say that Negroes feel superior to the whites because they have better schools. . . .

> Note that the [second] time Doris speaks she has an opportunity to question the evidence for the prior assertion, yet does not do so. She may know *how* to question evidence, but not *when*. Note also how Bill, in effect, claims that the issue of how good the Negro schools are is irrelevant, but Jean misses Bill's meaning. It may be that she has the ability to "identify the problem" but does not recognize that she has missed an opportunity to do so here.[16]

The Harvard staff's attempts to improve on the critical-thinking tests currently on the market resulted in the development of the other two varieties of tests mentioned.

One type offered the student an excerpt of a dialogue on a controversial issue and, in one version, asked him to select which of a series of evaluative comments about the dialogue were most valid. In other words, it was a multiple-choice test to assess the pupil's skill at analyzing thinking processes revealed by the dialogue. In another version of the multiple-choice

---

[16]Oliver and Shaver, *Teaching Public Issues in the High School*, pp. 184-185.

test the student was asked to identify which replies in a transcript of a debate were the best ones to support a particular debater's position. Following tryouts of these multiple-choice measures, the project directors concluded that they represented a "marked improvement" over the typical critical-thinking test. However, these new evaluation instruments still tested the student's ability merely to identify adequate responses in debates rather than to produce analytical comments or adequate responses himself.

To correct the shortcomings of the multiple-choice tests, project personnel devised a further set of tests—ones that required students to make oral analyses of arguments over social issues. The nature of this variety of appraisal device is suggested by the following directions, which the teacher gave to the students who were about to take the test.

> We are going to read an imaginary conversation between two men (Bob and Don). Then I am going to ask you to describe the main points of disagreement between the two men, and I am going to ask you how you would go about settling or clarifying these points of disagreement. In analyzing these main points of disagreement try and use any critical thinking skills or knowledge you may have learned about the analysis of controversial issues.[17]

For purposes of the experiment, the pupil-teacher interview was taped so that each student's line of logic in analyzing the imaginary conversation could be assessed later on a rating sheet. Oliver and Shaver concluded that the rating sheet, on which a complex content analysis of student thought patterns could be recorded, furnished a more convincing appraisal of students' progress in analyzing controversial issues than did any of the paper-and-pencil tests.

But the question remains: Can teachers in typical classrooms go to the bother of assessing pupils' achievement by means of individual, tape-recorded dialogue analyses? Oliver and Shaver have observed:

> There is . . . no denying the impracticability of careful, complex content analysis for the day-to-day measurement needs of the average classroom. Teachers in general have neither the research competence nor the time to learn or use such a complex system.[18]

How, then, can the elementary-school teacher who chooses to use some jurisprudential teaching best evaluate the achievement of his pupils?

---

[17] Oliver and Shaver, *Teaching Public Issues in the High School*, p. 204.
[18] Oliver and Shaver, *Teaching Public Issues in the High School*, p. 225.

In our opinion, the most practical approach is for the teacher to pay close attention to the pattern of logic that each child displays during classroom discussions of social issues. After the class period, notations can be made about strengths and weaknesses different children evidenced in their contributions. Such judgments will likely be more valid if the teacher can develop some simple rating scale or check sheet on which to record how well pupils handled key steps in the discussion of social conflicts. The kinds of items that might be included on such a scale or sheet are suggested in Oliver's and Shaver's own report on content analysis of dialogues.[19]

In summary, the typical teacher will probably find informal observation of pupils' participation in classroom debates to be the most practical form of appraising children's progress under jurisprudential teaching.

Conditions Affecting
Adoption of Jurisprudential Teaching

Most of the factors determining whether a jurisprudential approach will be adopted in a given classroom have already been described in earlier sections of this chapter. In these final paragraphs we shall briefly review the most crucial of these factors and shall mention a few additional ones.

The most important element in implementing a jurisprudential curriculum is clearly the classroom teacher. A jurisprudential program requires his commitment to the debate of political issues and a considerable skill at directing children in constructive disputation. Since there are no established textbooks for children in this field, the teacher must be willing to develop or collect the resource materials and case studies needed to interest children in arguing public issues and to furnish them the background information required for understanding the complexities of the issues. As Oliver and Shaver have written:

> This is not a curricular pattern to be dictated from the central office. It requires a certain type of teacher, open to the exploration of ideas, to the examination of the legal and ethical principles underlying policy decisions, able to think in other than categorical terms and to tolerate the conflict of ideas and ideals. . . . He must have a tentative-probabilistic view of knowledge. He must be aware of symbol-referent relationships and be able not only to distinguish the emotive from the cognitive connotations of words but to deal with words as

---

[19] Oliver and Shaver, *Teaching Public Issues in the High School,* pp. 203-226.

representations of concepts rather than manifestations of reality. . . . And, of course, the teacher must also have a good general background in history and the social sciences if he is to deal with public issues adequately in the classroom and be able to direct students to the proper sources of information. . . .

The teacher must be willing to interact freely with his students in the interchange of ideas, accepting their contributions as valuable and worthwhile to build upon.[20]

This array of demands on an instructor's ability and dedication is so substantial that it seems improbable that many elementary-school teachers will choose to make jurisprudential teaching a very large part of their social-studies program, if, indeed, they are willing to try it at all.

Two other important factors affecting the adoption of Oliver's system are the intellectual maturity of the pupils and their interests. Some children seem easily bored or confused by arguments over political issues. When many such uninterested pupils are in a class, the teacher may weary of the effort to engage them in discourse. In some instances the children's boredom and frustration arise from a poor choice of issues; the children are simply unmoved by problems remote from their everyday lives. In these cases, wiser selection of topics may improve the success of classroom disputation. But in other cases the pupils apparently are too immature intellectually to comprehend the complexity of social issues. Their arguments display such faulty logic that the discussion sessions seem a waste of time. With such children, jurisprudential teaching would appear far less practical than other kinds of social studies.

Even when teacher and pupils are willing and able, a jurisprudential approach may be rendered impossible by a school administrator or school board that requires teachers to dedicate the entire social-studies program to some other approach, such as descriptive geography or a type of narrative history that adheres to a single interpretation of events of the past. Many administrators, school-board members, and parents believe that the elementary social-studies program should be dedicated to the inculcation of specified *American values* and historical facts rather than to the disputation of social problems. When such people exercise decisive power over the school's subject matter and teaching methods, it may be impossible for a teacher to mount a jurisprudential approach.

But there are elementary classrooms in which Oliver's legal-ethical procedures will succeed. Given a capable teacher with interested pupils under an innovative administration, jurisprudential teaching may well ". . . bring the conventional curriculum more in line with the needs and commitments of a democratic, pluralistic society."[21]

---

[20]Oliver and Shaver, *Teaching Public Issues in the High School*, p. 240.
[21]Oliver and Shaver, *Teaching Public Issues in the High School*, p. 241.

9

Confluent Education

For many people who believe that a prime goal of elementary education is to promote children's personal-social well-being, the typical American school has been a considerable disappointment. Critics point out that despite new and better school buildings, higher academic requirements for teacher certification, and greater varieties of teaching media, many thousands of pupils appear to hate school or hate themselves or both. Even before completing their first decade of life, great numbers of children view themselves as failures. Fearful and confused, they react in a variety of unbecoming ways. They are rebellious, despondent, antagonistic, introverted, aggressive, submissive, indecisive, irresponsible, or overdependent on adult supervision. Their poor performance on schoolwork earns them low grades. In some cases they earn satisfactory school marks—perhaps even excel—but at the price of constant worry. They always feel that something will soon go wrong.

According to some observers, a key cause of this unhappy state has been the curriculum's exclusive emphasis on the cognitive or intellectual facet of the child's personality to the neglect of his affective or emotional development. Over the years a variety of solutions have been proposed for righting this ostensible imbalance. Some people—educators and parents alike—say the school should not be expected to concern itself with children's personal-social adjustment and their emotional problems. The school's task, they say, is to focus on the cognitive and leave the affective to home and church.

But others—educators, psychologists, and parents—are convinced that it is impossible to separate cognitive from affective development. It is not a question of whether the school should meddle with the child's emotional life. The child and his inseparable emotions spend so much time in the classroom that the school inevitably influences his affective being. So, it is said, teachers had better learn to do their influencing in a conscious, constructive manner rather than, as in the past, contributing unwittingly to children's feelings of inadequacy, indecisiveness, antagonism, and despondency.

In recent years a variety of movements have grown up—in different sections of the United States and abroad—as attempts to care for children's emotional growth within the regular school program. They are not attempts at special education for the handicapped or seriously disordered child. They are plans for the positive emotional development of all children. Included among these efforts are the work of Gerald Weinstein at the University of Massachusetts, Al Alschuler at the State University of New York in Albany, and George I. Brown of the University of California, Santa Barbara. The general goals of the programs are similar even though the work has progressed under different labels in different places: humanistic education, sensitivity training, affective learning, and teaching for personal-social awareness. The various movements do not represent a unified plan. However, leaders of several programs have shared experiences and teaching materials, so that one program has often influenced the direction of others.

In this chapter we focus on one representative approach, the *confluent education* of George I. Brown.

The Beginnings

Confluent education is a term adopted by Brown from the experiential work of Esalen Institute at Big Sur, California, and from the work of Gestalt Therapist Fritz Perls. Its purpose is to suggest that learning should be so conducted that it encourages the harmonious flowing together of cognition and affect. Brown's teaching procedures, drawing heavily on Esalen approaches and Gestalt therapy techniques, are the result of nearly a decade of experimentation at the University of California, Santa Barbara, and at Esalen Institute.

Unlike many curriculum designs, which begin with a theory or rationale that dictates what form classroom practice should take, confluent education began as personal encounters among people in university classes, primarily classes preparing students for careers as elementary-school teachers. The sessions originally aimed at improving participants' creativity, in the sense of opening their minds to new ways of viewing themselves and the world—new sensations, perceptions, and emotions. A variety of personal and group sensitivity techniques were employed to accomplish this goal. But no technique involved the use of drugs, since Brown considered it a serious error to use chemical-escape devices as substitutes for what he believed should be a heightening of awareness while people are in normal physical states.

Although some objective testing was performed to reflect the kinds of creativity changes achieved in the group sessions, it was primarily testimonials from participants and the instructor's observations of their behavior that suggested that a great many of them were seeing life in remarkable new dimensions.[1] The experiments in stimulating creativity were then tried out with elementary-school pupils[2] before Brown expanded his interests to encompass a broad range of cognitive-affective relationships.

Over the 1967-69 period he organized a team of investigators to comb the literature of psychology, psychotherapy, group processes, and counseling in order to find techniques that might be adapted for regular classroom practice. The intention was not to perform psychotherapy in the classroom. It was to identify and to create approaches that would encourage a consonant integration of intellect and feeling. Several teachers who were members of the team tried out the more promising techniques with their elementary- and secondary-school classes. Results of the project, sponsored by the Ford Foundation through the Esalen Institute, were reported in *Human Teaching for Human Learning*.[3] A further project was launched in 1970 to advance the program.

The Values Sought

In its present state, confluent education is still more a cluster of classroom practices that appear to increase pupil awareness than it is a

---

[1] George Isaac Brown, "An Experiment in the Teaching of Creativity," *The School Review*, 72, No. 4 (Winter 1964), 437-450; George Isaac Brown, "A Second Study in the Teaching of Creativity," *Harvard Educational Review*, 35, No. 1 (Winter 1965), 39-54.

[2] George Isaac Brown, *Operational Creativity: A Strategy for Teacher Change*. Unpublished paper presented at the meeting of the American Educational Research Association, February 1966.

[3] George Isaac Brown, *Human Teaching for Human Learning* (New York: Viking, 1971).

tightly ordered theory that logically determines what classroom practices should be like. Its practitioners have been far more concerned about making their techniques work than in explaining why they work. Thus the rationale for, and interpretations of, confluent education are still evolving. It is a clear case of theory coming after practice. This incomplete state of the theoretical side of their work has not particularly disturbed the project staff, for they have come to trust their feelings for guiding their activities as much as they trust logical analyses.

The attention that Brown's staff has given to rationales has been primarily directed at the outcomes or values they seek. The state of their thought about these matters in 1969 is indicated by Brown's comments in *Human Teaching for Human Learning.*

> ... undergirding the actual work of the Ford-Esalen project was a continuing dialogue among the staff as to a philosophical rationale to justify what we were trying to do. A number of issues or themes emerged from time to time, but three issues seemed central to our reflections. These were freedom and responsibility, innovation versus revolution, and Americanism and patriotism.
>
> Although it is not possible in the space of this short chapter to describe in detail the progress of our thinking about these themes, here are some of the conclusions and positions we reached.

Freedom and Responsibility

> When we confronted the basic questions, "Why introduce affective experiences into the classroom?" and "Why is it important to integrate the affective and cognitive domains and, accordingly, modify the curriculum?" we became aware that something besides our own prejudices was involved, especially if we were to answer these questions reasonably when they were put to us by people not in the project.
>
> One dimension of these questions is that of the relationship between freedom and responsibility in a democratic society. A goal we were striving for in our work was to help students become both *more free* and *more responsible.* We believed this could be done by increasing the student's sense of his own power to take responsibility for his behavior. Further, by providing experiences that made available ways to become free, followed by the actual experience of increasing freedom, we could help the student attain the personal satisfaction that is unique to feeling free. It was crucial that the two qualities, freedom and responsibility, be thought of as existing in an indivisible relationship. Just as we tried to achieve a balance between affective and cognitive learning, we also sought for ourselves and our students a balance between freedom and responsibility.
>
> In the kind of society which for the individual overstresses responsibility— and this is what our schools seem to do—it is likely that totalitarian conditions will rapidly emerge. It is true that one is responsible to someone or something or some group unless one is responsible only to oneself, which can lead to anarchy. However, when responsibility is stressed at the expense of freedom to make

changes, the repression of freedom also suppresses any possibilities for change. As a consequence, the status-quo situation or establishment becomes entrenched, and the prevailing rules and regulations continue to be enforced, resulting in a totalitarian or authoritarian society.

On the other hand, when individual or collective freedom is stressed without an accompanying appropriate emphasis on responsibility—when one is responsible only to oneself—chaos and anarchy can swiftly follow. Some current examples are riots and, to a degree, certain aspects of the hippie movement. . . .

Interestingly, in our language we do not say "I think responsible" but, instead, "I feel responsible." And yet when we teach responsibility in school, we teach it as thinking, not as feeling. Furthermore, we usually begin by stressing responsibility to others. Before one can be responsible to or for others, one must know what feeling responsible is like, what it means. The meaning that makes most sense to an individual, whether child or adult, is personal meaning. It follows, then, that one must begin with learning to feel responsible and to take responsibility for oneself. From here one can move meaningfully into the experience of taking responsibility for others, and can recognize when this is important and when it should be avoided. There are times when taking responsibility for someone else deprives him of the opportunity to stand on his own two feet, thereby interfering with his own learning of the first step.

Among the techniques we used, Gestalt-therapy experiments were especially productive in teaching the relationship between freedom and responsibility.

Innovation versus Revolution

Following the theme that freedom and responsibility are essential and inseparable values to be learned by members of a democratic society in order for that society to continue to flourish, the next question is, "What if the educational system in a democracy is not teaching these and other important concepts? Do we throw the whole thing out, as some demand, or do we attempt innovation within the present system?"

We are sympathetic with such critics as Paul Goodman, who cry out that the present curriculum is anachronistic or even, in some instances, archaic. However, believing that significant change can occur within the educational establishment, we hold that it does not make sense to throw everything out and begin again. Change should be brought about through commitment and involvement rather than by edict or revolution. The democratic process is not merely a chauvinistic cliché. Nor is it *just* a political theory. As a political and social process, democracy provides a system that is psychologically sound in its potential for allowing healthy and gradual change.

Change occurs when frustration is (1) encountered, (2) confronted, (3) experienced, and (4) worked through. When life is experienced as smooth and easy, there is no need for change. There is no dissatisfaction with what is. However, when frustration does exist, reality-based resolutions of the frustration occur, again when emotion and intellect work together.

Too much overbalance toward emotional reaction, or the affective, can lead to violent revolution. Though, historically, violent revolution may have been unavoidable in some cases, in regard to the improvement of the educational system the wasteful destruction that inevitably accompanies violence could now be avoided if there were at least a modicum of foresight and action.

We say foresight *and* action because too much overbalance on intellect, or the cognitive, leads to discussion and the development of theories and usually stops there—with little action. Moreover, discussion and theories tend to be about an abstract rather than a real set of conditions. This is because those specialists engaged in the discussion, having chosen an occupation that centers on discussion and the intellect, have often at the same time rejected a mode of existence that involves less pleasant and less manageable work—the so-called "world of hard knocks." The contrast between the world of the authors of the following abstract of a study and the world of the author of the next excerpt is obvious.

> Switching attention from one source of information to another requires time. . . . In this experiment, nonsense syllables were learned in a serial learning task in which syllables could be presented either visually or auditorially and under conditions that involved different frequencies of switching modality. . . . [The] procedure yields an estimate of switching time of 168 milli-seconds—a value closely in accord with those previously derived from entirely different procedures (Reid and Travers, 1968).[4]

The following account of how a Gestalt technique is used in a classroom is from *Anger and the Rocking Chair*, by Janet Lederman, a member of the Ford-Esalen project staff who taught a special class of children who could not be maintained or "contained" in regular classrooms in a school in an urban poverty area.

"I don't want to read that dumb book!"

Books are of little value to you as they do not relate to your present world.

"I hate my fucking sister. She beats me up."

You have just told an explicit story with words that have explicit meaning for you. I suggest that you write your story.

"I don't know how to spell the words."

I write the words on a separate piece of paper and you write them on your paper. I give you the words as you ask for them. This is also proof that I am listening to you. If you are ready, the same story can be expanded into fantasy. You may find other emotions available to you. As a result, your real works may expand.

"What would you like to do to your sister?"

"I can't do anything. She is bigger than I am."

"She is not here and this is just pretend. Tell her what you would like to do to her."

"I'd like to hit you."

"What else would you like to do?"

"I'd like to kick you."

---

[4] I. E. Reid and R. M. W. Travers, "Time Required to Switch Attention," *American Educational Research Journal*, 5, No. 2 (March 1968), 203-212.

"What else?"

"That's all, I'm finished."

Now you begin to write your story. You are full of energy. You are completing unfinished business.[5]

Here is a professional teacher confronting a real problem where control of the situation is tenuous at best, but where a crossroads in a child's life is encountered. This contrasts clearly with the carefully controlled but manufactured problem described in the abstract. . . .

For learning to take place at all the learner must open himself to new experience. The nature of the experience may vary from the concrete to the abstract, but before he can learn anything a learner must be willing to expose himself to new experience. Teachers use a variety of methods, from enticement and reward to threat and reproof, to motivate students to take this step. There is unavoidably always some risk when one moves into the unknown, or not-yet-known, worlds of new experience. The most primal risk is that one will change. And the status quo is comfortable. Security, no matter how false or how well sustained by the denial of reality, seems preferable to "what might happen."

The ideal pedagogical condition is where a learner, fully possessed of feelings of personal adequacy as an explorer in the universe of experience, finds the adventure of new experience a prospect of challenge and excitement. . . .

Americanism and Patriotism

What can be chauvinistic clichés, slogans deviously used to hide some scoundrelly act, or superficial verbalisms about what it means to live in a democracy make sense to us and were supported by the work in the project.

Discipline should be taught in the schools. To us this means a quality of discipline that emphasizes personal responsibility so that one respects law and order because one is committed to the democratic process that produces *and*, as needed, changes laws and the order that follows. The disciplined person that we hope will emerge as the result of confluent education will not need a policeman standing over him to see that he does not break the law. He will, however, be vitally concerned for the justice of our laws and will act and vote accordingly.

The individual comes before the state. We believe that the uniqueness of the individual is a precious commodity and that for the state or any institution of the state to repress, inhibit, or distort the enormous potential of each individual for learning to do for himself and for his society is evil and wasteful. We believe that confluent education is an approach to the development of the individual's potential—not as a self-centered, greedy, manipulative malcontent, or as an unthinking member of a mob or movement, but as a whole person who thinks and feels for himself and who is also aware and capable of, in Buber's words, an "I-thou" relationship with others—a relationship all human beings need to help manifest their humanness.

---

[5] Janet Lederman, *Anger and the Rocking Chair* (New York: McGraw-Hill, 1969), pp. 43-44.

Democracy is unreservedly preferable to a totalitarian state. The comments in the earlier part of this chapter make quite explicit our commitment to this position.

Concern for preserving the freedom of our country must permeate the very being of every citizen. Yes, *permeate.* Because a student can feel what it means to be free, as a citizen he will have a genuine understanding of the democratic process both as a theoretical construct and as an operational system with strengths and weaknesses. Furthermore, he will be committed to an open society for his fellow men not because he has *been told* to value the society but because he has *experienced* authentic contact with those who make up the society and knows the profound satisfaction of honest and open communication within that society.[6]

The foregoing set of values, then, represents the general cluster of objectives that confluent or humanistic education attempts to promote.

Scope and Sequence

We have labeled Brown's confluent education a *partial* program because it does not propose to teach all the social skills and understandings that children are expected to acquire in elementary school. Although no explicit rationale has been offered to define the scope of confluent education, the activities of its practitioners in classrooms imply that the scope is determined by three principles or value statements:

1. Children should be given direct experiences with ways to become more aware of themselves and of their relationships with others.
2. Anytime a pupil's actions suggest that he can profit from expressing and comprehending (emotionally as well as intellectually) his feelings, the teacher should use methods suitable for promoting such expression and comprehension.
3. When social-studies topics are pursued, activities that elucidate the affective factors involved in social phenomena should be employed along with the more traditional methodology aimed at cognitive learning.

[6]From *Human Teaching for Human Learning* by George Isaac Brown, pp. 227-237. Copyright © 1971 by George Brown. All rights reserved. Reprinted by permission of Viking Press, Inc.

Later we shall illustrate these three principles in action.

Since the original Ford-Esalen project was exploratory in nature, it did not produce a master scope-sequence plan to cover all grades or even a series of two or three grades. Each teacher in the project developed his own order of experiences for children at a single grade level.

The best organized of these programs at the elementary-school level was that developed by Gloria A. Castillo, a first-grade teacher who served on the project staff from 1967 to 1969. We shall inspect a series of the lessons she tried out with her class. In doing so, we can better understand the nature of confluent education in practice and can observe her application of the principles that guided the sequence in which she ordered activities. The principles are reflected in the introduction to Unit One of Mrs. Castillo's program:

> A great deal of the educational process as we know it emphasizes the past or the future, the "then." We build upon concepts developed in the past, and we develop new ones for their use in the future. All of this has a time and place in education. But one dimension that is almost completely ignored is that of the present—the "now." It is usually only when a child cannot or will not deal with the "then" (what he already knows or what he will have to learn) that we take the time to discover where he is now. . . .
>
> In this process it seems to me that we are telling the child that all that is worth knowing is outside of him—in books, in films, in the mind of the instructor. One important source of information is ignored—that of the child himself. Children are not expected to know what is important to them, what is happening to them. Therefore, it is necessary to begin an awareness of now on a fairly simple level, on something that does not involve too much risk. The following lessons are presented in an order of risk-taking as far as possible, the first involving the least risk. The fifth lesson, however, is different and not in sequence. It is a re-enforcing mechanism and is to be used throughout the school year. The lessons that follow it deal with an awareness of others as the focus, rather than the individual. . . .
>
> After self-awareness and awareness of another individual, the child should explore the possibilities of extending his awareness even farther to include such things as the group, the family, and the community. There should be many daily opportunities for the child and the teacher to respond to "What am I doing now?" and "How do I feel?"[7]

The objectives of these lessons are to enable the child to recognize the present tense of *now* and to respond more adequately to *now*. This

---

[7]Gloria A. Castillo, *Left-Handed Teaching* (Santa Barbara, Calif.: unpublished manuscript, 1970), pp. 16-17.

response includes verbalizing answers to "What am I doing now?" and "How do I feel about what I am doing?" Furthermore, the child is to discover new ideas about what is happening now, to identify certain peers as friends, to differentiate between reality and fantasy, to increase his response to imaginative situations, and to make more creative use of fantasy.[8]

The first five lessons in the sequence are described in the following paragraphs:

Lesson One—I Share What I Know About Me: Have the class sit in a circle. Teacher begins by saying, "I'm going to share what I know about me right now. I am sitting down, I see you looking at me." Continue with statements that are true of the moment you say them. Examples: "I can hear my voice. I see Judy come into the room. I hear the heater turn on." After enough examples are given to show the children what is expected, ask, "Who wants to do it now?" Listen carefully as the children speak, helping only when and if it is necessary to keep their remarks in the present tense. This may be difficult for them at first.

Lesson Two—Looking: Sit with the children in a circle. Remind them of what they did in Lesson One. Say, "Today I want you to look at yourself, the parts you can see right here and now. What do you see?" Begin the game yourself to set the example. Be sure to keep it in the present tense and begin each sentence with the words "I see my . . . ." Examples: "I see my shoes. I see the mole on my hand. I see my ring. I see the hair on my arm." As the teacher, listen and help the children keep their observations in the "here and now." Also help them, if necessary, to use the word "my," urging them to restate "I see the shoes" as "I see my shoes."

Lesson Three—Touching Now: Sit with the group in a circle. Ask, "Who can tell me how they are right now?" If the children make the kinds of statements encouraged in Lesson One, continue to the next step. If they do not, review Lesson One activities briefly. Next ask, "Who can find something about yourselves today that you could not find yesterday?" After a few responses, begin to focus on touch rather than sight. "Touch something cool. Touch something soft. Touch something warm. Touch something cool. Touch something wet. Touch some hair." And so forth. After several such directions, encourage children to touch whatever they wish and to describe the act aloud, following the pattern of Lesson Two. Examples: "I am touching my lips. I am touching my shirt. I am touching my chair."

Lesson Four—I Am in Control of Myself: Sit in a group. Ask, "Who makes you do things?" Accept their answers that other people make them do things. Examples: "My mother makes me do my piano lesson. My father makes me rake the leaves. My sister makes me clean up the mess we make playing house."

---

[8]Castillo, *Left-Handed Teaching,* p. 17.

Then ask, "How do these people make you do things?" Again accept all of their answers. Using the children's examples, get them to see that they do what other people want for a variety of reasons. Examples: "I practice my piano lessons so I won't get a spanking. I rake the leaves so I can get my allowance. I clean up the mess because my sister helped me have fun. I set the table so I can help my mother."

Ask again, "Who makes you do things?" Hopefully the child will begin to see that he alone has the ultimate decision to make himself do something or not. If he still answers that others make him do things, ask, "What do I make you do?" Accept all answers. Choose a response that can be demonstrated within the room. Example: "You make me do math." Now play a game called "(Insert teacher's name) makes me do math." To play the game, the teacher first says, "David, it is time for math. Get your book and do page 34." David must say everything *he* is doing. It might go like this: "I am getting my math book. I am putting it on the desk. I am turning to page 34. I am getting a pencil. I am thinking 'what is $7 + 6$?' I am writing 13. I am doing my math." By means of discussion, help the child see he is actually the one who is doing the action. He is the one who ultimately has to take the responsibility for what he does, even though others have expectations for his behavior.

The foregoing is a difficult concept for children, who are used to having adults responsible for what happens to them. It is also difficult for teachers, who often feel overly responsible for what the child does and does not do in the classroom.

Games to Play with Lesson Four:

"I am a robot." Ask the children to pretend they are robots. They can do nothing unless they are told to do it. Teacher begins as "Master Controller." Give the class specific instructions. Before children can begin anything new, they must be told to stop the former action. Example: "Walk forward. Stop. Walk backwards. Stop. Wave your right arm. Stop. Wave your left arm. Stop." After giving a few directions, give two together without the stops to see if the children stop the first one on their own. Example: "Walk forward. Sit down." If they do what you say, stop them and remind them that a robot cannot do a thing for itself, and on that most recent command it would walk forward AND sit down. How can you do both at the same time? Give them a few more clear directions, one thing at a time. Then appoint a child as "Master Controller." Help the children do exactly what the "Master Controller" says, nothing more, nothing less.

The children can then write a story about being a robot. "How does it feel to be controlled?" "How does it feel to be the Master Controller?" These are suitable topics for discussion.

"I am in control of myself: follow the leader." Have the children stand in a circle. Explain, "In a little while I am going to ask someone to go into the middle of the circle and be IT. The one who is IT says, 'I am in control of myself. I can jump.' Then he shows that he can make himself jump. Then all of us in the circle say and do the same thing. He then chooses another child to be IT." Discuss, "How does it feel to control the whole group?" "Would you rather be controlling the group or have some one control you?"

Lesson Five—What Are You Doing Now? This lesson is not intended to follow the pattern of the ones preceding it. The lessons before it were really a readiness for the following. It is hoped that this one will continue throughout the day, week after week, through the year.

While the children are at regular activities—such as sharing, social studies, language arts, and the like—ask, "What are you doing?" At first they may think they have done something "wrong" and will stop all activity. Keep questioning the child until you get a complete sentence, beginning with the word "I." The following is an example of what might happen on the first try.

"Irene, what are you doing?"

"Nothing."

"Who is doing nothing?"

"Me."

"Now can you put that all together in one sentence beginning with the word *I?*"

"I am doing nothing."

"David, what are you doing?"

"Working on my math."

"Who is working on math?"

"I am working on math!"

"How are you working on your math?"

"Quietly, not bothering anyone."

"Who is working quietly, not bothering anyone?"

"I am working quietly, not bothering anyone."

"Now what are you doing?"

(Quizzical look) "I don't know."

"I see you smiling at me."

"I am smiling at you."

The following are examples of statements after the child is used to responding in a way that reflects his present being.

"What are you doing?"

"I am hitting Philip."

"I am reading my book."

"I am scribbling in my book."

All of these are ways of helping the child get in touch with his reality. They also help him take responsibility for his actions.[9]

The foregoing set of lessons, then, represents one sequence of activities for first-graders, founded on a rationale that moves them

---

[9] Castillo, *Left-Handed Teaching*, pp. 18-23.

gradually from familiar experiences to less familiar ones and from understanding themselves to understanding one other child, then to understanding groups further removed from the individual in terms of intimacy and age. Other teachers using humanistic- or confluent-education techniques devise different sequences of experiences.

Materials and Methods

Confluent education does not depend upon a particular set of materials, such as textbooks, films, or study prints. It relies more on a point of view or a quality of teacher-pupil interaction in any social situation or in any case of the individual child seeking to understand how he is feeling at the time. The closest things to materials produced by the Brown project have been patterns for lesson plans or activities, like those for first-graders previously reproduced.

To suggest something of the range of methods encompassed by humanistic or confluent approaches, we shall describe activities in several classrooms, organizing them under the three convictions or principles mentioned earlier.

Principle 1: Experiences should be designed specifically to teach awareness of self and others in current reality. The series of five lessons described by Castillo above were of this type. As a further illustration, we shall describe a lesson on communication as it was used by a sixth-grade teacher. Although the lesson in this case was not conducted as part of the Ford-Esalen project, it was adapted from confluent-education approaches and introduced by Dale L. Brubaker in schools in the Milwaukee area.

The teacher intended the lesson to help pupils comprehend:

1. ways that communication between individuals depends on: (a) the use of words, (b) body movements or gestures, and (c) eye contact.
2. the contrast between feelings which result from believing you are not understood or are not understanding and those feelings which result from believing you are communicating well.

To introduce the five-stage lesson she told her pupils they should choose a partner for conducting an experiment on communication. Partners should stand straight, back to back. Without turning around, they should think of their partner and try to tell him something without talking. After the pupils tried this, she asked, "How well did you understand each other?"

Typical responses from students:

"You can't understand what they're saying."

"You can't see him."

"He was hitting me and seemed to tell me to move."

"He poked me in the back so I didn't do nothing. I just tried to get his message."

Stage 2: The teacher said, "Stand straight, back to back. Don't turn your head, but you may talk to the person behind you." Following this experience, she asked again about their ease of understanding.

Typical responses from students:

"You could hear if he talked loud enough."

"We had to shout."

"I couldn't see him talking, so I didn't know who he was talking to."

Stage 3: The teacher said, "Stand facing each other and communicate without talking." Following the activity, she asked about how well their communication succeeded.

Typical responses from students:

"If he moved his lips you could see it."

"Some hand signals you can get."

"He told me I was crazy."

Stage 4: The teacher said, "Stand facing each other with your eyes shut, and talk to each other." When asked how well this worked, students responded:

"I didn't like it because I thought I was talking to nobody."

"It didn't seem like it was normal."

Teacher: "Did you notice what else you did besides use your voice?"

"Our hands were moving."

"I held onto the person."

Teacher: "Why did you think you wanted to touch the person?"

"The person might leave, and then you'd be standing there talking to yourself."

"You can't know when you're supposed to talk, because everyone talks at the same time."

Stage 5: The teacher said: "Stand and face each other. Keep your eyes open, you do not have to keep silent. Now, communicate with each other." When questioned about the effectiveness of this method, pupils said it was the best. When asked "why?" they responded:

"You can see his eyes."

Teacher: "Why do you suppose eye contact is so important?"

"To make sure he's looking at you and probably listening."

"You know when it's your turn to talk."

"Well, when a person makes movements with his hands, you can tell."

"Sometimes I don't look at their face. I look at their stomach to see if tney're done breathing."

"I can see what kind of person they are."

"If you're lookin' at this one guy and he sounds real good, but he looks tired with big sacks down all over his eyes, so maybe you want to leave him alone."

"Lots of times when you look puzzled, you wrinkle your head a lot."

Principle 2: The teacher should respond spontaneously to the child anytime the child's actions suggest that he can profit from comprehending (emotionally as well as intellectually) his feelings. In the Ford-Esalen project the best example of this methodology was perhaps that reported by Janet Lederman, who taught in a special ungraded class for children from a predominantly black neighborhood who would ordinarily be in kindergarten through fourth grade. The special class was composed entirely of *behavior problems*—children that other teachers could not handle in regular classrooms.

Often I am asked how I evaluate the "techniques" I use with children. How do I know what to do? How do I know if I am succeeding in my efforts to "teach" effectively? My first impulse is to answer, "I have no elaborate system of evaluation." I wonder if this is so. I am an affective being; that is, I have and use such emotions as love, anger, grief, and joy. I have a great deal of cognitive information stored and ready for use—information accumulated from study and experience. Therefore, when I am teaching I am affectively (emotionally) and cognitively (thoughtfully) encountering the child who is also responding both affectively and cognitively. The balance and the percentage of each component is a constantly changing sum within me and within the child. We are formed by both affective and cognitive domains as a sculpture is formed by both positive and negative space. There is no way in reality of separating the two without changing the "beast." Therefore, I use both in a continuing evaluation system.

I would like to take you with me, in reflection, as I expose my "system": my attitudes, my expectations, my intuitive responses, and my computations—my affective and cognitive domains.

I do not plan for children I have not met. How can I? I have no idea of "where they are" in either domain. I have enough teaching experience to be able to pass out paper; I have enough teaching experience to be able to create a lesson on the spot or lead a discussion or a game until the true needs of the children make themselves apparent. It is then that real educational environment begins to develop. With some children the time of waiting is almost nonexistent; with others the time of waiting is long. I will wait. The children come into a barren room. The room begins to fill as they begin to *live* within the environment we create together.

Now I ask the reader to enter inside of me and listen in to my senses, my intuition, and also my computations. I shall not address you now, for I am directing my attention to the children.

Roderick, you walk into the classroom. It is your first day. You hit every child in your path as you cross the room. There are several toys on the floor, and you step on each one of them. You do not sit in the circle with the other children. You sit just outside the circle. You are in touch with being "angry," and that you are able to communicate. You seem busy protecting yourself. I imagine you could use some help. I want to find ways of showing you I want to protect you. Words won't do. Then I imagine you will *allow* me to protect you (trust) and then perhaps some of your energy will be released for other things—like learning to write. Now you need to be a big shot or bully. This way you imagine you are safe. I won't get too close to you. I will give you space. I watch you until I discover something that you like to do. Something you do well. It takes awhile and I wait. You like to work with wood. I ask you to saw many pieces for me. You do. I don't let anyone take the job away from you. I only ask you to do things in which you will succeed. Your experience with frustration is ample. One day after recess some bigger boy chases you into the room. I have no idea whether you provoked the situation. This is the time to protect you. I do. We don't talk about it. The action stands for itself. I am beginning to feel love for you. I enjoy your aggression. When you start to take over the class, I do not respond with pleasure. I do not tolerate your violence. I don't imagine you want that kind of power. You are testing to see if I am strong enough to take care of you. Yes, I am. We even wrestle to prove it to you. You are very much in your senses. Words have little meaning for you. I use very few words. My messages to you are through action. We will build words after our relationship has developed a meaning. How will I know? You begin to arrive at school on time. If you need to go play for a while, you put your lunch bag by the door for me to see you are here. You begin to call me by my name. You have your temper tantrum in the room instead of stealing something and running away. Your body begins to relax, and you smile now from time to time. You begin to work on numbers when I sit with you. You begin to learn to print when I sit with you. I am not going to push you to work away from me yet—not until you are ready. The first time I will ask you to work on something I know you can do and that *you know* you can do. How will I know you are ready? You will not mind if I am giving attention to some other child when you sit next to me. I might get up and move away for a few minutes, and you will keep working. I am watching you. I am listening with my eyes and ears, all the time thinking what the next step is to be. I watch for the first time you make a mistake and are able to go on instead of tearing up your paper. I assume you feel safe in the room when I see that you don't have to be a bully for the entire time. I begin to send you on small errands, and I give you points for returning right away. I mark down the time you leave and return so that you have some structure. I know you are beginning to trust *you* and me when you don't need that structure. And I imagine you trust me when you are in stress and ask for it back from time to time—before disaster strikes. I do not ask you to do things that are impossible for you. You have enough contact with frustration and you don't need more! You begin to trust that I will not ask the impossible of you; therefore, you begin to take a few risks—such as writing a story. I make sure you succeed. Soon you are willing to try arithmetic, and you find you love adding numbers. You do pages of adding. Then comes a crisis. You have been doing what you thought impossible and this scares you. How do I know? You become a bully once again. You try all your old techniques—almost to make sure that they are still there. I won't let you use them in the classroom any more. This time I tell you, "Roderick, I won't accept this kind of behavior any more. You needed it when you came. You knew no other way to behave. Now you do. I have seen you. I won't let you stay in class today." I send you home. You want to stay. You cry. I send you home and hope you get the message. The next day you return. You got the message. You left the bully outside the door. We don't talk about what happened. We go on. I felt you wanted someone to control that bully. You begin to use other things available to you in the room—puzzles, games, the chalk board. You sit with us in the circle. You like to sit next to me while I read stories. You like to select the book, and you begin to make your wants known—not by fighting but by asking. You can even wait and take turns. You put your arms around me, and you allow me to hold and comfort you and play with you. You begin to say, "This is my teacher, my room, my school."

Stanley, you spent two years with me. I am remembering when you first arrived. You are sullen. You do no schoolwork. You steal things from the room. I say nothing yet. I give you time to be wherever you are. I will meet you there first. You cry a great deal. You have no friends. I am wondering if you remember this day? You are frowning and angry. You walk over to the chalk board and you write in large letters, "FUCK." You look at me. You see I am looking at you. I accept your message. You stand there for a time, then you slowly erase the word. You do not steal anything today. Thereafter you use that technique to show me your anger. Sometimes the letters are huge, sometimes they are very tiny. You start to print, and then you want to write stories. You love to paint and build boats. At the end of the second year you are ready to move on to a regular room. A room you have tested and found to be comfortable for you. You come back for visits. Your visits become shorter and shorter. Soon you visit only when there is a substitute teacher or when you are under stress. Then comes the time when I push you from the nest. I tell you, "Stanley, you are too big to visit during the school day. Come see me after school and tell me what you are doing." You are ready, and somehow that gives you more confidence in yourself. Then comes the *day*, that wonderful day your teacher and I stopped you from reading. Your eyes were red-rimmed. Were you "reached," as they say? I think so. Do I have a systematic test to prove it? No![10]

Principle 3: When social-studies topics are taught, activities that elucidate affective factors in social events should be employed along with the more traditional methods aimed only at cognitive understanding. Most of these activities place the pupil in the position of either simulating other people's feelings or experiencing conditions he has never actually met before. Typically the activities include discussions that aim to help children express the feelings that arise in such situations. For example, pupils can role-play incidents from history, confrontations between

---

[10]Janet Lederman, "Confluent Learning—Personal Viewpoint," in Brown, *Human Teaching for Human Learning*, pp. 219-222.

present-day political figures, and experiences of children in cultures different from their own. Furthermore, the teacher can formulate class-room activities that generate emotions similar to those generated by a variety of social environments of the everyday world. To illustrate this last type of instructional technique, we shall describe two lessons. The first was taught by a second-grade teacher for the purpose of simulating crowded living conditions. The second was developed by a fourth-grade teacher to illustrate how people rejected by a group feel as compared to those who are accepted by a group. Thus the second lesson simulated emotions encountered under conditions of ethnic or religious prejudice. Though neither teacher was associated with the Ford-Esalen project, both used methods that were in harmony with confluent education's approach.

Second-Grade Lesson on Crowding

In discussing problems that different people experience in daily living, the class talked about *slum* and *tenement* and *ghetto*, but the teacher guessed that the pupils had no real feeling for crowded living conditions, since all came from middle-class homes. Thus she organized an activity to convey the affect resulting from crowding.

She taped three chairs together to form a tight circle, each chair facing outward. Then she drew a chalkline on the floor defining the narrow boundaries of the circle. Above these chairs in the corner of the room she hung a radio. She gave three pupils the special privilege of sitting there for ten minutes to hear a radio program. Every two or three minutes she sent a few more pupils to join them, specifying that they had to stay within the circle to listen. Eventually sixteen children were forced into the area. At the end of ten minutes all of them were allowed to return to their desks, and the teacher initiated a discussion of what had occurred and how they had felt about it. The following pupil responses resulted.

Teacher: "How did it feel to be in a confined area that you weren't per-mitted to leave?"

Pupils: "It was hot." "It was squishy." "I couldn't get in because there was no more room." "No one had any respect for anyone." "They were pushy and noisy." "I didn't like to stand." "I wondered why we were doing this."

Teacher: "Did you enjoy being crowded?"

Pupils: "No, it wasn't fun—too warm." "Someone was always pushing." "It was so noisy we couldn't hear the radio." "Yes, it was fun," said some of those who had pushed and shoved.

Teacher: "How did you like more people coming into your circle?"

Pupils: "I didn't feel happy about it."

"I didn't like to stand."

Teacher: "How did you feel being one of the last to join the circle?"

Pupil: "I felt bad. There wasn't room for me. I had to force myself in."

The teacher then shifted the discussion to the matter of people having to live in crowded quarters which were often dirty, and they could not be alone or leave. She explained that these people lived in a small section in the center of their own city.

Pupil: "Why don't they leave?"

Teacher: "They have no money."

Pupil: "Not even enough for a bus?"

Teacher: "Maybe that much, but where would they go?"

Pupil: "To the woods?"

Teacher: "Could you live in the woods for a long time?"

Pupils: "No. We'd get cold." "Nothing to eat." "What would you do there?"

Pupil: "Do they have beds?"

Teacher: "Yes, but not enough. How do you think they could sleep?"

Pupils: "Buy other beds." "Buy sleeping bags." "Sleep on the floor." "Maybe more than one could sleep in a bed."

Teacher: "Yes, they sleep several in a bed. Would these children get enough sleep to be alert in school?"

Pupils: "No!"

Pupil: "How do they undress with all those people around?" All pupils giggled. Some covered their faces. Others blushed.

Teacher: "It's embarrassing, but that's the way some people in the center of the city live, even though they don't want to."

Fourth Grade Lesson on
"In" and "Out" Groups

Objectives: As a result of the lesson, children should be able to express verbally the feelings of what it is like to be a member of an "in" group and an "out" group.

Procedure: The teacher asked six boys and one girl to leave the classroom for a few minutes. While they were out, she told the class they were going to try an experiment. Two of the boys remaining in the classroom were selected as captains of teams to be chosen. They were instructed not to choose Allen and Tom, who were among those that had left the room. They were even to select a girl in preference to those boys. The captains should offer to give Allen and Tom to the opposite team, for they were not good players.

The seven pupils were invited back into the classroom, and the team selections began. During the choosing, one captain told the other, "You pick Allen. He's a rotten kid." The other captain said, "I don't want Tom. He's a sissy." Some class members agreed.

The teacher observed that at the beginning it was apparent from Allen's and Tom's facial expressions that they were completely stunned by the class's adverse verbal assessment of them. After the initial shock wore off, the boys tried to act nonchalant. Both started to laugh. Later, as the choosing and the rejection continued, Allen became angry. His remarks suggested he wanted to walk out as a way to escape the pupils' comments. Tom's expression suggested curiosity mixed with a desire to be accepted, even if he had to be silent.

Class members showed varied emotions. Some enjoyed playing their roles. Others, such as Carol, looked unhappy, nearly on the verge of tears. Some did not enter the role but observed like spectators at a game. Several appeared concerned over the two boys' feelings, but this concern seemed to become indifference as the activity progressed.

After the teams had been selected, the teacher explained to the seven pupils that it had been a social experiment, and the captains and class members were just playing roles to demonstrate what it felt like to be included in a group and to be rejected. During the ensuing discussion the following comments were made:

Allen: "I felt kind of let down by my friends."

Tom: "Sure felt funny inside."

Carol: "I would have felt lonesome if I were them."

Glen: "I felt terrible."

Denise: "Good. I really felt good."

Carol: "I felt queer because we didn't let the two in."

Davy: "Not me. I was happy about it."

Brenda: "It felt good not to be left out like them."

To summarize the breadth of methods in confluent education and in similar approaches, we can say that it encompasses all techniques that promote the pupil's awareness of emotional aspects of his own life and others' lives—that is, promote such awareness in a constructive, mentally healthy setting. The methods are intended to free the child to experience a broader range of emotions and to understand their role in his life. At the same time he is directed toward accepting the responsibility for his affective states and their consequences.

Assumptions about Pupils and Teachers

The humanistic educator's most obvious assumption is that the intellectual and emotional facets of a child's life are inextricably intermeshed. And unless teachers understand cognitive-affective integration, they may fail to provide learning experiences that enable the child to mature as a healthy personality. Or even worse, teaching techniques employed to hasten intellectual progress may so violate principles of affective growth that whatever emotional stability the child displayed upon entering school degenerates rather than improves.

Another key assumption is that children of a given age level vary in their intellectual skills, their emotional maturity, and their awareness of self and others. The strength of this assumption as it may affect classroom methodology was suggested throughout Lederman's description of her approach to ghetto children who had been expelled from regular classrooms and assigned to her special group.

Confluent education further assumes that teachers who are to be successful with this approach need:

1. Tolerance for children's varied perspectives toward life.
2. Sensitivity to children's feelings and to their different stages of emotional development. Such sensitivity is enhanced by the teacher's stimulating a heightened awareness of both verbal cues and nonverbal communication factors such as gesture, facial expression, and posture.
3. Ingenuity in spontaneously reacting to pupils' behavior or moods in ways that promote affective-cognitive growth. The teacher needs to be clever about taking advantage of unplanned situations as opportunities for fashioning activities that will move children to a higher level of awareness.

In effect, it is not enough for the teacher to follow the steps of a lesson plan systematically. To succeed as a humanistic or confluent educator, he must also establish a special quality of emotional understanding with the children.

Evaluation Techniques

Children's progress toward the objectives of cognitive-affective harmony is not measured by written or oral tests or by rating scales. Rather, the teacher appraises children's progress through observations of their behavior and through his feelings or intuition. Upper-grade children may be asked to keep a diary of their feelings and thoughts during the time they are following a series of intensive confluent-education activities. The teacher can use the diaries as part of the material on which to base his appraisal of the child's growth toward greater awareness, freedom, and responsibility.

The Adoption of Confluent
or Humanistic Approaches

In one sense, instituting confluent education in a classroom should be relatively easy, since this curricular innovation is not proposed as a complete program that would displace an entire set of present practices and materials. Rather, confluent or humanistic practices can be added to an existing structure. Furthermore, since it does not depend upon a given set of books, films, or charts, no expenditure of funds for expensive materials is required.

However, in another sense, the difficulties of inaugurating humanistic activities are considerable. The sensitivity to children's feelings, the tolerance for varied points of view and for freedom to be individualistic, and the ingenuity and confidence required to create activities spontaneously to suit the unplanned occasion are traits not possessed by all teachers. According to the protagonists of confluent education, teachers can take part in workshops that will enhance their awareness and perhaps their tolerance. But it is clear that many teachers would not submit themselves to such sensitivity training, for it requires time and possible alterations in their personalities, and they regard such changes as personally threatening. Thus a key obstruction to the widespread adoption of humanistic approaches is the lack of preparation among teachers to handle the techniques successfully. Although some teachers, by the nature of their personalities, would seem to be "natural" confluent educators, others require personal experiences in sensitivity or awareness training in order to conduct a confluent-education program successfully. Still others, by the nature of their established personalities, might never be able to carry out such a program.

Another problem faced in the conduct of programs focusing on emotional as well as cognitive factors is that of parent reaction. Some parents may not like the changes they observe in their children's behavior or attitudes as a result of confluent-education experiences. Consequently, they may object to the teacher's including emphases on affect in the curriculum. And in the hands of an inept practitioner, certain confluent approaches may indeed upset some children and warrant the complaints parents may register with the teacher or school principal.

In sum, the essential ingredients for the successful inclusion of confluent-education practices in the school program are the individual teacher's skill at analyzing children's cognitive-affective needs, the teacher's ingenuity in devising activities to suit these needs, and the school principal's understanding of the contributions humanistic approaches can make to the child's personal-social development.

10

Current Social Themes and Problems

For many years teachers have sought to keep their social studies up to date by appending to their regular program a periodic current-events day. This activity typically consists of assigning each pupil the task of bringing to class a news story, the essence of which he relates to the other pupils. In some cases teachers require that the story be in the form of an article clipped from the daily paper or a weekly news magazine. In other cases they allow pupils to describe news events obtained from any media—television, radio, newspaper, or news magazine.

The purposes of such current-events activities are several. Perhaps the most common is to acquaint pupils with the key local, national, and international events of the day so that they are aware of what is going on in the world beyond their own immediate lives. A second is to acquaint them with the sections of news media, such as the various sections of a newspaper, and with the varieties of events reported in those sections. A third is to alert pupils to methods of interpreting news reports, including methods of recognizing bias and propaganda. Allied to each of these purposes is a fourth—to engage children in the study of current social problems so that they better understand the origins, effects, and possible solutions of difficulties that beset their society. This focus of school studies on present-day personal and social problems is what older youth mean when they urge educators to make schooling more relevant.

The partial plan described in this chapter not only fulfills typical goals of traditional current-events programs but goes far beyond such programs in organization and purpose. The plan is one being constructed at the University of North Carolina, Greensboro, and the University of Wisconsin, Milwaukee, under the direction of Dale L. Brubaker and James B. Macdonald, with both in-service and preservice teachers playing important roles in the development and testing of classroom activities. The pattern concerns itself with four central themes, each theme encompassing social problems. It focuses on both the cognitive and affective facets of the themes and problems. In other words, children's classroom activities are designed to improve their skills of social analysis at the same time that the pupils experience emotions typical for people facing social problems in their real lives.

The Value Orientation

A key conviction that has determined the selection of themes and problems is that social studies should focus on significant happenings of the day. The term *significant* in this case means events that affect large numbers of people in either positive or negative ways. Attention to current events apprises us of what the significant happenings are. The University of North Carolina, Greensboro, and the University of Wisconsin, Milwaukee (hereafter abbreviated UNCG-UWM), staff established five major interdependent themes under which they believed the most important social changes and problems could be subsumed: (1) urbanization, (2) technological change, (3) survival, (4) intergroup relations, and (5) intragroup relations.

A second conviction has centered on the rights and responsibilities of the learners. Pupils should (1) identify their own values, (2) analyze their values in relation to information presently held, newly acquired information, and alternative forms of action, and (3) either reconstruct their values in light of this analysis or defend those values they consider still valid. These three steps are what the project staff have meant by *critical inquiry*.

A third conviction is one suggested by John Dewey: a problem must be felt by the learner before he will become actively engaged in the inquiry process. According to the UNCG-UWM project members, this emotional or affective dimension of learning has been given too little attention in the more traditional social-studies curricula. Whatever emotional content has been included in the typical program has been in the form of sermonizing by the teacher or the textbook author to persuade children to accept the teacher's or author's own values. But, according to the project staff, such sermonizing has done more to frustrate than to promote critical inquiry. In contrast, the UNCG-UWM program attempts to obtain an emotional commitment on the part of the learner by placing him in situations that enable him to experience emotions similar to those of people faced with real-life social problems. Therefore, many of the teaching methods in the program use simulation materials or situations, particularly sociodrama or role playing.

Another value held by builders of the UNCG-UWM program is that curriculum materials should be conceptually oriented. The term *concept* here refers to an abstract and general quality. Each of the four themes around which the program is organized is a broad concept. Each lesson is designed to teach one or more concepts as well as to provide the child with an opportunity to experience emotions related to a social or personal problem. For example, illustrative lesson plans described later in this chapter focus on such concepts as *values, factual claims, multiple causation, "in" groups, "out" groups, power, economic affluence, poverty, stereotype, alienation*, and *ghetto*. Concepts within lesson plans are often common to more than one social-science discipline, so that the conceptual approach of the project can be labeled interdisciplinary. The project staff adopted such a conceptual approach because it provides for efficiency of organizing lessons, and once the learner understands a concept in one setting he should be able to use it as an analytical tool in other situations.

A fifth conviction is that the teacher, along with the pupils, is a learner and searcher for understanding and for solutions to problems. "This is in contrast to the more typical situation in which the sermonizer, the person with predetermined conclusions, makes an emotional appeal in order to convince students of the validity of his biases. The teacher is expected to be a coordinator, catalyst, and learner rather than a more authoritarian moral judge and dispenser of knowledge."

A final belief is that traditional classroom methods have restricted communication among pupils and thus have limited the ways in which children might influence each other's ideas and behavior. Consequently, the UNCG-UWM curriculum encourages more interaction among pupils. Dialogue is not mediated constantly by the teacher, as is often true when the instructor, as the center of attention, directs question-answer or discussion sessions. In addition, the program encourages nonverbal as well as verbal means of communication, giving more attention to gestures, facial expressions, postural cues, and tonal qualities of the voice than does the typical social-studies methodology.

Viewed another way, the UNCG-UWM proposal is a reaction against several characteristics of social-studies teaching that the project's leaders regard as both typical and undesirable: (1) lack of attention to current social movements and problems, (2) insufficient guidance in critical inquiry,

(3) lack of an emotional commitment by the learner, (4) the teacher's assuming the role of an authoritative fount of knowledge and values rather than of a co-searcher for understanding and solutions to problems along with the pupils, and (5) restricted communication within the classroom.

Scope and Sequence

The scope of the UNCG-UWM program is defined by the four overlapping themes and their constituent social problems as they intersect with social-science concepts. This structure is pictured in Table 10-1.

Early in the project's work some staff members argued for a social-problems structure. However, others held that a theme approach furnished opportunities to study positive factors in social change as well as problems, so the broader scope of themes was adopted.

Since the UNCG-UWM project is still in the developmental stage, it does not involve a set sequence of activities or lessons. Rather, the staff is still experimenting with the ordering of lessons in different patterns. The program is properly labeled *partial* because the staff views its materials as supplementary to existing curriculum patterns. Teachers at a variety of grade levels can adapt the sample lesson plans for use with their pupils at various times of the school year. So the recommended lesson plans might be inserted into an expanding-environments or a history-geography organization wherever a teacher might deem it profitable.

Materials and Methods

The UNCG-UWM materials consist of lesson plans organized around themes (such as intergroup relations) and around problems subsumed under themes (such as intergroup conflict involving blacks and whites or alienation of an older from a younger generation). At the end of each series of lesson plans is a bibliography of suggested materials.

Each lesson involves three elements intended to promote critical inquiry and, in most cases, to evoke emotional insights: (1) a problem to be solved, (2) concepts to comprehend, and (3) a social setting. The following lesson plan designed for upper-grade pupils will illustrate these three elements. The realm from which the plan has been drawn is that of intergroup relations. The problem is that of arranging a compatible

TABLE 10-1   Curriculum Structure—Current Social Themes and Problems

THEMES—Sample Lesson Titles (+ = Lesson centers on positive action.) (− = Lesson centers on problems.)	Related Social-Science Disciplines				
	Social Psychology	Geography	History	Polit. Sci.	Economics
I. URBANIZATION					
+ Loyalty to community	X		X	X	
+ City knowledge, rural knowledge	X	X			X
+ Back to nature	X	X	X		
+ Art in the city	X				
− Noninvolvement with others' lives	X	X			
− Commuter attitudes	X	X		X	X
− Trouble in schools	X	X		X	
II. TECHNOLOGICAL CHANGE					
+ Information: storage and retrieval	X	X			X
+ Influencing the media	X	X		X	X
+ Use of leisure time	X				X
+ Vocations	X	X	X		X
− Traffic	X	X	X	X	X
− Dehumanization	X		X		
− Technological unemployment	X	X	X	X	X
III. SURVIVAL					
+ Recycling cans and papers	X			X	X
+ Information summarizing	X	X		X	X
− Overcrowded territory	X	X		X	
− Air pollution	X	X	X	X	X
− Noise pollution	X	X		X	X
IV. INTERGROUP RELATIONS—GROUP INTERACTION					
+ Facts and values	X				

TABLE 10-1   Continued

	Social Psychology	Geog-raphy	His-tory	Polit. Sci.	Eco-nomics
∔ Compromising 2	X			X	X
∔ Feeling black or white	X	X	X		
∔ Comparing cultures	X	X	X	X	X
∔ Diplomacy	X			X	
− Ethnic stereotypes	X	X	X		
− Landlord-tenant confrontation	X			X	X
− White police in a black ghetto (authority representative in hostile group)	X			X	
− Informers in society	X			X	X
− Preferential treatment	X			X	X
− Marginality: immigrants vs. Anglo-Saxon Americans	X	X	X	X	X
− Marginality: parents vs. peers	X				X
− Marginality: male and female roles	X		X	X	X

V. INTRAGROUP RELATIONS— PERSONAL BEHAVIOR

	Social Psychology	Geog-raphy	His-tory	Polit. Sci.	Eco-nomics
∔ Verbal-nonverbal communication	X				
∔ Positive reinforcers—smiles and nods	X			X	
∔ Positive reinforcers—comments	X			X	
∔ Respecting the rights of others	X			X	X
∔ Compromise 3	X				
− Confronting someone you dislike	X			X	
− Intolerance	X				
− Dealing with anger	X				
− Dealing with jealousy	X				

agreement between a landlord and a tenant. The central concept is that of multiple causation. The social setting is a confrontation between landlord and tenant. The emotions to be evoked are those arising in a landlord when he feels he is being faced by a demanding tenant and those felt by a tenant who thinks he is being exploited.

Lesson Plan 1:   Landlord-Tenant Confrontation

Objectives:

As a result of this lesson, pupils should conclude that:

1. A given action or event has many causes.
2. People concerned with an event interpret what occurs according to their own priority of values (belief systems).
3. People who wish to influence the outcome of an event behave on the basis of their own priority of values.
4. Landlords commonly have a different priority of values than do tenants.

Methods and Materials:

1. Announce to the class that a landlord has just asked his financially poor tenant's family to leave their apartment. The class's task is to identify reasons that this confrontation has occurred. Tell them that two pupils will be chosen to act out the meeting between the landlord and tenant, and by viewing this scene the class may be able to estimate why this event happened.
2. Select one pupil to play the role of landlord. Hand him a card labeled *Landlord* citing some reasons for why he is evicting the tenants. Tell him that he is also permitted to think up other reasons as well.
3. Select one pupil to play the role of tenant. Hand him a card labeled *Tenant* citing some reasons he has not paid the rent. He can also think of other reasons.
4. Before the role-playing begins, ask each pupil to divide a sheet of paper into two columns, one titled *Landlord* and the other *Tenant*. As the scene is acted out, they are to write in these columns apparent reasons for the actions of the two characters.
5. Have the two actors come before the class. Describe the setting somewhat in this fashion: "We'll imagine that the landlord has just knocked on the door of the tenant's apartment. When the tenant opens it, the landlord steps in and says that the family will have to move. When the tenant asks why, the landlord starts to give his reasons. Then the tenant answers back. Now, let's begin with the landlord knocking on the door."

6. When the sociodrama has gone far enough to elicit a variety of reasons or arguments on both sides, ask the two characters to switch roles and play the scene again.

7. After the second playing of the scene, conduct a discussion of the reasons for the event's occurring. After listing reasons on the board, ask, "What was the one real reason this incident happened?" This question should elicit the response that there was no one real reason. The causes were multiple. Ask "Why did the landlord push these arguments and not accept those of the tenant? And vice versa. Why did each of them feel this way?"

Evaluation Procedures:

Observe pupil responses in the role playing and discussion. Take a controversial event from the newspaper and ask pupils to write a brief paper telling why the event may have occurred. They should suggest more than one cause.

In sum, the UNCG-UWM project materials propose to teach both concepts, such as *multiple causation*, and feelings or sensitivities, such as the affect generated in the combatants during the landlord-tenant confrontation.

The aim of the cognitive aspects of the program is to teach broad concepts and generalizations that might be applied in interpreting a variety of social situations. This aim is in contrast to the goals of certain traditional curricula that have stressed the acquisition of specific historical and geographical facts.

As noted in the landlord-tenant example, the UNCG-UWM materials spell out in considerable detail the steps for conducting lessons. The purpose of this specificity is to make clear to teachers the sequences of steps that have proven successful in try-outs of the lessons. Furthermore, it was assumed by the project staff that teachers would make wider use of the materials if lesson plans were detailed, for most elementary-school teachers have very little time to build their own approaches in every subject-matter area, and therefore they appreciate detailed plans that are "ready to go." The project staff assumed that the inexperienced teacher would more likely succeed with these new ventures if precise directions were given. On the other hand, experienced teachers would feel free to deviate from the suggested plan in ways they were convinced would better suit their particular group of pupils and their own style of teaching.

One characteristic of the UNCG-UWM materials is that several lessons are designed to focus on a particular problem or concept in several different settings and with different mixtures of people. This feature can be illustrated by three lessons dealing with discrimination and prejudice. The lessons have been used with pupils of a single ethnic category—all blacks, all Anglos, all Latin-Americans—and with ethnically integrated classes. The first lesson stresses conditions in a society that accords preferential treatment to people with a given trait. The second focuses on the plight of a distrusted authority figure in a hostile group. The third treats the feelings engendered within a society in which informants or spies play a prominent role.

Lesson Plan 2:   Preferential Treatment

Objectives:

The following experiences should enable pupils to:

1. Give a working definition of stereotype, such as "what you think a person is like just from seeing him or hearing what group he belongs to."
2. Tell what *preferential treatment* means, either by giving a definition or by giving several examples of such treatment.
3. Describe the feelings frequently experienced by people who enjoy preferential treatment (pleasure, a desire to retain preferred status, a psychological distance from those not accorded such treatment, guilt) and by those who do not (anger, puzzlement, loneliness, rejection).
4. Tell advantages of stereotypes (such as ease in deciding how to treat a person) and their disadvantages (such as the possibility of treating a person in an unfair or harmful way).

Methods and Materials:

1. Divide the class into two groups according to some physical characteristic, such as those who wear glasses versus those who do not (or those with blue eyes versus those with eyes of a different color, those with dark hair versus those with light, those who are taller versus those who are shorter). Tell the pupils the basis for the division, and move those with one characteristic—for example, those who wear glasses—to the desks on the right side of the room and the rest of the pupils to the desks on the left side. Do not inform them of how this division will be used.
2. Pass out worksheets to each group. The sheets should be related to some learning task the class is pursuing in arithmetic, reading, social studies, or science. The worksheets given to the people with glasses are very legible. Those given to the non-glasses group are nearly illegible.
3. Explain the worksheet assignment to the entire class, but accept questions from and give explanations to only the glasses group. If the non-glasses pupils ask questions or complain about the illegible worksheets, tell them: "Just do your work. Get busy and no complaints." If glasses-wearing pupils ask questions, give them clear, pleasant answers.

4. As the pupils begin work, circulate among the glasses-wearing pupils, helping them complete their work. Ignore the non-glasses pupils, except to discipline those who talk or are unruly.

5. Since the glasses-wearing pupils will finish first, give them five or ten minutes of free time to chat and have a good time. If non-glasses children finish early, tell them to check over their answers or get to work on arithmetic problems.

6. Following the glasses-wearing children's brief recess, conduct a general class discussion. Ask the class: "What happened? What were we doing? How did it feel?" Write the opinions on the chalkboard under the categories *Haves* (for the glasses-wearing pupils) and *Have-Nots* (for the non-glasses group).

7. Ask whether anyone knows what *stereotype* means. If no one knows, give a simple definition and ask children for some examples of stereotypes (such as those based on skin color, church affiliation, age, sex, hair style). Give additional examples of your own. Explain that some of them were receiving *preferential treatment* on the basis of a physical characteristic rather than on the basis of their personal behavior. Ask for other examples of people receiving preferential treatment for some group characteristic.

8. Ask whether stereotypes are ever useful. Are they ever harmful? If pupils cannot cite examples, give some of your own.

Evaluation:

Observation of pupils' responses during the discussion:

Lesson Plan 3:   Authority Representative in Hostile Group

Objectives:

As a result of this lesson, pupils should:

1. Identify the feelings that might be experienced by an authority figure, such as a white policeman, in a hostile or fearful group, such as a black neighborhood. The feelings might include self-consciousness, loneliness, fear, anger, and hostility toward the group.

2. Suggest ways that barriers between the authority figure and the group might be reduced.

Methods:

1. Explain to the class that they are going to act out a spontaneous play. Ask one pupil to leave the room. Before he goes out, hand him a card explaining that he is a white policeman assigned to a black neighborhood. Some other policemen have told him the people in the neighborhood cannot be trusted and that they hate policemen.

2. While the policeman is out of the room, tell the class that they are blacks living in a neighborhood that has no whites. A new policeman has been assigned to their area. You hear that he is tough and he has been sent to arrest, or maybe beat up, as many blacks as he can. He is just waiting to accuse someone of doing something illegal. When the policeman returns to the room, the pupils are free to move around. But they should always keep a watch out for the policeman as they go about their business.

3. Bring the policeman back, and explain that everyone is free to do what he likes for the next ten minutes but not to leave the room.

4. After the ten minutes of freedom, ask the policeman how he feels. What did he experience? How did the rest of the class feel about him and about themselves? Note the responses on the chalkboard.

5. Ask for other instances in which an individual is in a strange or hostile group. If no suggestions are given, give your own examples (immigrant new to the country who does not speak the language well, a new child who comes to school in the middle of the year, an older adult among young people who consider him "a drag").

6. Ask what might be done to improve the feelings between the white policeman and the black neighborhood.

Evaluation:

Have each pupil write about a situation in which he was in a strange group and about how he felt. Have him indicate whether he was a representative of outside authority when he was in the group.

Lesson Plan 4:   Informers in Society

Objectives:

As a result of this lesson, pupils identify:

1. Feelings many blacks harbor toward police and toward others in their own group because police solicit blacks to inform on activities of their fellow community members (feelings of fear, hostility, social distance or alienation).

2. Advantages and disadvantages of informers for the work of police and for the welfare of the individual who lives in the black community.

Methods:

1. Explain to the class that one reason for conflict between the police and such groups as blacks living in urban centers is the use of black informers to get information about other blacks. Say that you are going to play a game to help the class identify and understand what feelings might arise in a group because of informers.

2. Have each pupil write his own name on a slip of paper. Collect the slips and redistribute them so that no one has his own name. Tell the pupils not to let anyone know whose name they have. However, this name identifies the pupil who is their target. For the next ten minutes, each child is to watch his target so as to gather mental notes that would be useful in telling what the person looks like, what his habits are, and how he is likely to act. He should collect this information without the target child realizing who is watching him.

3. Permit pupils to follow their own interests in the classroom for ten minutes, moving wherever they desire.

4. After the period of free movement, conduct a general discussion. Either you or a student can function as a policeman who asks each informer what information he has collected about the target individual.

5. When a variety of informers' descriptions have been collected, ask class members what it felt like to be "spied on." List responses on the chalkboard.

6. Ask for advantages and disadvantages to the police and to the black community of using black informers. List these on the chalkboard.

7. Ask for other situations in which informers are used (in school, in business organizations where people vie for promotion, on teams involving competition for positions).

Evaluation:

Observe pupils' responses during the discussion.

Characteristics of
Learners and Teachers

One key assumption underlying the UNCG-UWM materials is that pupils learn most effectively when they actively grapple with problems— that is, when they are both cognitively and affectively involved in working through a learning task.

A second assumption is that the individual differences in reading and writing abilities of pupils are more varied than their abilities to express themselves orally. Thus, the methodology places far greater emphasis on oral than on written or printed communication, enabling a greater proportion of the pupils to take part successfully than is often true when reading and writing serve as the prime instructional media.

A third assumption is that children come to a better understanding of the thoughts and feelings of other people when they share a common experience and then discuss the cognitive and affective aspects of the experience.

Fourth, the project's methodology assumes that the application of a generalization to other life situations after it is derived from a specific incident is not automatic but is best applied in interpreting other events when the teacher focuses pupil attention on a broad range of similar situations. For example, the lesson on informers focused initially on police informers in a black community, but during the follow-up discussion the teacher directed attention to other applications of the same concepts illustrated in the black-community example.

The UNCG-UWM materials assume that the individual teacher is the best judge of whether a given activity is suited to his own class. Therefore, no lesson is relegated to a certain grade level or kind of pupil.

Evaluation Procedures

The objectives for each lesson plan in the UNCG-UWM project are stated as specific behavioral outcomes, thus rendering the task of appraisal of pupil progress much easier. The teacher has a clear idea of what kinds of pupil actions will serve as evidence that the children have achieved the goals.

In most lesson plans the children's responses during discussion sessions or sociodramas furnish information about their attainment of the objectives. However, in some cases the children are expected to respond individually in the form of a written essay or short written answer to a question. Such objective-type test items as true-false, multiple-choice, and matching are not recommended. However, in some instances a worksheet requires fill-in responses from pupils. The worksheet is both part of the teaching methodology and part of the evaluation. For example, the following lesson aims at giving children practice in distinguishing factual from value statements. Since the lesson was designed for use with pupils in an all-black urban school, the individuals whose pictures are displayed are all Negroes. In an all-white school or one with an ethnically mixed student body, the pictured celebrities might be whites or members of various racial groups.

Lesson Plan 5:   Facts and Values

Objectives:

On an evaluation sheet, pupils should demonstrate their recognition of the distinction between factual claims and value claims by:

1. Writing F in front of factual statements and VC in front of value claims.

2. Underlining words that help identify value claims, such as *good, bad, better, best.*

Methods and Materials:

1. Hand the students a sheet containing the following material:

. . . .

A. Look at the pictures of the two football players.
   Player Number 1 is named _____ .
   Player Number 2 is named _____ .
   Who is the better football player? _____
      Why is he better? _____
B. Look at the pictures of the two actors.
   Actor Number 3 is named _____ .
   Actor Number 4 is named _____ .
   Who is the better actor? _____
      Why is he better? _____
C. Look at the pictures of the two actresses.
   Actress Number 5 is named _____ .
   Actress Number 6 is named _____ .
   Who is the better actress? _____
      Why is she better? _____
D. Write *F* in front of *facts.* Write *VC* in front of *values* or *opinions.*
   _____ Diahann Carroll is a television actress.
   _____ Jim Brown was a football player who became an actor.
   _____ Harry Belafonte is a singer.
   _____ Jim Brown is a better actor than Harry Belafonte.
   _____ Gail Fisher is a better singer than Diahann Carroll.
   _____ O. J. Simpson cannot dance as well as Harry Belafonte.
   _____ Diahann Carroll and Gail Fisher have both been on television.

. . . .

2. Hold up a picture of Jim Brown and place it on the blackboard chalk tray below a number 1. Hold up a picture of O. J. Simpson and place it below number 2. Ask the pupils to write answers to the questions under A on the worksheet. When they answer the question "Why is he better?" write some of their oral responses on the chalkboard.

3. Follow the same procedure in having them fill out section B using photographs of Jim Brown as an actor and Harry Belafonte. Do the same for section C with photographs of Diahann Carroll and Gail Fisher.

4. Ask whether they can tell which statements under A, B and C are facts and which are opinions or values. If they cannot make this distinction, explain the difference between facts and value claims.

5. When all pupil questions have been answered, have each child complete section D on his own. Then ask him to underline each word in a value claim that helped him decide it was an opinion.

6. Discuss with the class the correct answers to the statements and questions.

Conditions Conducive to Adopting the UNCG-UWM Pattern

The University of North Carolina, Greensboro, and the University of Wisconsin, Milwaukee, social-studies program is inexpensive to adopt, for it involves no purchase of books, filmstrips, or charts. Thus, budget limitations in a school system would serve as no barrier to its implementation.

Furthermore, the UNCG-UWM approach focuses on the solution of current social problems, which a substantial number of educators and citizens say should be a prime concern of the school. This focus suggests that the approach would be a welcome supplement to more traditional programs that are organized around textbooks or a county or city curriculum guidebook.

On the other hand, the fact that the lesson plans in many cases treat socially sensitive or controversial issues may frighten some teachers or administrators from adopting the plan, for fear of upsetting pupils or their parents. In addition, the activities place more responsibility in the hands of the pupils, and the outcome of a lesson involving role playing is not nearly so predictable as that of a lecture or reading assignment. Therefore, teachers who feel that they have a somewhat tenuous hold on the class may not wish to invite possible conflict and disorder in the classroom by introducing activities that stimulate the expression of emotions and debatable opinions. But these same elements of controversy and the eliciting of affect attract the more venturesome teacher who wishes to conduct class sessions that he considers more lively and relevant to daily living than many traditional lessons.

In-service education focusing on the UNCG-UWM type of lesson would encourage more teachers to attempt these current-social-problems methods. The UWM project staff has found that audio tapes and video tapes of the use of sample lessons with different kinds of teachers and different classroom populations are perhaps the most successful materials for explaining to teachers successful ways to implement this kind of program.

11

The Georgia Anthropology Project

In recent years, educators' efforts to improve children's social-science skills have resulted in a variety of curriculum projects, each centered on a particular discipline, such as economics, social psychology, anthropology, political science, or history. These new departures are properly dubbed *partial* programs, for they supplement rather than replace existing curricula.

As an example of such a single-discipline design, we have chosen to review one of the best-known of the endeavors financed by U.S. Office of Education grants in the 1960s: the Anthropology Curriculum Project at the University of Georgia. The project began in the early 1960s with anthropologists from the University's Department of Sociology and Anthropology joining specialists from the College of Education in developing and field-testing a variety of one-month study units for elementary and junior-high pupils. Although the federal grant terminated in mid-1969, new units were still being issued in 1970.

The Project's Value Orientation

Unlike many social-studies programs, which seek to inculcate values deemed suitable for American citizenship, the Georgia plan is designed to teach the academic discipline of anthropology—that is, the search for a set of principles that *describe* and *explain* man's physical and cultural conditions.

> Any field of knowledge, such as anthropology, consists of a system of concepts, or word labels, which are used to express ideas and describe relationships. An understanding or mastery of any field of knowledge begins with an understanding of the concept system, the meaning of which expands and develops as the knowledge of the discipline is extended.[1]

It is the purpose of the University of Georgia materials to teach such a concept system so that the child can ". . . organize and interpret in a more meaningful manner the world in which he lives."[2]

In a sense, the Anthropology Curriculum Project is a reaction against the general trend of elementary social studies of the progressive-education era. To contrast their approach with interdisciplinary and problem-centered curricula of the 1930-1960 period, project members have written that:

> For almost thirty years the social studies movement has contended that a subject approach to the transmission of social studies is inappropriate for the elementary grades. [But we believe] . . . that any type of organization of material, irrespective of its method, is designed to transmit knowledge, and that there is nothing incompatible, except preference and tradition, with a subject presentation of a social science in the elementary grades.[3]

Scope and Sequence

The scope of concepts encompassed by the Georgia curriculum is reflected in the list of categories within which the study materials have been developed: evolution, fossil man, race, culture, old world prehistory, new world prehistory, technology, economics, kinship, political and

---

[1] *Anthropology Curriculum Project* (Athens, Ga.: Anthropology Curriculum Project), p. 1 (advertising brochure).

[2] Pauline Persing, Wilfrid C. Bailey, and Milton Kleg, "Introduction," in *Life Cycle* (Athens, Ga.: Anthropology Curriculum Project, 1969), p. viii.

[3] Persing, Bailey, and Kleg, "Introduction," p. vii.

non-kin groups, religion, and the life cycle.[4] In addition to comprehending concepts and generalizations associated with these categories, pupils are expected to ask the kinds of questions anthropologists ask, including both general queries (Why is it that clothing may be worn for different reasons in different cultures?) and more specific ones (Why do many Americans wear jewelry and neckties?).

As for sequence, project personnel originally thought that an analysis of the concepts of anthropology would provide a hierarchic structure of complexity that would serve as the framework for constructing a sequential curriculum from the lower to the upper grades. However, as materials were developed and tried out with children, "it was found . . . that complexity is a function of the level of explanation, rather than of the concept *per se*."[5] Even though the final curriculum materials were designed for use at specified grade levels, project members believed that any of the units could be used at any grade level if appropriate modifications were made in the way concepts are explained.

> The sequencing . . . reflects merely the logic of the curriculum builders, and no claim is made that grade unit arrangement is inherent in the concepts of anthropology. For example, the Grade 7 unit "Life Cycle" might just as well serve as a point of entry to anthropology in Grade 1 instead of "The Concept of Culture," except that "culture" is a more significant organizing concept than is "life cycle."[6]

Materials and Methods

The instructional materials issued by the project are of several varieties. Nearly every unit includes a teacher's manual that contains background material about the anthropological concepts to be studied and, to some extent, suggestions for directing the pupils' activities. Text materials for the pupils may be either sets of pictures or paperback textbooks illustrated with pen-and-ink drawings. A unit on language includes a recording of 13 foreign languages and eight American dialects. Several of the units are accompanied by written tests. Teachers are asked to

[4] Norris M. Sanders and Marlin L. Tanck, "Anthropology Curriculum Project, University of Georgia," *Social Education*, 34, No. 4 (April 1970), 409.
[5] Marion J. Rice, "Materials for Teaching Anthropology in the Elementary School," *Social Education*, 32, No. 3 (March 1968), 254.
[6] Rice, "Materials for Teaching Anthropology in the Elementary School," p. 254.

supplement these basic materials with others of their own devising, such as artifacts, pictures, and models.

The contents of the materials are suggested in the following descriptions of the several units that compose the overall program. As noted earlier, each unit typically takes four or five weeks for a class to complete. The basic program consists of one unit for the kindergarten, three for primary grades, three for intermediate grades, and one for the junior high. Four additional units can be used with intermediate or upper-grade pupils.

Concept of Culture: An Introductory Unit (kindergarten). A picture-text and activity book with daily lessons extensively outlined in the accompanying teacher's manual.

The Concept of Culture (primary). Ethnographic description with emphasis on oral presentation by the teacher and the use of a picture text by the pupils. Three ethnographies—the American, Arunta, and Kazak—are studied as comparative cultures. The . . . topics are: how we study people, housing, material culture, earning a living, social organization (family and community), and religion.

Development of Man and His Culture: New World Prehistory (primary). Introduces archeological methods by presenting Indian life in five stages of cultural development: paleo-Indian, archaic, formative, classic, post-classic.

The Changing World Today (primary). Case studies of modernization in Japan, Africa, and India.

The Concept of Culture (intermediate). Repeats and enlarges on ideas developed in the primary unit of the same name. Chapters in the pupil texts and study guides treat: how we study people, concepts of culture, cultural universals, cultural variation, enculturation, culture dynamics.

Development of Man and His Culture: Old World Prehistory (intermediate). Chapters on archeological methods, evolution, fossil man, and Old World prehistory. A programmed text to parallel the narrative text in this unit emphasizes archeology as a science. It is accompanied by a pronunciation guide and tape recording to aid children in acquiring the new vocabulary. A 30-minute 16-mm color sound film on pre-Columbian Indian sites in Georgia shows ways archeological methods help man gain insights into past cultures.

How Change Takes Place (intermediate). Case studies of modernization and planned change in Latin America and the United States are supplemented by a major section on theories of change.

Life Cycle (junior high). Life from birth through old age is traced for Chinese, American, Tiv, and Balkan peasant cultures.[7]

The four additional units are about (1) political anthropology: values, socialization, social control, and law, (2) urban communities, (3) language, and (4) race, caste, and prejudice.

---

[7] *Anthropology Curriculum Project* (advertising brochure), p. 1.

In contrast to so many of the newer national social-studies projects, the Georgia approach does not emphasize inquiry in the sense of the pupils' using inductive methods to derive concepts and generalizations of their own. Rather, the didactic strategy is principally a deductive one, though some of the later units in the series do include activities requiring inductive techniques. The deductive approach, as defined by a project member, is a ". . . closely directed, explanatory process by which children are given generalizations along with supporting evidence and are helped by the teacher to draw valid conclusions."[8]

What this deductive approach means in classroom practice is illustrated in the lesson plans found in some of the teacher's manuals. The teacher's task is not to pose open-ended questions intended to stimulate children's own ideas about a topic. Rather, the questions are designed to lead the children to an understanding of definitions and generalizations evolved by professional anthropologists. When the teacher asks "What is anthropology?" the response he wants is the one provided in the lesson plan: "Anthropology is the study of man." In effect, pupils and teachers are thought to lack the expertise for building their own system of organizing observations about man. They are to learn the anthropologists' systems.

The following lesson plan from the teacher's manual accompanying *Concept of Culture: An Introductory Unit* shows the pattern of teaching that the project staff recommends for kindergarten children.

Lesson 3
Man Needs Shelter[9]

Learning objective

All men need shelter, but all men do not have the same type of shelter.

Materials and their use

1. A picture of an American house brought by each child (to be shared by pupils to examine and discuss)

2. Pupil Activity Book Pictures 13, 31, 35 and 54 of Kazak yurt, Kazak winter house, Arunta lean-to and windbreak for teacher (for sharing with class and discussion)

---

[8] Oscar T. Jarvis, "The Deductive Method of Teaching Anthropology," in *Teaching Anthropology in the Elementary School* (Athens, Ga.: Anthropology Curriculum Project, 1967), p. 1.
[9] Jean Blackwood, Anne Hunt, and Frances Emmons, *Concept of Culture: An Introductory Unit* (Athens, Ga.: Anthropology Curriculum Project, 1968), pp. 10-11.

shelter
yurt
sod
lean-to
windbreak

Prerequisites

Each student should bring to class a picture of an American house, either a photo or drawing of his own house or a cut-out picture from a newspaper or magazine. It's usually a good idea to allow the child this choice.

Procedure

Teacher, through a series of questions, guides students to an understanding of man's need for shelter. Why do we live in houses? (place to eat, sleep, protect us from rain, sun, etc.).

Man needs a shelter to protect him from the weather or from any kind of nearby danger. Can you think of anything we would want to keep out of the house? (pests, fire, etc.).

Are all American houses alike? (No.) I'm going to let you show the class the picture you brought of an American house. As the children show their pictures, be sure to point out that many kinds of materials are used; it will also be easy to compare the various sizes and shapes.

When all the children have had a chance to share each other's pictures, ask whether or not anyone has ever seen a house being built. Give a few children a chance to explain their particular experience along those lines. Be sure to stress that most Americans have skilled workers to build our houses, in contrast to some cultures in which the families build their own houses. Remind the children, however, that American families go camping. In this case, the family often has to work together to get the shelter up.

If time or weather permits, it is a good idea to take the children outside and look at some nearby houses together, noting the materials used, shape, size, etc.

You have had a chance to share your pictures of American shelters. Now I would like to share some pictures with you; these are not American shelters, however; they are shelters used in some other culture. The teacher shows the pictures of the Kazak yurt and sod houses.

The Kazak have two types of shelter. Their summer house, a yurt, is made with a wooden frame and covered with felt. The winter house has wood to help support it and is covered with sod. The Kazak family works together to build their house. "How is this house made?" can be answered while the children look at the Activity Book pictures showing the family working together.

Next show the pictures of the Arunta shelters in the Activity Book. The Arunta make their shelters—lean-to and windbreak—from the brush found around the particular location where they happen to be staying. The Arunta family works together to make the shelter and plans to leave it behind when a move becomes necessary. Discuss (as with the other cultures) how the shelters are made, the materials used, and the people who make them.

Summary

We have seen that man needs shelter to protect him and his household from weather and danger. Who would like to tell me about some of the materials used to build American homes? (Be sure children remember that a variety of materials are used.) Thank you. Now who would like to tell us the materials used in a Kazak yurt? (wood and felt. Note: it would be good to have a small piece of felt for the children to feel. This experience makes a lasting impression.)

Follow same procedure, allowing children to tell the materials used in Kazak winter home (wood and sod); and the materials used in Arunta lean-to and windbreak (brush).

I wonder who can remember who builds American homes? (workmen) Kazak homes? (members of family) Arunta homes? (members of family)

Review activity (optional)

We have been talking about shelters in three cultures, haven't we? Who would like to help me make some shelters for each other? (Each child could choose the kind of shelter he would like to make. If any particular kind of shelter is not chosen, a child who finishes his chosen task quickly can be asked to make the shelter not allotted to anyone.) We could put all the models on a table or counter. Maybe another day we could make some people and animals to go along with the shelters.

Review materials and their use

A variety of paper, clay, dirt, straw, sticks, glue, small pebbles, and other relevant material (to make shelters for three cultures).

Whereas the kindergarten teacher's manual offers detailed lesson plans, the manual for first grade sketches only the specific objectives (concepts) and some review questions that might be used. At the second-grade level and above, the manuals accompanying the units are mainly composed of more elaborate anthropological information than that found in the pupils' textbooks. Consequently the teacher can prepare himself to discuss, with some measure of confidence, concepts and examples that go well beyond the contents of the children's books.

Because the upper-primary and intermediate teachers' guidebooks contain anthropological subject matter rather than detailed instructional techniques, the classroom teacher must depend primarily on his own initiative for devising ways to interest pupils in the subject and to communicate the anthropological concepts without distortion. In some social-studies programs, the teacher's burden of motivating pupils and communicating subject matter is rather light, for the teaching materials themselves (textbooks, workbooks, filmstrips, recordings) are carefully designed to appeal to children and to explain concepts in ways that are easy to understand. However, such planning does not appear to have been used in the children's basic texts in the Georgia program. Particularly in the primary grades, the teacher must go to considerable effort to render the contents of the children's texts both interesting and comprehensible.

For example, the pages from the second-grade text in the Georgia series that are reproduced as Figures 11-1, 11-2, and 11-3 would appear to require far more of the teacher than simply asking the children to read the pages themselves and answer review questions. One educator, after analyzing the project's teaching materials, wrote:

> In the judgment of this reviewer this project places too much emphasis on the vocabulary and methodology of anthropology in the elementary grades. However, a paper by Marion J. Rice [coordinator of the Anthropology Curriculum Project] states that a comparison of pretest and post-test scores for grades one, two, four and five indicates a significant increase in achievement in anthropology. . . . An open-ended questionnaire given to fourth and fifth grades yielded a preponderance of positive over negative responses. Some pupils complained about the vocabulary but more often this complaint came from teachers. . . .
>
> The fourth-grade cycle on culture again takes up the Arunta and Kazak in comparison to the children's own lives but the description of the cultures is subordinated to anthropological constructs. . . . The [pupil] text does a remarkably good job in defining these ideas in simple language but even so there is doubt in this reviewer's mind that a broad range of fourth-graders are intellectually or psychologically ready for such a concentration on abstract ideas.[10]

In summary, the basic methodology recommended for teaching toward the anthropology-curriculum objectives is a deductive one. The instructor's goal is to help children understand the terminology and methods of anthropologists as well as generalizations derived from anthropological studies. Teacher's manuals offer suggestions for classroom activities and recommend review questions to be asked throughout the unit. The publications for teachers also offer a wealth of supplementary anthropological information beyond that in the pupil textbooks. Teachers are expected to supplement the recommended activities with ones of their own creation.

---

[10]Sanders and Tanck, "Anthropology Curriculum Project," p. 410.

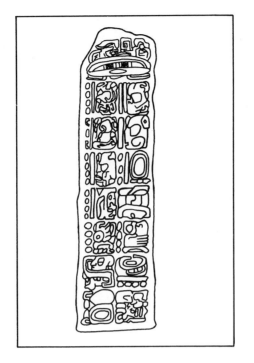

Absolute dating gives a more or less fixed date. Among the methods are *calendrical, dendrochronology*, and *Carbon 14*.

Calendrical dating is dating by a calendar. The problem is to take some other calendar and make the years the same as our calendar. The problem is to find the *base* year.

In the picture is a Mayan calendar stone. It is called a *stela*. A stela is a stone with writing. Also there are *glyphs* which stand for numbers. A *glyph* is a picture in the Mayan writing that stands for something.

It is thought that the *base* year in the Mayan calendar is 4 Ahau 8 Cumhu. It is thought to be the same as our calendar date 3113 B.C. Archeologists do not agree on this date. We cannot change Mayan dates to our calendar. Archeologists can read the Mayan numbers. They do not know how to read the calendar. Carbon 14 methods are helping to solve this problem.

FIGURE 11-1   Page from Pupil Text, Grade 2: Methods of Absolute Dating: Calendrical Dating*

*Marion J. Rice, The Development of Man and His Culture: New World Prehistory (Athens, Ga.: Anthropology Curriculum Project, 1966), p. 21.

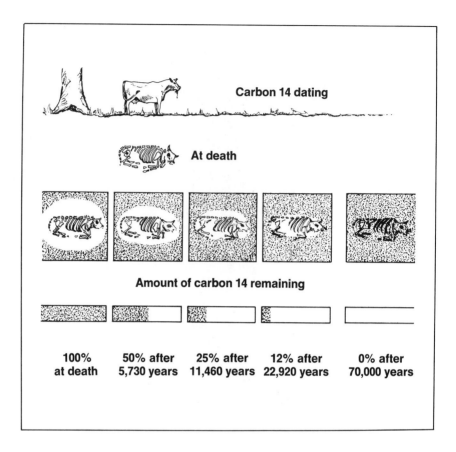

Carbon 14 dating

At death

Amount of carbon 14 remaining

| 100% at death | 50% after 5,730 years | 25% after 11,460 years | 12% after 22,920 years | 0% after 70,000 years |

Carbon 14 is a method of radio carbon dating. It is done in a laboratory. Much special equipment is needed. An archeologist does not do the dating. It is done by another kind of scientist.

Carbon 14 dating can be used on any organic (plant and animal) material. All organic material has Carbon 14. The older the piece of material, the less Carbon 14 it has.

Carbon 14 dating is the most used method of dating. It cannot date things older than 70,000 years. After that time, too much of the carbon has disappeared.

This method of dating can be used on such different things as parchment made from animal skins, charcoal, and fossil remains.

FIGURE 11-2   Page from Pupil Text, Grade 2:
Absolute Dating: Carbon 14*

*Rice, The Development of Man and His Culture, *p. 23.*

1. The Five Stages of New World History

The study of New World Prehistory is divided into five stages. A stage is a level of cultural development. The five stages are:

Paleo-Indian.   This Indian was a hunter of big Ice Age animals.

Archaic Stage.   This Indian hunted smaller game and gathered seeds, roots, and berries.

Formative Stage.   This Indian was primarily a village farmer. In North America his main crop was corn (maize).

Classic Stage.   This Indian lived in farm villages and had ceremonial centers.

Post Classic Stage.   This Indian had military governments and built large cities.

The Eskimo and the Plains Indian do not fit these stages.

All five stages are found only in Nuclear America. Many Indians did not progress beyond the Archaic Stage. In the United States, most Indians of the Southwest and Eastern Woodlands reached the Formative Stage.

FIGURE 11-3   Page from Pupil Text, Grade 2: The Development of
Man and His Culture: New World Prehistory*

*Rice, The Development of Man and His Culture, p. 29.

Characteristics of Learners

As implied earlier, the content of the Georgia curriculum is based upon the assumption that rather young pupils can adequately comprehend a large number of anthropological terms and generalizations. However, the exact amount of material that children are expected to master at particular grade levels is not entirely clear. For example, a surprisingly long, complex series of anthropological concepts is listed for children to learn at each step in the first-grade unit, but the accompanying directions state that teachers are not expected to teach all of these terms. This may well leave the teacher puzzled about how much the pupils really are expected to master. Perhaps the listing of an extensive series of terms is the curriculum designer's way of providing for individual differences in the abilities of pupils. For instance, the entire series might be presented to the children, with the most apt and interested pupils expected to comprehend much of the material, the average pupils less, and the slower children only a small amount. Whatever the rationale, this factor of a heavy vocabulary load has concerned teachers and curriculum coordinators who have examined or used the University of Georgia materials.

Regarding the socioeconomic differences among children, project personnel have apparently assumed that all, or nearly all, of the ideas and examples in these anthropology units will be new to pupils of all social-class backgrounds. In other words, none of the children will have a marked advantage over their classmates because of their superior background in the field of anthropology. In view of the somewhat exotic cultures that are studied in the units, this assumption may well be correct, particularly for primary-grade pupils. However, variations among children in the richness of home facilities (books, motion pictures, educational television programs, magazines) and in opportunities for travel might be expected to result in some intermediate- and upper-grade children having a better experiential background than do their classmates.

Characteristics of Teachers

One obvious assumption underlying the structure of the Georgia project is that teachers without special training in anthropology should be able to use the curriculum materials successfully. Project personnel tested this assumption by comparing the classroom performance of teachers who had undergone a special six-week training session in anthropology with the performance of those who had not. The results of this assessment indicated that those who had not attended the training program but who had read the project materials were as successful in using the curriculum as those who had attended.

We noted earlier that the materials themselves are not adjusted for individual variations among children in reading skill or experiential background. Thus, it seems apparent that the staff has assumed that teachers themselves will be able to accommodate for individual pupil differences without suggestions or materials from the project. Perhaps the staff's recommendation of multiple media of communication—such as a pupil textbook plus a teacher demonstration plus a film—is intended to aid pupils in mastering the anthropological concepts despite the children's differences in learning style. A child who does not read well might still grasp the ideas from the teacher's demonstration or the film. However,

---

[11] Sanders and Tanck, *"Anthropology Curriculum Project,"* pp. 409-410.

two questions about this assumption remain inadequately answered in project publications: Are most elementary-school social-studies teachers capable of making the necessary adjustments for pupils' individual differences without the help of specialists? Do most teachers have the time to alter the more difficult materials to suit the children's varied levels of comprehension?

Evaluation Procedures

The evaluation techniques furnished with the University of Georgia program are of two varieties.

First, the teacher's guidebooks suggest review questions, which the teacher asks during discussion sessions to obtain a general impression of how adequately the children have comprehended the material just studied. Such question sessions also provide an opportunity for children who have not mastered the information to clear up their misconceptions. By way of illustration, here is the set of seven questions suggested for use following the "economics: housing" portion of the first-grade unit on *Concept of Culture.*

1. Why does man need shelter?
2. What function or functions does housing serve?
3. What are some basic house types?
4. Is there any relationship between house type and the type of economy prevailing in a culture? Explain.
5. How can the physical environment influence housing types?
6. Can culture influence housing type? Explain.
7. What types of shelter do Americans, Arunta, and Kazak utilize?[12]

The second kind of evaluation device in the Georgia plan is a set of multiple-choice tests to accompany each of the regular units above the kindergarten level. These are intended either as pretests (to measure children's anthropological knowledge before studying the

---

[12] *Teacher's Guide, Grade One, Concept of Culture* (Athens, Ga.: Anthropology Curriculum Project, 1965), p. 12.

unit), as post-tests (to measure their achievement at the end of the unit), or as both. A typical test is comprised of both verbal and pictorial items. Here are samples of two verbal items from a test designed for grade 0.

Item 1: The FIRST stone tools were:
1. burins.
2. hand-axes.
3. pebble tools.
4. projectile points.

Item 2: Suppose that there is an island on which there are 20 white rabbits and 20 brown ones. The rabbits eat the food in people's gardens, so the people try to kill as many of the rabbits as they can. They kill some rabbits of each color. However, they find that the brown rabbits, which match some of the colors in the woods, are harder to see.

Suppose that you were to go to that island 50 years from now. Which sentence below tells what you would MOST LIKELY find on the island?

1. There will be more brown rabbits than white ones.
2. There will be more white rabbits than brown ones.
3. All of the rabbits will be white.
4. There will be about the same number of white rabbits and brown ones.[13]

Two kinds of pictorial items from this same grade-0 test are illustrated in Figure 11-4.

As the sample items suggest, some of the test questions assess the pupils' memory of technical terms. However, many other questions require the children to apply concepts or principles in analyses of data or in making predictions.

When the concept load and vocabulary load outlined in the teacher's manuals and pupils' texts are compared with the test questions, it appears that the tests do not make as heavy demands on the pupil as the basic vocabulary lists in the lesson plans. In short, the tests seem better suited to the typical abilities of children at each grade level than do many of the lessons.

---

[13] Marilyn J. McCrary and Robert L. Turknett, *A Sequential Curriculum in Anthropology, Test Form 5*, revised edition (Athens, Ga.: Anthropology Curriculum Project, 1968), pp. 3, 8.

Here are drawings of the skulls of four fossil men. Use these pictures to answer the question next to them.

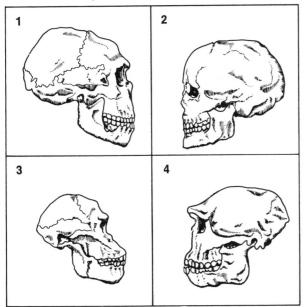

27. Which of these men lived AFTER the other three?

   1. Man 1

   2. Man 2

   3. Man 3

   4. Man 4

Here is a picture of the side of a cliff where a river has cut away much rock. Different kinds of rock are marked with different patterns so that you can tell them apart. The locations of fossils are marked with capital letters. Use the picture to help you answer the question next to it.

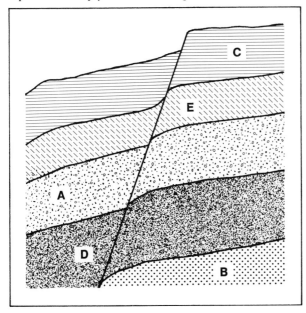

34. Fossil A is OLDER than

   1. Fossil B only.

   2. Fossils C and E only.

   3. Fossils B and D only.

   4. Fossils B, C, D, and E.

FIGURE 11-4   Sample Pictorial Test Items*

*McCrary and Turknett, A Sequential Curriculum in Anthropology, *pp. 6, 7.*

Conditions Influencing the Adoption
of the Georgia Anthropology Curriculum

The fact that the Georgia curriculum is designed to supplement rather than replace existing social-studies programs would seem to enhance its chances for adoption, since it can be used as a segment of several different curriculum patterns. For instance, a school that wishes to retain its present overall social-studies program can shorten one or two of the existing units to provide time for the intensive study of anthropology. Or, as another alternative, one unit of the existing curriculum can be replaced with the Georgia curriculum materials. If a school system wishes to assemble its own social-science curriculum by adopting a series of partial programs focusing on individual disciplines, the Anthropology Curriculum Project materials can represent a one-month portion of the overall plan. Other national programs in economics, social psychology, geography, and political science might furnish materials for the rest of the year's work.

Because the Georgia program offers at least one unit per grade, kindergarten through junior high, a school can use the project's complete set of units for the sequential study of anthropology from one grade level to the next. On the other hand, each unit is sufficiently independent of the others to permit a single teacher successfully to adopt a unit for his grade level, even if the rest of the teachers in the school do not include the study of anthropology in their social-studies offerings.

As noted earlier, the vocabulary and concepts that form the chief content of the Georgia materials appear somewhat more difficult and greater in number than those found in the typical social-studies or science curriculum. The increased difficulty, coupled with the rapid pace at which technical words are introduced in the children's textbooks, suggests that the classroom teacher must display a good deal of ingenuity in providing life-like examples, classroom demonstrations, and pupil activities that will both sustain the children's interest and accurately communicate the anthropological concepts. Without a variety of clear examples and activities that illustrate the concepts, the program could well deteriorate into vocabulary drill that results in the rote memorization of definitions rather than real comprehension of concepts and principles.

The Anthropology Curriculum Project appears to have done a good job of aiding the classroom teacher in expanding his understanding of anthropology well beyond the level required of the pupils. The teacher-background booklets about anthropology at each grade level appear interesting and clearly written.

In summary, the Georgia program depends heavily for its success on the dedication and initiative of the individual classroom teacher. For most pupils, the text materials do not "teach themselves."

12

Units in Social Psychology

The analysis of how people act and why is hardly a novel aim for an elementary social-studies program. Indeed, all "social study" involves some sort of examination of human behavior. However, it is somewhat unusual for a program to concentrate almost entirely on the tools and concepts of the discipline of social psychology, as do the Social Science Laboratory Units. These units were published by Science Research Associates in 1968, after several years of development at the University of Michigan's Institute for Social Research under the direction of Ronald Lippitt (social psychologist), Robert Fox (professor of education), and Lucille Schaible (educator and writer).

The Michigan plan is properly considered a partial program, since its seven units can either serve as a full year's social studies in one of the intermediate grades (4, 5, or 6) or be divided up so as to supplement a basic social-studies pattern in any or all of these grades.

The Authors' Value Position

The laboratory units belong in the mainstream of innovations in curriculum designs of the 1960s, for they represent a reaction against what the authors consider shortcomings of existing elementary social studies.

First, social studies have been frequently considered primarily a body of information to be mastered by the students. The curriculum has emphasized memorizing facts rather than critical and analytical thinking.

Second, little attention has been given to value inquiry.

Third, we've been inclined to underestimate the learning potential of children. With the advent of the new mathematics and physical science curricula, children have demonstrated that they can understand and use concepts traditionally reserved for high school or even college students.

We've also assumed an obligation to protect children from the "harsh realities" of life.

Finally, many current social studies curricula do not adequately represent the disciplines that deal with man and his social world. . . .

More important, every teacher knows that students can't help but learn about human behavior each day. They interact with the members of their families, with their classmates, with members of their peer groups, churches, and clubs. Each day they make generalizations about human behavior and take value positions. But we must question some of these unguided, incidental learnings. Can they be adequate?

The classroom can and should be a laboratory for guided learning about human behavior.[1]

Scope and Sequence

The following overview of the issues considered in each of the units suggests the range of topics and intellectual skills encompassed by the Michigan program.

Unit One—Learning to Use Social Science: Are social scientists like other scientists? How do they conduct experiments? This basic unit presents some of the tools and methods the social scientist uses. Children learn how to approach the study of human behavior with the objectivity of scientists. This unit is a prerequisite to study of all other units.

Unit Two—Discovering Differences: What are some ways that people are different? Are differences important? Pupils identify biological and cultural

---

[1] Ronald Lippitt, Robert Fox, and Lucille Schaible, *The Teacher's Role in Social Science Investigation* (Chicago: Science Research Associates, 1969), pp. 5-6. ©1969, Science Research Associates, Inc. Reprinted by permission.

differences between individuals and between groups. They inquire into the causes and effects of making prejudgments about differences. In this way, they discover how and why stereotypes develop.

Unit Three—Friendly and Unfriendly Behavior: What are some causes and effects of kindness and cruelty, acceptance or rejection? . . .

Unit Four—Being and Becoming: What does it mean to grow up? Are there different ways of growing up? This unit gives the student an opportunity to study his own development. . . . A major inquiry concerns ways in which heredity and environment influence development.

Unit Five—Individuals and Groups: What is a group? How does it function? . . . Three types of group leadership (autocratic, democratic, laissez-faire) and three types of group members (dissenter, mode, slider) are subjects for inquiry.

Unit Six—Deciding and Doing: How do we make decisions? Do we always carry them out? Students . . . attempt to establish the causes of successful and unsuccessful efforts.

Unit Seven—Influencing Each Other: How do we influence each other? Pupils examine five bases of social power to learn why some influence attempts are more successful than others. They also discover that while children and adults have the ability to influence each other, not all influences are intentional.[2]

The sequence in which the seven units are studied is highly flexible. Although Unit One, which introduces the learner to social-science procedures, should be the initial step in the pupil's experiences, the six subsequent units can be arranged in whatever order the teacher considers most convenient. Ordinarily a unit takes from four to six weeks to complete.[3]

Materials and Methods

The laboratory units, as packaged by Science Research Associates, consist of three kinds of materials for pupils and three kinds for teachers.

A *Resource Book* for pupils includes illustrated stories of social situations and research reports from scientific journals as adapted for children. The book, which contains readings for all seven units, also furnishes expository materials with definitions of scientific terms as the groundwork for a particular inquiry project. The writing style and reading-difficulty level of the resource materials is suggested by the following excerpt, which is a chapter entitled "Multiple Causation."

---

[2] Lippitt, Fox, and Schaible, *The Teacher's Role in Social Science Investigation*, pp. 3-4.
[3] Lippitt, Fox and Schaible, *The Teacher's Role in Social Science Investigation*, p. 7.

You have studied causes and effects in several behavior specimens. You have learned the difference between inside and outside causes and the difference between starting and in-between causes.

So far we have dealt with behavior that has just one or two causes. As you have probably guessed, a behavior can have many causes. In fact, it usually does. If any one of the causes is missing, the behavior frequently will be different. Usually all the causes must come together for a person to behave in a certain way.

When a behavior, another way of saying an effect, has several causes, social scientists speak of *multiple causation*. Multiple causation means that there are usually many causes for one effect.

Think of multiple causation as a bracelet with many links. All the links are important if there is to be a certain effect. If one of the links is lost or broken, the effect—or the behavior—might be different.

Read the following behavior specimen, "The Carnival." As you read, think about the many causes acting on Dottie. Some of them are inside, and at least one is an outside cause.

The Carnival

Dottie and her friend Katie went to a carnival with Dottie's older sister. As the three girls walked down the midway, they heard music blaring from loudspeakers and screams of laughter coming from the people on the amusement rides. The bright lights were dazzling. What a crowd! Dottie couldn't remember when she had seen so many people in one place.

"Golllleeee, look at all those cute stuffed animals," Katie said, pointing.

Dottie tried to see where Katie was pointing. "Where?" she asked.

"Over there, where the man with the mustache is standing. See?"

Dottie looked again in the direction that Katie was pointing to and she finally saw the stuffed animals. Oh, they must be the prizes for winning the dart game, she thought. They look just like they are waiting to be won. Boy, would I ever like to have one!

"Do you think we could try to win one of them?" Dottie asked her sister, Mary.

"Why not?" Mary answered. "Mom gave us the money to spend. Besides, it would be fun and that's what a carnival is for. Come on, let's go."

Dottie gave a quarter to the man with the mustache in the booth. He handed her three darts. She looked at the pretty colored balloons pinned to the back of the booth. She aimed, then threw her first dart. A yellow balloon broke!

"Yippee!" cried Katie. "You got one, Dottie!"

Dottie aimed the second dart and let it sail. Bang! She broke another balloon.

"Come on, Dottie, only one more to go!" Katie urged.

Dottie took a deep breath and aimed the third dart very, very carefully. She hurled it at a red balloon with all her might. Thunk! It quivered in the wood, just missing the third balloon.

"Oh, no," Dottie wailed. "What terrible luck!" She had come so close to winning one of the stuffed animals. Dottie just *knew* she could break all three.

"Too bad," Katie said. "You almost had your pick of the prizes."

Then the man with the mustache held out three more darts. "Three for a quarter," he said invitingly. Dottie looked at her sister for a second.

"I'm going to try again," Dottie said. She gave the man another quarter.

How many causes can you find in this story to explain why Dottie tried a second time to break all three balloons?

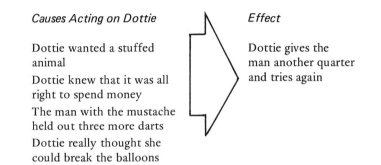

Causes Acting on Dottie

Dottie wanted a stuffed animal

Dottie knew that it was all right to spend money

The man with the mustache held out three more darts

Dottie really thought she could break the balloons

Effect

Dottie gives the man another quarter and tries again

You'll notice that three of the causes listed are inside causes acting on Dottie. One of them is an outside cause. You can probably think of other outside causes that were also working on Dottie.

Dottie's behavior is an example of multiple causation. Multiple causation means that a group of causes must be present if the effect is to occur. Let's suppose that Dottie didn't want a stuffed animal. Even if the other causes were present, she wouldn't have tried to break the balloons.

Look at the second cause. Dottie could not have tried to break the balloons if she didn't have the money to spend. Look at the other causes. You will see that if any *one* of them had *not* been acting on Dottie, she might have behaved differently. All of these causes are necessary to explain why Dottie tried a second time to break the balloons.[4]

In addition to the *Resource Book*, the program includes a 30-page project book for each unit. The project book is a workbook in which the pupil records his observations or conclusions about the behavior incidents in the *Resource Book*.

Four phonograph records offer dramatic incidents for the pupils to analyze in relation to the seven units.

---

[4] Ronald Lippitt, Robert Fox, and Lucille Schaible, *Social Science Laboratory Units, Resource Book* (Chicago: Science Research Associates, 1969), pp. 31-34. ©1969, Science Research Associates, Inc. Reprinted by permission.

To aid the teacher in directing pupils' inquiry, the program furnishes two manuals (*Teacher's Guide: Social Science Laboratory Units* and *The Teacher's Role in Social Science Investigation*) as well as a phonograph recording that illustrates discussion problems that are often met in using this approach to teaching social studies.

In summary, these materials offer both incidents of human behavior and suggestions about how to analyze them as social scientists would. Teachers and pupils are expected to supplement the behavior incidents with examples from their own experiences.

The methodology advocated by the authors of the program has been called *laboratory experiential learning*. It consists of eight general steps in scientific inquiry: (1) exposure to or confrontation with a puzzling phenomenon, (2) formulating focused inquiries or questions, (3) deciding how to get the information needed to answer the questions, (4) collecting the data, (5) analyzing and interpreting the information, (6) identifying values and exploring their bases, (7) making generalizations about what has been discovered, and (8) raising new questions or checking the foregoing discoveries.[5]

Although this general configuration of steps runs throughout the units, certain lessons may place more emphasis on one stage of the process than on another. To illustrate, let us consider segments of Lessons 2 and 5 in the initial unit of the program. The unit is entitled "Learning to Use Social Science." In the teacher's manual, Lesson 2 (How Do Social Scientists Observe Behavior?) is described in the following manner. The *items* in the lesson plan are activities to be carried out in relation to the teaching materials provided with the program.

Purpose of Lesson 2

To explain the meaning and function of a behavior specimen and role playing.

To demonstrate different ways of making observations—descriptions, inferences, value judgments.

To produce a behavior specimen in class for observation.

Item 6

Behavior specimens—examples of typical human interaction—play an important part in the *Social Science Laboratory Units*. They serve as a stimulus for inquiry and provide opportunity for pupils to make observations.

---

[5] Lippitt, Fox, and Schaible, *The Teacher's Role in Social Science Investigation*, p. 9.

Behavior specimens are of three types—recorded, read, and produced in the classroom by some pupils for the rest of the class to observe. Pupils who take part in the behavior specimens produced in class are called role players. (Eventually your pupils will be able to create their own specimens of behavior to illustrate a particular kind of interaction.)

Direct the class to read the story in the Resource Book that explains the function of behavior specimens and role playing. Then instruct them to do some simple kinds of role playing at their desks—eating ice-cream cones, an ear of sweet corn, or a lollipop, for example.

Appoint pairs of students to demonstrate interaction by role-playing such activities as a phone conversation, an imaginary game of ping-pong, a game of cards, or catch.

Instruct the rest of the class to observe each role play and then describe only what he *saw*. This will provide some introduction to the important business of recording observations accurately.

(Read "What Is a Behavior Specimen?" on pages 7-9
of the Resource Book.)

Item 7

Pupils are about to learn the very important distinctions that social scientists make when they report their observations of behavior. They are *descriptions, inferences*, and *value judgments.*

Stress the fact that the scientist constantly strives for objectivity. When he records his observations about a specific behavioral interaction, he reports (*describes*) only the facts. . . .

After a social scientist has collected many observation reports about a similar behavior, he will want to guess *why* it happened. He supposes or guesses the reasons the people behaved as they did . . . he is making an *inference.*

Social scientists try hard to be objective even when they are making inferences about behavior. They rarely make *value judgments*—that is, label a behavior as good or bad, right or wrong.

Value judgments are important distinctions for children to make, however. They are encouraged to do so, in fact, as a basis for learning more about human behavior. The trick is knowing the difference between value judgments, inferences, and descriptions. . . .

When you have completed the reading assignment, divide the class into small groups. Select one student in each group to choose a behavior to role-play for his group, such as eating an ice-cream cone, peeling a banana, sharpening a pencil, or chewing celery.

After a behavior has been role-played, ask the rest of the group to make statements about it and then decide what kind of statement was made each time—a description, an inference, or a value judgment.

Another way to reinforce these concepts is to ask children to bring in pictures or comic strips from newspapers or magazines that illustrate human interaction. Then ask the class to make statements about the behavior in the pictures by first describing it, then making an inference about the reasons for it and, finally, making a value judgment.

(Read "Three Ways to Use Observation" on pages 11-13
of the Resource Book)

Item 8

An exercise in Project Book 1, page 4, "Descriptions, Inferences, and Value Judgments," will provide practice in making distinctions about statements that refer to a photograph. Read over the exercise before doing it in class.

Answers

D	1.	Margo is smiling.
D	2.	Margo is holding the kitten.
I	3.	The kitten feels warm to Margo.
V	4.	Everyone should have a pet.
D	5.	The picture was taken inside a house.
I	6.	The kitten is a birthday present for Margo.
I	7.	Margo likes kittens.[6]

After presenting the answers to the remaining 13 items in the exercise, the lesson-plan guidebook suggests ways to handle discussion of the exercise with the class. Then the guidebook describes Item 9, which is "the first behavior specimen to be produced in the classroom. It is a sample of unfriendly behavior that it is hoped will become a stimulus for inquiry. One boy intentionally rips another boy's poster. What happened? Why did it happen? Should anyone have acted differently?"[7] The manual subsequently tells what the role-playing situation is to be, who the characters are, and how the action starts. Then children in the class are chosen to play roles in the spontaneous playlet, securing cues to their actions from "briefing sheets" that describe for each actor his initial behavior as one boy rips up another's newly completed poster. Then the selected children are set loose to act out the scene while their classmates observe the action and categorize their observations as descriptions, inferences, or value judgments.

The foregoing example from Lesson 2 illustrates several general points about the Lippitt, Fox, and Schaible program. The lesson

---

[6] Ronald Lippitt, Robert Fox, and Lucille Schaible, *Social Science Laboratory Units, Teacher's Guide* (Chicago: Science Research Associates, 1969), pp. 13-14. ©1969, Science Research Associates, Inc. Reprinted by permission.

[7] Lippitt, Fox, and Schaible, *Social Science Laboratory Units, Teacher's Guide*, pp. 15-16.

concentrates on one aspect of behavioral-science inquiry. It introduces children to the central concepts and skills by means of reading and discussion. It furnishes practice in using the skills in a controlled situation represented by a workbook exercise. Then it gives them additional practice in a less controlled situation, the role-playing incident.

Let us now turn to Lesson 5 of the same unit to see how a different subskill of behavioral-science inquiry is taught. The key question for this lesson is "How Do Social Scientists Ask Questions?"

Purpose of Lesson 5

To introduce the interview and questionnaire as methods of collecting information about behavior.

To illustrate how social scientists make and test their predictions about behavior.

To review previous concepts.

Item 22

The material presented in this reading selection briefly describes two additional methods of collecting information about behavior. The first, of course, is direct observation. The others are the questionnaire (a list of written questions with space for answers) and the interview (directly asking a person questions and writing down the answers). Pupils will use both in their data collection projects.

*(Read "Special Ways of Asking Questions" on
pages 39-41 of the Resource Book.)*

Item 23

Social scientists make special kinds of guesses about how people *will behave* in a given situation. Scientific guesses are given a special name—predictions. Predictions made by social scientists are neither wishful thinking nor wild guesses. Their predictions are based on facts they have collected in their past investigations about similar kinds of behavior. Even so, they always check their predictions to find out how well they understand behavior.

*(Read "Asking Questions About the Future" on pages 43-44
of the Resource Book.)*[8]

---

[8] Lippitt, Fox, and Schaible, *Social Science Laboratory Units, Teacher's Guide*, p. 26.

Subsequent items in the lesson require the pupil to answer questions in the Project Book relating to the foregoing reading passages.

In Lesson 6 the pupils learn the "dos and don'ts" of successful interviews by listening to interviewing procedures on a phonograph record. The children assess the interviewers' techniques by use of a rating scale in the Project Book—that is, in the pupils' workbook.

In summary, the *laboratory experiential learning* of this social-studies plan finds pupils alternately reading examples of behavior and ways to study it, testing out their own understanding of the concepts by doing exercises in a Project Book, conducting and analyzing role-playing sessions, considering behavior specimens on records, and analyzing people's actions observed in everyday life. The emphasis, then, is on activities that stimulate the pupils to think in the manner of social psychologists, as far as possible.

Assumptions about Pupil Characteristics

Two of the central assumptions about children on which the Lippitt, Fox, and Schaible design has been based were mentioned at the beginning of the chapter: (1) ". . . children have demonstrated that they can understand and use concepts traditionally reserved for high school or even college students"[9] and (2) ". . . students can't help but learn about human behavior each day. They interact with the members of their families, with their classmates, with members of their peer groups, churches, and clubs. . . . But we must question some of these unguided, incidental learnings. . . . The classroom can and should be a laboratory for guided learning about human behavior."[10]

In addition to assuming that elementary-school pupils can and should study human behavior scientifically, the authors believe that children profit most from first confronting a "behavioral phenomenon that is puzzling. . . ."[11] Such confrontation motivates them to solve the puzzle through formulating questions, gathering data, analyzing the data, and drawing conclusions. In effect, the authors are convinced that the child learns best when he actively solves problems.

A further assumption is that children can and should examine the values they and other people hold. Therefore, the teaching materials in the

---

[9]Lippitt, Fox, and Schaible, *The Teacher's Role in Social Science Investigation,* p. 6.
[10]Lippitt, Fox, and Schaible, *The Teacher's Role in Social Science Investigation,* p. 6.
[11]Lippitt, Fox, and Schaible, *The Teacher's Role in Social Science Investigation,* p. 7.

program press the learners to analyze what they regard as good and bad, desirable and undesirable, and why they regard it as they do.

Occasional comments throughout the teacher's guidebook indicate that the authors of the plan recognize that there will be differences among pupils in ability and interest. For instance, in Lesson 5 of Unit One, the guidebook suggests that the passage on "How Social Scientists Test Predictions" should be read aloud "if you have slow or very young readers, or if you think the concepts are too advanced."[12] In Lesson 9 the authors write: "The final data collection project, C, will take more time to complete and greater sophistication on the part of students. It is not recommended if pupils have had difficulty in completing either Project A or Project B."[13] In Lesson 4 of Unit Three, the guidebook instructions include the following recommendation: "Instruct the class to read the story silently or have several of your better readers read sections aloud, or read it aloud yourself."[14] However, other than such infrequent references to the way children's limitations in reading or analytical skill might affect teaching methods, the instructor's manual gives no attention to individual differences among learners. Either the authors believe that all children will be able to succeed with virtually all of the suggested methodology, or else they think the classroom teacher can accommodate for differences without aid from the program's designers.

Assumptions about Teacher Characteristics

In the Lippitt, Fox, and Schaible materials, the most evident belief about teachers is that the program's rationale and key teaching methods cannot be comprehended adequately by the typical teacher without some special instruction. To furnish such instruction, the authors have provided not only the teacher's guidebook to individual lessons but also a phonograph recording that introduces the structure and purposes of the plan and a 152-page booklet explaining *The Teacher's Role in Social Science Investigation.* These materials may be used either by an individual teacher or by a group engaged in in-service training within a particular school. The booklet offers detailed guidance for (1) conducting value inquiry in class, (2) producing behavior specimens for study, (3) teaching observation skills,

---

[12] Lippitt, Fox, and Schaible, *Social Science Laboratory Units, Teacher's Guide*, p. 27.
[13] Lippitt, Fox, and Schaible, *Social Science Laboratory Units, Teacher's Guide*, p. 39.
[14] Lippitt, Fox, and Schaible, *Social Science Laboratory Units, Teacher's Guide*, p. 87.

(4) formulating questions and questionnaires, and (5) organizing groups for laboratory learning.[15]

Evaluation Procedures

This curriculum plan offers the teacher two forms of aid in assessing children's achievement. First is the series of exercises in the pupil workbooks known as *project books.* Second is the part of the instructional booklet for teachers (*The Teacher's Role in Social Science Investigation*) that suggests different steps in the evaluation process and gives examples of assessment devices that teachers can create. The following examples from these two sources indicate the nature of the materials they contain.

The most typical variety of evaluation item in the project books is a set of questions the child is to answer about some classroom activity, such as a reading passage, a segment of a recording the children have heard, an investigation the class has carried out, or a role-playing incident produced in class. For instance, here are items from a lesson in Unit Seven, "Influencing Each Other."

> *Directions:* Your will play the second part of this record (I Need a Dry Rag). Listen carefully. Then complete your observation report.
>
> 1. Why doesn't Brian want to get the dry rag?
> 2. Why doesn't Jack get it himself? . . . .
> 4. What does Brian have to say about Jack then?
> 5. Brian liked doing errands when he wasn't busy. Do you agree?

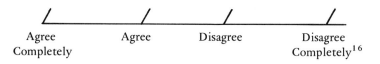

| Agree | Agree | Disagree | Disagree |
| Completely | | | Completely[16] |

The foregoing evaluation device obviously assumes not only that the child can read adequately but also that he can formulate answers in

---

[15] Lippitt, Fox, and Schaible, *The Teacher's Role in Social Science Investigation,* p. vii.
[16] "Influencing Each Other," *Project Book 7/Social Science Laboratory Units* (Chicago: Science Research Associates, 1969), p. 10.

written form. However, other items in the project book only require the pupil to choose between two or more possible answers or to fill in blanks with words he chooses from a list of possibilities. An example of the multiple-choice variety combined with short written answers is drawn from the project book accompanying Unit Three, "Friendly and Unfriendly Behavior." The incident to which the children are to respond is that of a doctor giving an injection to a screaming child.

1. Do you think the child perceives the doctor's *behavior* as

   _____ friendly   _____ unfriendly

2. Why did you answer the way you did? What *inference* did you make about the doctor's behavior?

   _____

   _____

   _____

3. The doctor's *intentions* are probably _____ friendly
                                            _____ unfriendly

4. Why did you answer the way you did? What *inference* did you make about the doctor's intentions?

   _____

   _____
                                                    [17]
   _____

A different sort of multiple-choice item requires the child to circle or underline appropriate words in a list. In Project Book 1 the children are instructed:

Circle the tools that the social scientist uses:

eyes	microscope	pen	paper	X-ray machine
mind	ears	test tube	questionnaire	interview[18]

[17]"Friendly and Unfriendly Behavior," *Project Book 3/Social Science Laboratory Units* (Chicago: Science Research Associates, 1969), p. 7.

[18]"Learning to Use Social Science," *Project Book 1/Social Science Laboratory Units* (Chicago: Science Research Associates, 1969), p. 22.

In the project books the pupil also occasionally faces true-false or completion exercises that indicate how adequately he has understood the concepts of the lesson.

Although the project books offer a diversity of evaluation items for each lesson, the authors of this social-psychology program do not consider these items sufficient measures of pupil progress. The classroom teacher is expected to create his own evaluation techniques as well. Aid with this task is offered in the form of "guidelines for evaluation" in the instructional booklet for teachers. The booklet illustrates ways of writing learning objectives and of constructing various devices to assess children's achievement of the objectives. For each kind of objective, the authors give examples of alternative assessment techniques. For instance, the following examples are cited as possibilities for evaluating pupils' abilities to apply skills they have learned:

> Read the question and then select one of the alternatives listed below. Explain your reason for choosing it in the space provided.
>
> "If you were a member of a club in school that wanted to raise money for a trip with another club in school, which of the following ways would you suggest for raising money?"
>
> 1. The clubs compete to see which one can raise more money.
> 2. The clubs work together to raise the money.
>
> Why? _____
> _____

A more complex problem would be to ask students to indicate one or more value judgments in a behavior specimen and then to support their choice with reasons, as follows:

> Katie was eager to get through the long line at the store so that she could be home in time to help her mother prepare supper. She noticed that two people at the head of the line were talking while the line moved forward. There was room and they weren't paying any attention, so she cut in front of them.
>
> How do you think this story should end? _____
> _____
> _____
>
> Why do you think so? _____
> _____
> _____

Another objective in this category is to obtain indications of specific attitudes and values. One of the most common ways of measuring attitudes is to develop scales ranging from very positive to very negative, as shown following:

How do you feel about school? Make a check (✔) on the rating scale.

/	/	/	/	/
Like it a lot	Like it some- what	Neutral	Dislike it some- what	Dislike it a lot

A series of simple faces works well with younger children.

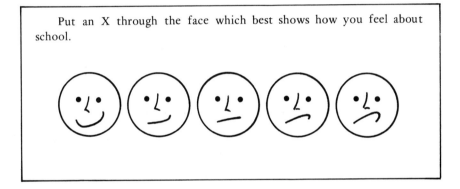

Put an X through the face which best shows how you feel about school.

Another approach is more indirect because it asks for a choice between activities and infers the attitudes from these choices:

Which do you prefer?

_____ reading a book   _____ walking in woods

_____ visiting a museum[19]

Not only does the Lippitt, Fox, and Schaible booklet recommend ways of evaluating pupil progress, but it also suggests techniques for the

---

[19]Lippitt, Fox, and Schaible, *The Teacher's Role in Social Science Investigation*, pp. 137-139.

teacher to use in assessing his own effectiveness or, more broadly, the influence of the classroom learning environment.

The following items have been used by teachers to ascertain what student attitudes toward specific learning periods in the classroom reveal about themselves and the teacher.

---

1. How do you feel about how much you learned today?

    /⎯⎯⎯⎯⎯⎯/⎯⎯⎯⎯⎯⎯/⎯⎯⎯⎯⎯⎯/

Don't think I learned much	Learned a little bit	Learned quite a lot	Learned a lot

Please say why you feel the way you marked. ⎯⎯⎯⎯⎯⎯⎯⎯⎯

---

2. Was it clear to you why we did ⎯⎯⎯⎯⎯⎯⎯ in class today?

                    (activity)

    /⎯⎯⎯⎯⎯⎯/⎯⎯⎯⎯⎯⎯/⎯⎯⎯⎯⎯⎯/

Very clear to me	Pretty clear to me	Not so very clear	Not at all clear to me

What do you think is the reason we did what we did in class today?

⎯⎯⎯⎯⎯⎯⎯⎯⎯⎯⎯⎯⎯⎯⎯⎯⎯⎯⎯⎯

---

3. Did you feel lost during the class activity?

    /⎯⎯⎯⎯⎯⎯/⎯⎯⎯⎯⎯⎯/⎯⎯⎯⎯⎯⎯/

Never lost at all	Lost a couple of times	Lost quite a few times	Lost most of the time

What made you feel lost? ⎯⎯⎯⎯⎯⎯⎯⎯⎯⎯⎯⎯

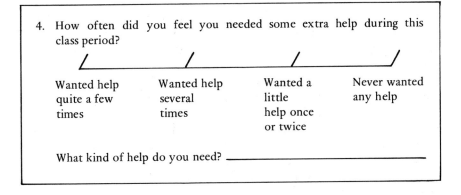

4. How often did you feel you needed some extra help during this class period?

| Wanted help quite a few times | Wanted help several times | Wanted a little help once or twice | Never wanted any help |

What kind of help do you need? _____

Some teachers have felt that their pupils might feel restrained in responding to the preceding questions in a way that could be critical of the teacher. So, in beginning this procedure, those teachers appointed a committee of respected pupil leaders to collect and tabulate the class responses and report the results without involving individual pupils.

The main point is that the pupils will learn to be honest and to use this opportunity seriously if they perceive that the teacher is objective about the facts and shows interest in doing something about what the surveys show.[20]

All in all, this social-psychology program offers teachers rather extensive guidance and numerous devices for evaluating the adequacy of pupils' learning.

Conditions Affecting the Adoption of the Units in Social Psychology

The seven units that compose the Lippitt, Fox, and Schaible plan conveniently fit into either of two kinds of upper-elementary-grade social-studies programs: (1) those that use an entire year for the intensive study of social psychology and (2) those that dedicate one or two months during each of two or three years to such study.

[20]Lippitt, Fox, and Schaible, *The Teacher's Role in Social Science Investigation*, pp. 139-141.

This flexibility of use is made possible by the fact that after the initial unit, which introduces children to behavioral-science methods, the remaining six units can be taught in any order and at any upper-grade level the teacher chooses.

As a *laboratory experiential* approach, the program is designed to meet the needs of teachers who want children's social-studies learning to go well beyond reading about social psychology. Children actively use methods of behavioral scientists to conduct their own studies. They observe behavior specimens, compose and administer questionnaires, conduct interviews, perform sociodramas, record data, and draw interpretations from the information they have gathered. In short, the plan stresses actual investigation of social-psychological phenomena.

The Lippitt, Fox, and Schaible plan also suits the needs of teachers who like to have all of their teaching materials furnished with the program. In contrast to some curriculum designs, this plan does not require the teacher to search for resource materials on his own. The necessary textbook, workbooks, and recordings are part of the curriculum package that the school purchases.

On the other hand, this program is not appropriate for teachers who feel insecure using such instructional techniques as role playing, group work, and social-psychological investigations. These methods require some ability to judge the adequacy of the pupils' "research methods" and of their solutions to research problems they encounter. In effect, the laboratory units succeed best at the hands of a teacher who exhibits a rather venturesome spirit.

Four

Other Variations

Earlier we noted that Chapters 3 through 12 are not proposed as a thorough survey of elementary social-studies curriculum patterns. Rather, they represent only a sampling of published programs drawn from the pool of hundreds of plans available in today's schools.

Limitations of space prevent us from examining additional patterns in detail. However, in the following pages we offer some impression of the nature of 11 other innovative curriculum proposals by surveying a series of their key features. So that the characteristics of one program can easily be compared with those of the others, we have organized the treatment of each plan according to the following topics: (1) identifying label, (2) source of the curriculum materials, (3) principal authors, (4) period of development or publication of the program, (5) grade levels for which it is designed, (6) the rationale, philosophy, or key purposes underlying the program, (7) the kinds of teaching methodology that are featured, (8) the materials furnished for teachers, (9) the materials furnished for pupils, and (10) the kinds of evaluation procedures recommended or implied in the plan.

The 11 designs, in the order of their presentation, are:

1. Developmental Economic Education Program (DEEP)
2. Development of Guidelines and Resource Materials on Latin America
3. Educational Research Council Social Science Program
4. Elementary Economics Program
5. Focus on Inner-City Social Studies
6. Franklin Social Sciences Program
7. Intergroup Relations Curriculum
8. Materials and Activities for Teachers and Children (MATCH)
9. Providence Social Studies Curriculum Project
10. Project Social Studies, University of Minnesota
11. Washington University Elementary Social Science Project

1.	Identifying label	D E E P—*Developmental Economic Education Program*
2.	Source of the curriculum materials	Joint Council on Economic Education, 1212 Avenue of the Americas, New York, N.Y. 10036
3.	Principal author	S. Stowell Symmes
4.	Period of development or of publication	1964-1971
5.	Grade levels	K-12
6.	Rationale, philosophy, or key purpose	To promote economic education throughout the elementary and secondary grades, the program furnishes many resource units intended to encourage school systems to develop their own approaches to curriculum change. Upon request school systems may enroll in the Cooperating Schools Program.
7.	Stresses what teaching methods?	Bibliographies furnished in teacher's guidebooks refer to many different methods. Teachers are to select their own methodology from the suggested alternatives.
8.	Provides what materials for teachers:	

8.1	General teaching strategies?	In the form of alternatives in teacher's guidebooks.
8.2	Specific lesson plans?	No.
8.3	Social-science subject-matter background?	Some in teacher's guidebooks.
8.4	Lists of books, films, recordings?	In teacher's guidebooks.

9. Provides what materials for pupils:

9.1	Textbooks?	Paperback readings.
9.2	Workbooks, activity books?	No.
9.3	Supplementary resource books?	No.
9.4	Films?	Filmstrips.
9.5	Audio recordings?	No.
9.6	Separate pictures, charts?	No.
9.7	Separate maps?	No.

10.	Suggests what evaluation techniques?	Teacher observation of pupil success with learning activities.

1.	Identifying label	Development of Guidelines and Resource Materials on Latin America
2.	Source of curriculum materials	Dr. Clark C. Gill, 403 Sutton Hall, University of Texas, Austin, Texas 78712
3.	Principal authors	Clark C. Gill and William B. Conroy
4.	Period of development or of publication	1966-1969
5.	Grade levels	1-12
6.	Rationale, philosophy, or key purpose	To identify and sequentially organize social-science content about contemporary Latin America, focusing primarily on comparative studies of families, schools, and communities.
7.	Stresses what teaching methods?	Teacher questioning, class discussion, individual and group projects.

8. Provides what materials for teachers:

8.1	General teaching strategies?	In primary- and intermediate-grade resource units for teacher use.
8.2	Specific lesson plans?	In resource units.
8.3	Social-science subject-matter background?	Some in resource units.
8.4	Lists of books, films, recordings?	In resource units.

9. Provides what materials for pupils:

9.1	Textbooks?	Some unit materials.
9.2	Workbooks, activity books?	No.
9.3	Supplementary resource books?	No.
9.4	Films?	No.
9.5	Audio recordings?	No.
9.6	Separate pictures and charts?	Yes.
9.7	Separate maps?	Yes.

10. Suggests what evaluation techniques?   Teacher questioning, teacher observation of pupil progress in projects.

1.	Identifying label	Educational Research Council Social Science Program
2.	Source of the curriculum materials	Educational Research Council of America, Rockefeller Bldg., 6th Floor, Cleveland, Ohio 44113; also Allyn and Bacon, 470 Atlantic Ave., Boston, Mass. 02210
3.	Project director	Raymond English
4.	Period of development or of publication	1960s-1971
5.	Grade levels	K-9
6.	Rationale, philosophy, or key purpose	Concepts from various social science disciplines were identified

6. (Continued)

by social scientists, then organized for teaching in an interdisciplinary pattern. Instructional materials stress mastery of subject matter and development of healthy emotional attitudes and social relationships. The analysis of values is highlighted.

7. Stresses what teaching methods?

Teacher questioning, class discussion, pupil inquiry and projects, simulation activities. Methods assume considerable faith in pupils' ability to carry out independent study.

8. Provides what materials for teachers:

8.1 General teaching strategies?

In teacher's manual.

8.2 Specific lesson plans?

In resource-unit form in teacher's manual.

8.3 Social-science subject-matter background?

Background information in teacher's manual.

8.4 Lists of books, films, recordings?

In teacher's manual.

9. Provides what materials for pupils:

9.1 Textbooks?

Soft binding, colored illustrations.

9.2 Workbooks, activity books?

No.

9.3 Supplementary resource books?

Yes.

9.4 Films?

Filmstrips.

9.5 Audio recordings?

Tapes.

9.6 Separate pictures, charts?

Yes.

9.7 Separate maps?

Yes.

10. Suggests what evaluation techniques?

Discussion questions from teacher's manual, tests furnished in supplementary publication. D. Beck, Administrative Assistant, ERCSSP

1. Identifying label	Elementary Economics Program
2. Source of the curriculum materials	Elementary Economics Program, Industrial Relations Center, 1225 East 60th St., Chicago, Ill. 60637
3. Principal author	William D. Rader
4. Period of development or of publication	1960-1971
5. Grade levels	4-9
6. Rationale, philosophy, or key purpose	To provide economics materials to supplement existing social-studies in grades 4-6. Emphasis on simulation games shows project staff's interest in approximating real-life situations.
7. Stresses what teaching methods?	Reading, discussion, simulation games.
8. Provides what materials for teachers:	
8.1 General teaching strategies?	In teacher's resource book.
8.2 Specific lesson plans?	Teacher's Guide to Daily Lessons.
8.3 Social-science subject-matter background?	In teacher's resource book.
8.4 Lists of books, films, recordings?	In teacher's resource book.
9. Provides what materials for pupils:	
9.1 Textbooks?	Units of study.
9.2 Workbooks, activity books?	No.
9.3 Supplementary resource books?	Pupils' units of study are essential resource materials.
9.4 Films?	No.
9.5 Audio recordings?	No.
9.6 Separate pictures, charts?	Yes.
9.7 Separate maps?	Yes.
10. Suggests what evaluation techniques?	Only grade 4 and 5 programs furnish pre- and post-tests for each unit; tests measure mostly for memory, some for interpretive skills. Oral questions by teacher

10. (Continued)	in discussion sessions also used. Upper grade test currently being revised. Economic Man (formerly entitled Exchange) is published by Benefic Press, Westchester, Ill. 60153. Economic Man in the Market is a short four week unit based upon Economic Man. The game MARKET is an intrinsic part of this program.

1. Identifying label	Focus on Inner-City Social Studies (Project FICSS)
2. Source of the curriculum materials	FICSS, c/o Dr. Melvin Arnoff, Room 121, College of Education, Kent State University, Kent, Ohio 44240
3. Principal author	Melvin Arnoff
4. Period of development or of publication	1968-1971
5. Grade levels	K-12
6. Rationale, philosophy, or key purpose	Emphasizes social studies appropriate for urban U.S.A. Stresses family structure in cities, Afro-Americans in U.S. History, minority power in U.S. FICSS units can be integrated into existing social studies program.
7. Stresses what teaching methods?	Children read resource materials, case studies; teacher leads discussion, asks questions.
8. Provides what materials for teachers:	Specific minimum essential resources needed to teach each unit. Teachers' guides available and include objectives, outline of content, suggested learning activities and resources.
8.1 General teaching strategies?	Unit approach emphasizing student directed-teacher guided inquiry.
8.2 Specific lesson plans?	Some suggested daily lesson plans.
8.3 Social-science subject-matter background?	Drawn from all of the social sciences that focus upon the particular unit topic.

8.4 Lists of books, films, recordings?	Included in unit guide.
9. Provides what materials for pupils:	
9.1 Textbooks?	Does not suggest a text but rather a mix of pertinent books, film-strips, transparencies, etc.
9.2 Workbooks, activity books?	No.
9.3 Supplementary reading books?	Yes.
9.4 Films?	No. (Suggested in resource section of unit)
9.5 Audio recordings?	(Provided as useful in some kits)
9.6 Separate pictures, charts?	Yes.
9.7 Separate maps?	Yes.
10. Suggests what evaluation techniques?	A formal evaluation program has been developed using experimental and control classrooms to assess pupil attitudinal changes and information acquisition. Teachers keep a daily log of activities and comments, which will be useful in revising the unit, assessing the utility of the kit materials, the appropriateness of content, and the effectiveness of the suggested sequence of daily lesson plans.

---

1. Identifying label	Franklin Social Sciences Program
2. Source of the curriculum materials	Franklin Publications, Newport Beach, Calif. 92660
3. Principal authors	Margaret Johnstone Lenz, Penrod Moss, Mary S. Reed
4. Period of development or of publication	Mid-1960s–1971 +
5. Grade levels	K-6
6. Rationale, philosophy, or key purpose	To develop children's skills in investigating and understanding significant concepts of social-science

6. (Continued)	disciplines, including history, geography, political science, economics, anthropology, sociology, and social psychology.
7. Stresses what teaching methods?	Presentation of problems or questions that pupils are to work out with teacher's aid; questioning and class discussion emphasized.
8. Provides what materials for teachers:	
8.1 General teaching strategies?	In teacher's guidebooks.
8.2 Specific lesson plans?	In teacher's guidebooks.
8.3 Social-science subject-matter background?	No.
8.4 Lists of books, films, recordings?	In teacher's guidebooks.
9. Provides what materials for pupils:	
9.1 Textbooks?	Yes, illustrated in color.
9.2 Workbooks, activity books?	No.
9.3 Supplementary resource books?	Yes, called *Data Resources, Findings from Research*
9.4 Films?	Sound filmstrips.
9.5 Audio recordings?	With filmstrips.
9.6 Separate pictures, charts?	No.
9.7 Separate maps?	No.
10. Suggests what evaluation techniques?	Teacher observation of pupil answers in discussion and pupil success on individual and group projects.

---

1. Identifying label	Intergroup Relations Curriculum
2. Source of the curriculum materials	Lincoln-Filene Center for Citizenship and Public Affairs, Tufts University, Medford, Mass. 02155
3. Principal author	John S. Gibson
4. Period of development or of publication	1950s-1971+

5. Grade levels

1-6

6. Rationale, philosophy, or key purpose

To improve democratic human relations through education, the curriculum emphasizes the child's developing a positive self-concept, squarely facing socially sensitive issues, and acquiring a thought structure to treat such issues. Ideas integrated through study of government or social control. Includes stress on children's affective reactions.

7. Stresses what teaching methods?

Reading, discussion, teacher questioning, role playing, and simulation games.

8. Provides what materials for teachers:

8.1 General teaching strategies?

In teacher's guidebooks.

8.2 Specific lesson plans?

In teacher's guidebooks.

8.3 Social-science subject-matter background?

No.

8.4 Lists of books, films, recordings?

In teacher's guidebooks.

9. Provides what materials for pupils:

9.1 Textbooks?

Pamphlets and paperbacks.

9.2 Workbooks, activity books?

No.

9.3 Supplementary resource books?

Yes.

9.4 Films?

Filmstrips, motion pictures.

9.5 Audio recordings?

Tapes and discs.

9.6 Separate pictures, charts?

Yes.

9.7 Separate maps?

Yes.

10. Suggests what evaluation techniques?

Teacher questions, teacher observation of pupil success in activities.

---

1. Identifying label

MATCH—*Materials Activities for Teachers and CHildren*

2. Source of the curriculum materials	Developed by The Children's Museum, Jamaicaway, Boston, Mass. 02130; Published by American Science and Engineering Inc., 20 Overland St., Boston, Mass. 02215
3. Principal author	Frederick H. Kresse, Children's Museum, Boston
4. Period of development or of publication	Development 1964-1968 Publication 1968, 1969 Developed under U.S.O.E. Project
5. Grade levels	"The City" grades 1-4; "A House of Ancient Greece" grades 5, 6; "Japanese Family" grades 5, 6.
6. Rationale, philosophy, or key purpose	Emphasize the use of real objects as mediators of learning of predominantly non-verbal subject matter. Children should be actively involved with models, artifacts, films, and the like.
7. Stresses what teaching methods?	Children—often in small groups—learn directly from interacting with real materials. Emphasis is placed on student-directed learning, though some activities are teacher-led. The teacher acts at times as a leader, consultant, organizer, observer, etc. His role varies over a wide range depending on the particular activity.
8. Provides what materials for teachers:	Each unit is a self-contained, multimedia instructional system activated by the teacher and children. Units come in kit form with all the materials a teacher and class of 30 will need for 2-3 weeks of in-depth use.
8.1 General teaching strategies?	In teacher's manual.
8.2 Specific lesson plans?	In teacher's manual.
8.3 Social-science subject-matter background?	In teacher's manual and in books that come with the unit.

8.4 Lists of books, films, recordings, realia?	Provides some references, but generally the kits contain all the materials the teacher will need.
9. Provides what materials for pupils:	
9.1 Textbooks?	No. Real artifacts rather than books.
9.2 Workbooks, activity books?	Some—to guide individual and small group activities.
9.3 Supplementary resource books?	Yes.
9.4 Films?	Motion pictures, filmstrips.
9.5 Audio recordings?	Yes.
9.6 Separate pictures, charts?	High-quality pictures and charts.
9.7 Separate maps?	Yes.
10. Suggests what evaluation techniques?	Teacher observation of pupil performance on small-group projects, in discussions, role-playing situations, individual interactions. No written tests provided.

---

1. Identifying label	Providence Social Studies Curriculum Project
2. Source of the curriculum materials	Providence Social Studies Curriculum Project, Rhode Island College, Providence, R.I. 02908; also Rhode Island College Book Store, Providence, R.I. 02908
3. Principal author	Ridgway F. Shinn, Jr.
4. Period of development or of publication	1964-1969
5. Grade levels	K-12
6. Rationale, philosophy, or key purpose	The most suitable social-studies curriculum is one developed by specialists from six disciplines (human growth and development and learning theory, social-studies curriculum theory, administration, classroom teaching, history, geography). History and

6. (Continued)

7. Stresses what teaching methods?

8. Provides what materials for teachers:
   8.1 General teaching strategies?
   8.2 Specific lesson plans?
   8.3 Social-science subject-matter background?
   8.4 Lists of books, films, recordings?

9. Provides what materials for pupils:
   9.1 Textbooks?
   9.2 Workbooks, activity books?
   9.3 Supplementary reading books?
   9.4 Films?
   9.5 Audio recordings?
   9.6 Separate pictures, charts?
   9.7 Maps?

10. Suggests what evaluation techniques?

geography serve as the integrating disciplines.

Questioning, discussion, small-group projects.

In teacher's manual.

Some are sketched in teacher's manual for illustration.
Some in form of resource units in teacher's manual.
In teacher's manual.

No.
No.

No.

No.
No.
Yes.

Yes.

Teacher observation of pupil responses to questions in discussion sessions and of pupil performance on projects.

---

1. Identifying label — University of Minnesota, Project Social Studies

2. Source of the curriculum materials — Project Social Studies, 130 Peik Hall, University of Minnesota, Minneapolis, Minn. 55455; also Green Printing Co., 631 8th Ave. North, Minneapolis, Minn. 55411

3. Principal author — Edith West

4. Period of development or of publication — 1963-1968

5. Grade levels	K-12
6. Rationale, philosophy, or key purpose	Interdisciplinary teaching of major social-science concepts, generalizations, and inquiry techniques; increased emphasis on behavioral sciences and non-Western world.
7. Stresses what teaching methods?	Questioning, discussion, case studies, simulation games, reading text materials.
8. Provides what materials for teachers:	
8.1 General teaching strategies?	In teacher's manual.
8.2 Specific lesson plans?	As resource units in teacher's manual.
8.3 Social-science subject-matter background?	Some in form of resource units in teacher's manual.
8.4 Lists of books, films, recordings?	In teacher's manual.
9. Provides what materials for pupils:	
9.1 Textbooks?	No.
9.2 Workbooks, activity books?	Readings and study sheets.
9.3 Supplementary reading books?	No.
9.4 Films?	No.
9.5 Audio recordings?	No.
9.6 Separate pictures, charts?	Yes.
9.7 Separate maps?	Yes.
10. Suggests what evaluation techniques?	Teacher observation of pupil success in learning activities, pupil answers in class discussion.

---

1. Identifying label	Washington University Elementary Social Science Project
2. Source of the curriculum materials	Metropolitan St. Louis Social Studies Center, Washington University, St. Louis, Mo. 63130

3. Principal authors	Harold Berlak and T. R. Tomlinson
4. Period of development or of publication	1960s-1971 development Publication 1971-1972, Singer Division of Random House
5. Grade levels	4-6
6. Rationale, philosophy, or key purpose	To develop pupils' analytical strategies for dealing with social and moral issues. To develop students' conceptual understanding of their social environment.
7. Stresses what teaching methods?	Role play, simulation games, small group discussion, use of A. V.
8. Provides what materials for teachers:	
8.1 General teaching strategies?	In teacher's guidebooks.
8.2 Specific lesson plans?	Yes, in guidebooks.
8.3 Social-science subject-matter background?	Yes, in guide work and references in guidebooks.
8.4 Lists of books, films, recordings?	In teacher's guidebooks.
9. Provides what materials for pupils:	
9.1 Textbooks?	Stories, text materials, photo essays.
9.2 Workbooks, activity books?	Yes.
9.3 Supplementary resource books?	No. Text materials are essentially resource information.
9.4 Films?	Sound filmstrips.
9.5 Audio recordings?	Yes.
9.6 Separate pictures, charts?	Yes.
9.7 Separate maps?	Yes.
10. Suggests what evaluation techniques?	Teacher questioning, teacher observation of pupil performance in classroom.

Author Index

Subject Index